ADVANCE PRAISE

A practical account of how to solve a vexing problem, viz. that of building engaged employees. This is a different kind of book that could change the approach to the issue of people engagement. Certainly worth the time and the price.

R. Gopalakrishnan, *CEO, The Mindworks*

For sustained business outperformance in the 'new normal', it is vital that we create an organizational culture which unleashes the human potential.

A critical determinant will be the level of employee engagement, and Dr Maheshwari does an excellent job of exploring employee engagement through a multidimensional and holistic lens. Readers will get an in-depth understanding of the seven accountability levels and the challenges posed at each level.

Be it a small-team leader or a C-level executive, all will be able to relate to this book and use the learnings to shift their performance to the 'next orbit'.

Rajeev Dubey, *Group President (HR and Corporate Services) and CEO (After-Market Sector), Member of the Group Executive Board, Mahindra & Mahindra Ltd*

Engage! vividly brings out the fact that while organizations are built mostly for economic value creation, they thrive only when the human 'spirit' is deeply engaged towards the fulfilment of the institutional purpose and objectives. A beautiful blend of logic and creativity, it delineates how the role holders at every accountability level must carry out their respective mandates in an appreciative cultural milieu. All this adds up creating a 'perfectly engaged organization'.

This text captures the best of Western as well as Indian philosophy of development in order to create an impeccable engagement paradigm. It brings out the true essence of a Sanskrit shloka: अमंत्रम् अक्षरम् नास्ति, नास्ति मूलमनौषधम्; अयोग्य: पुरुष: नास्ति, योजकस्तु तत्र दुर्लभ (There is no alphabet without meaning; no root without medicinal property; no person without ability. But rare is the manager or leader who can connect, organize and utilize immense human potential so as to harness latent human talent towards the creation of 'individual and organizational excellence').

D. V. Shastry, *Director (Personnel),*
Electronics Corporation of India Ltd

The book offers a novel vision to all individuals. In a world where being part of an organization is easy, but feeling like one is hard, it helps us to understand how the most benevolent organizations have the most engaged employees and self-fulfilled individuals. The book puts the idea of engagement as well as individual aims, wishes and health at the same level and gives insights on how both can be achieved simultaneously. The author never digresses from his objective and takes the readers step by step to the making of an engaged organization.

Navneet Saluja, *Managing Director,*
GlaxoSmithKline Consumer Healthcare Ltd

'Employees are nurtured by an appreciative culture that is deeply infor-med by the highest aspirations of human nature', as Dr Maheshwari rightly mentions in this book, is one of the essential takeaways for all the CEOs and CXOs who want to build ideal organizations. The book provides frameworks to architect an engaged organization without being preachy. Through well-researched case studies, Sunil brings life to his main theory that appreciative culture and holistic structure are the main pillars of an ideal, engaged organization. I would recommend this book to anyone wanting to understand how organizations excel.

Professor Debashis Chatterjee, *Author of Timeless Leadership*

ENGAGE!

ENGAGE!

ENGAGE!

Co-creating Organizational Vitality and Individual Fulfilment

SUNIL MAHESHWARI

Los Angeles | London | New Delhi
Singapore | Washington DC | Melbourne

First published in 2019 by

SAGE Publications India Pvt Ltd
B1/I-1 Mohan Cooperative Industrial Area
Mathura Road, New Delhi 110 044, India
www.sagepub.in

SAGE Publications Inc
2455 Teller Road
Thousand Oaks, California 91320, USA

SAGE Publications Ltd
1 Oliver's Yard, 55 City Road
London EC1Y 1SP, United Kingdom

SAGE Publications Asia-Pacific Pte Ltd
18 Cross Street #10-10/11/12
China Square Central
Singapore 048423

Published by Vivek Mehra for SAGE Publications India Pvt Ltd, typeset in 10.5/13.5 pt Adobe Caslon Pro and 10/13.5 pt Minion by Fidus Design Pvt Ltd, Chandigarh.

Library of Congress Cataloging-in-Publication Data
Name: Maheshwari, Sunil Kumar, author.
Title: Engage! : co-creating organizational vitality and individual fulfilment / Sunil Maheshwari, Dean, Samatvam Academy.
Description: New Delhi, India: SAGE Publications India, 2019.
Identifiers: LCCN 2018055319 | ISBN 9789353282714 (pbk) | ISBN 9789353282721 (epub 2.0) | ISBN 9789353282738 (ebook)
Subjects: LCSH: Employee motivation. | Organizational behavior. | Personnel management.
Classification: LCC HF5549.5.M63 M346 2019 | DDC 658.3/14—dc23
LC record available at https://lccn.loc.gov/2018055319

ISBN: 978-93-532-8271-4 (PB)

SAGE Team: Namarita Kathait, Sambhavi Shah, Mahira Chadha and Ritu Chopra

To

Dr Jayadeva Yogendra

The guiding light that shall continue to shine forever

Thank you for choosing a SAGE product!
If you have any comment, observation or feedback,
I would like to personally hear from you.

Please write to me at **contactceo@sagepub.in**

Vivek Mehra, Managing Director and CEO, SAGE India.

Bulk Sales

SAGE India offers special discounts
for purchase of books in bulk.
We also make available special imprints
and excerpts from our books on demand.

For orders and enquiries, write to us at

Marketing Department
SAGE Publications India Pvt Ltd
B1/I-1, Mohan Cooperative Industrial Area
Mathura Road, Post Bag 7
New Delhi 110044, India

E-mail us at **marketing@sagepub.in**

Subscribe to our mailing list
Write to **marketing@sagepub.in**

This book is also available as an e-book.

CONTENTS

Foreword by Dr Rajiv Kumar ix

Preface xi

Acknowledgements xv

Part I: The Quest 1

1. The Engaged Organization 2

 Case Study: Patagonia 10

2. The Engagement Imperative 26

Part II: The Foundations 41

3. The Individual Human Being 42

4. The Nature of Work 58

Part III: The Approach 67

5. The Appreciative Culture 68

 Case Study: The Tata Group 83

6. The Holistic Structure 98

 Case Study: Whole Foods Market 118

Part IV: The Architecture 133

7. Individual Excellence 134

 Case Study: Apple Inc. 152

CONTENTS

8. Supervisory Acumen   165

   Case Study: Narayana Health   179

9. Managerial Efficacy   190

   Case Study: The Aravind Eye Care System   203

10. Entrepreneurial Synergy   220

   Case Study: Interface Inc.   239

11. Transformational Leadership   261

   Case Study: ITC Limited   276

12. Mentorship Mastery   297

   Case Study: Jaipur Rugs   310

Epilogue   325

About the Author   329

ENGAGE!

FOREWORD

The level of engagement of employees in an organization is a good predictor of the success of an organization. Successful organizations must have engaged, involved and motivated employees who are also happy.

Sportspersons and artists experience the highest level of engagement and involvement or focused mental state. It has been described by the Hungarian-American psychologist Mihaly Csikszentmihalyi as getting into the 'flow', which he defines as an 'optimal state of consciousness where we feel our best and perform our best'. He lists a number of factors that accompany this state of 'flow' that include having clear goals, participating in an intrinsically rewarding activity, being able to judge your progress and receiving instant feedback, aligning skills to the goals set, as well as focusing on feeling control over the situation and outcome among many others.

Not all employees are expected to have the same level of engagement and not all the factors may always be present. However, emotions and responses are most often associated with the mental state required for optimum performance in any field.

Published employee survey results show that what is true of society at large is also empirically true of big organizations, that is, only a fraction of the employees feel engaged and even that limited sense of engagement is ephemeral. It waxes and wanes for most employees.

This book invites the reader to reflect on what it takes to make the phenomenon of engagement more present and stable for most employees in any organization.

The book explores what 'being engaged' means for individuals, managers, supervisor, leaders and organizations—the objective is to create a symbiotic environment and culture across the organization.

Engagement is a worthwhile individual goal for the sheer sense of joy and fulfilment it brings about. Building organizations that sustain engagement, besides the stupendous economic value that it can create, is a worthwhile objective in itself. This book points the reader towards this ideal.

I commend Sunil Maheshwari as well as Samatvam Academy for this effort, which will be valuable for executives and organizational leaders trying to build creatively engaged organizations.

27 September 2018

Dr Rajiv Kumar

New Delhi
Vice Chairman
National Institution for Transforming India (NITI Aayog)

PREFACE

Organizations employ people in order to fulfil their mandate. The hope is that the employees will give their heart and soul in order to enable the organization to succeed in achieving its aims and objectives. Indeed, the authentic engagement of employees with their specific jobs as well as the larger work context has been regarded as the ultimate source of competitive advantage for any organization.

The term 'engagement' refers to the degree to which employees feel passionate about their work, are committed to the organization and put in the additional discretionary effort. However, as organizations expand in size and scope, the psychological and emotional distance between the employees and the leadership of these organizations tends to progressively increase.

In the current times, employee engagement has become a major issue for large organizations. Digitization and globalization have only added greater complexity to the challenge of building sustainably engaged organizations.

This book is intended to be a guide for every organizational owner and manager who wants to build an organization that is both professionally effective and personally fulfilling. It explores how diverse individuals, as well as groups of people, may be innovatively unified as a symbiotic whole.

Human engagement comes about effortlessly when an organizational context simultaneously addresses the needs of the individual body, mind and the soul. Different dimensions of human personality then operate in unison for the benefit of all concerned. Aspirations and capabilities of each individual are spontaneously brought to bear upon the sustained accomplishment of the organization's vision or purpose.

Although the quest for engagement is universal, not many organizations have been able to achieve it. In all likelihood, there is no such thing as the perfectly engaged organization. Yet, it is (and should be) the Holy Grail that brings together and encompasses all leadership and management thinking along with the frameworks and technologies that go with them.

Common sense tells us that an engaged organization will be quick, agile, curious, innovative, learning- and knowledge-oriented, collaborative, supportive and much more. Perhaps most importantly, it delivers great results in a sustainable manner.

This book is about building such an organization. In order to be able to do this, we have peeled the engagement onion, tested every part of it, dug into the whys and wherefores of each, learned from the organizations that have done it well, iteratively developed the constructs for each element and then woven it all together into this paradigm of universality and truth.

This book is written as a pair of two complementary texts rolled into one. The first part appeals to the mind, whereas the second one engages the heart. The two modes of presentation are interwoven through alternate chapters, in order to provide a dialectic balance between the conceptual/theoretical and the pragmatic/practical facets of organization development.

The first text, so to say, comprises the conceptual chapters. The engagement challenge is systematically outlined at its outset. This is followed by the delineation of the basic foundations upon which engagement can take root. Next, the twin pillars of structure and culture upon which the edifice of an 'engaged' organization may be built are explained. Specifically, the culture of an 'engaged' organization needs to be appreciative in nature. Further, its structure should be a holistic one that provides for the performance of the entire set of job roles that enhances organizational vitality.

Finally, the architecture of such an 'engaged' organization is created. The text develops a set of result-oriented frameworks that utilize the appreciative paradigm in order to enhance the performance of work at every organizational level—from that of the individual contributor to the director. The process by which role holders at all levels and corners of the organization can carry out their respective work mandate so as to build engagement is described in detail.

The second text is inspired by the views of the twentieth-century French novelist Antoine de Saint-Exupéry. He said, 'If you want to build a ship, don't drum up people to collect wood. Rather, teach them to long for the endless immensity of the sea'. This literary genius also added, 'It is only with the heart that one can see rightly; what is essential is invisible to the eye'.

This second part comprises nine detailed case studies of contemporary and highly engaged organizational environments from around the world. Preceded by its respective conceptual chapter, each inspirational and enjoyable story shows how a uniquely engaged organization may be created.

Collectively, these illustrations establish that engaged organizations are founded and led by visionary people—who are relatively more transformational than transactional in their outlook and approach. These revolutionary businesspersons tap into every human being's innate desire to pursue a noble purpose that can help create a positive difference in the lives of his/her fellow human beings. Indeed, sustained engagement manifests only when the entire organization comes together to authentically serve chosen social needs in its own unique, but appreciative and synergistic, way.

Further, engaged institutions appear to be characterized by innovative business models that facilitate the delivery of large volumes of high-quality products/services—preferably at low cost and in an ecologically sustainable manner. The organizations covered in this text come across as being capable of innovatively creating or utilizing new technology without being constrained by its limitations.

This book is divided into four parts. The first part introduces the concept and quest for engagement and also how this may be fulfilled. The second part addresses the key concepts upon which employee engagement is built. The third part explains the twin pillars of culture and structure upon which engagement is based in actual practice. The fourth one vividly presents the detailed architecture of the 'engaged' organization. It identifies how role holders at every level must carry out their respective effectiveness mandates so that it all adds up and creates engagement across the organization.

The case examples have been prepared on the strength of extensive secondary research. The intent was to frame a strategic narrative of the development of these unique, but widely known and documented, institutions from a historical perspective. The organizations themselves have not been consulted in the framing of their respective tales. This was in order to avoid current biases and sidestep the distortions that usually arise from the 'recency' effect.

The synergy in comprehension that is created by the concepts and the cases working together is felt particularly in the later part of the book when the dots are collected and connected together into a holistic understanding. Taken together, the 12 chapters of the book comprehensively outline the contours as well as the skills that are vital towards architecting engaged organizations.

The Epilogue provides a closure to the book by summarizing how engagement may be built and the critical role that the chairpersons of institutions need to play in that process.

ACKNOWLEDGEMENTS

A book of this nature is not the result of any one person's labour; it is rather the product of an entire ecosystem. I am, therefore, thankful to all those who have been a part of my life for nearly half a century, in any capacity whatsoever.

In particular, my gratitude goes to my parents Mrs Meena and Mr Ratan Lal Maheshwari. They instilled a deep love of learning and education in the family, right from its very inception.

My dear wife Aarti has been equally supportive and encouraging. She has set very high standards of excellence and impact for Samatvam Academy as well as the book that has emerged from its work.

Professor Jay K. Mitra supervised my doctoral work at the University of Delhi, which acted as the precursor and the foundation of the present book in some ways. He has instilled high standards of research into my being. I cannot thank him enough.

While we were together at Wipro, Late Ranjan Acharya initiated me into the art and science of organization development. But for his constant support, ready wit and sheer presence during the initial years, I might not have been able to manage to stay the course.

Dr Daniel K. Saint, Dr Ashutosh Bhupatkar and Dilbag Singh—my faculty colleagues at Samatvam Academy—have been instrumental in the development of all the ideas, constructs and frameworks that form a part of this book. Dilbag was also tremendously helpful at all stages of the manuscript preparation.

My elder brother Dr Anil Maheshwari, Jehangir Ardeshir, Professor R. Ravi Kumar, Dr Vasant Bang, Mr V. N. Bhattacharya, Amitava

Mukherjee and Mr V. J. Rao reviewed the manuscript at various stages of its preparation and gave very helpful suggestions. I thank them all. Jehangir's dedication towards people engagement in general as a CEO, and the crafting of this text in particular, was especially inspiring.

Namarita Kathait, Sambhavi Shah and their colleagues at SAGE have done a splendid job of transforming a bulky manuscript into an appealing book.

Last but not least, my gratitude to the Almighty for guiding this 18-year journey to a fulfilling completion—through all the inevitable trials and tribulations.

ENGAGE!

PART I

THE QUEST

THE ENGAGED ORGANIZATION

1

> *Nature uses only the longest threads to weave her patterns, so that each small piece of her fabric reveals the organization of the entire tapestry.*

> — *Richard P. Feynman*

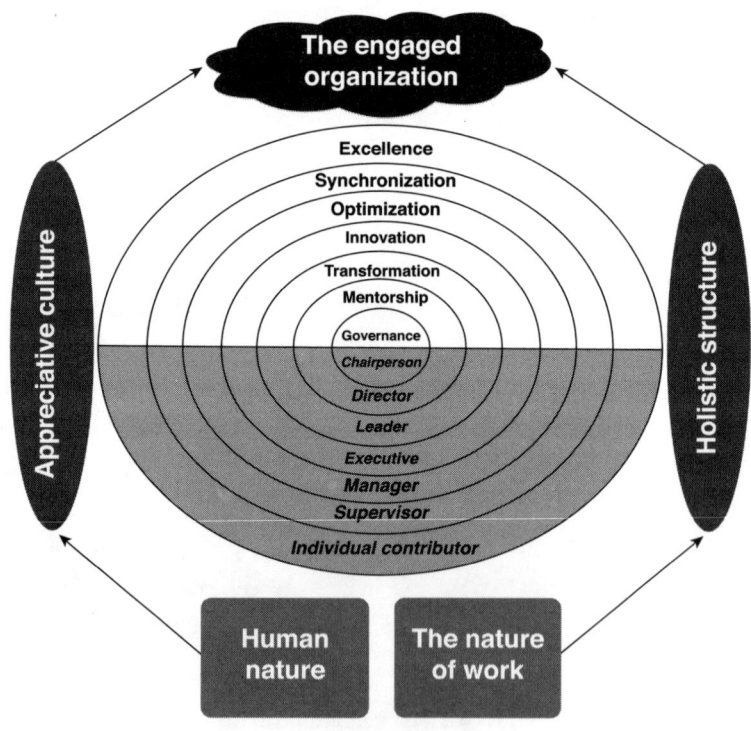

Figure 1.1

The Engagement Paradigm

Source: Samatvam Academy

Organizations are performance systems that are established, operated and developed by people in order to process unique ideas into frames of action and accomplishment. They help to secure performance at a scale and quality that cannot be matched by the best of individuals or small groups.

Organizations have evolved over the centuries. They make use of contemporary capabilities in order to produce the products and services needed at the time. An ideal organization is one that can mobilize a virtually unlimited number of people towards the creation of meaningful products, services and experiences—in ways that can help to fulfil the greatest aspirations of its stakeholders.

Such collaboration is best achieved by creating holistic mechanisms for coordination, which are in evolutionary harmony with the laws of nature. Employees at all levels of the organization then feel appreciated and are genuinely proud of their meaningful contribution to its purpose.

We call such a purposeful and synergistic collective context as an *engaged organization*. Figure 1.1 shows how an 'engaged' organization can be built as a coherent whole at many levels.

The Contours of the Engaged Organization

The salient organizational development challenge in modern times is that of building a highly engaged workforce that is happy and productive at the same time. The challenge becomes manifold, on account of the intensely dynamic socio-technological environment that serves as the external context in which engagement is to be accomplished.

An engaged institution is one that yields a high degree of organizational vitality, in conjunction with individual fulfilment. The cloud-shaped box at the top of Figure 1.1 represents the sublime endeavour to build such an organizational context.

The two square boxes at the bottom of the figure represent the two foundational factors upon which organizations may be built: (a) the nature of the human being and (b) the nature of the work that people are expected to perform. These denote the fundamental starting point for the design of any mode of accomplishment, in any organized setting whatsoever.

The depth of understanding of human nature that is imbibed by any group of people over a period of time is, naturally, reflected in its culture. Likewise, the internal structure of the organizational system corresponds most closely to the nature of work that the organization is expected to perform.

This book postulates that culture and structure are the two key inter-dependent attributes that determine the level of employee engagement in any organization. But what kind of culture and structure are conducive to the development of superior engagement? In the figure, the two oval boxes on either side of the concentric circles represent these two dimensions. They denote an 'appreciative' culture and a 'holistic' structure respectively.

Employees are nurtured by an appreciative culture that is deeply informed by the highest aspirations of human nature. On the other hand, a holistic structure facilitates the seamless accomplishment of the entire range of work elements that need to be performed, in a naturally ordered way. If the structure may be likened to the visceral body of the organization, the culture can be considered as its soul.

A holistically configured organization structure is characterized by seven primary roles: (a) individual contributor, (b) supervisor, (c) manager, (d) executive, (e) leader, (f) director and (g) the chairperson (of the Board). These are placed at progressively increasing levels of responsibility in a hierarchy of levels.

The accountabilities towards organization functioning that are respectively associated with these roles are (a) production, (b) synchronization, (c) optimization, (d) innovation, (e) reinvention, (f) executive development and (g) corporate governance. These responsibilities are best fulfilled when the person adopts a constructive approach to her work. This is facilitated by an appreciative organizational milieu.

The concentric circles at the centre of the figure represent these roles, accompanied by their specific accountabilities. The following table shows their correspondence.

Role	Accountability
Individual contributor	Excellence
Supervisor	Synchronization
Manager	Optimization
Executive	Innovation
Leader	Reinvention
Director	Executive development
Chairperson	Corporate governance

When capable people employed at the various levels of a holistically configured organization fulfil their respective accountabilities in a truly appreciative vein, an engaged work context naturally comes into being!

The Engagement of Employees

The primary objective of every institution is to create stakeholder value through the delivery of products, services and solutions. Its people create value by leveraging external resources, as well as the optimal utilization of their personal competencies and capabilities.

The finest employees are those that invest their complete being into the success of the enterprise. Their individual being gets aligned with the essence of the organizational mission and vision. When the head, the hand and the heart are integrated with the task, human effort is transformed in quality as well as quantity. So do the results that arise from it.

This phenomenon is beautifully captured in the construct of employee engagement, which refers to a positive, work-related psychological state that is characterized by a genuine willingness to contribute to the organizational success. Engaged employees are enthusiastic about their work. They take positive action to further the organization's reputation and interests.

Employee engagement is observable as adaptive behaviours that help to meet or exceed institutional expectations. Engaged employees and associates have been found to work harder, go beyond the call of duty more often and stay with the enterprise for a longer duration. They experience a blend of job satisfaction, commitment, job involvement and a feeling of empowerment.

The three salient aspects of employee engagement are (a) attitude, (b) behaviour and (c) outcome. An engaged employee might feel pride and loyalty (attitude), be a great advocate of the company to customers (behaviour) or go the extra mile to finish a piece of work (outcome). The outcomes may include lower accident and attrition rates, higher productivity and innovation, reduced sickness rates and other attributes. These three key aspects of engagement reinforce one another in a virtuous cycle.

Employee engagement has gained priority, because organizational performance is becoming less and less amenable to centralized regulation. The factors of production are increasingly getting standardized. Modern organizations rely upon the innate judgement, positive intent and momentary wisdom of the employees in order to deliver outcomes at the frontline, on the floor and in the field. The alignment of the task or job with the entire being of the employee is thus a critical imperative for organizational success. An engaged workforce thus becomes a key source of competitive advantage.

Multiple meta-analytic studies have demonstrated robust cross-sectional linkages between employee engagement and increases in profit, innovation, productivity, beneficial discretionary effort and customer satisfaction as well as retention.[1] Other studies have demonstrated that engagement also promotes a reduction in negative behaviour such as absence, voluntary attrition and sabotage.

The Twin Pillars of Engagement: Organization Culture and Structure

An organization is a social unit that is characterized by a management structure, which represents a relatively stable pattern of actions and interactions that people undertake for the purpose of achieving goals.[2] The organization structure determines the flow of internal communication, decision-making authority as well as accountability and how the institution gathers resources to achieve its objectives.

To fulfil their respective mandates, all organizations need at least a rudimentary structure that facilitates the division of work through the assignment of roles, responsibility and the authority to carry out different tasks.

Every organization is also marked by a unique culture, which encompasses the underlying beliefs, assumptions, values and ways of interaction that determine how things are accomplished therein. These attributes create a frame of reference for the perceptions, interpretations and activities of the people.[3] They influence the manner in which employees interact with one another and also with the external stakeholders of the enterprise. Culture thus has a significant impact upon all the organizational processes and outcomes. It plays a crucial role in determining organizational behaviour.

Organizational structure is an extrinsic factor that influences behaviour through formal limitations that are set by the division of labour, authority distribution, the grouping of units and coordination.[2] On the other hand, organizational culture is an intrinsic factor that guides the everyday actions of the people.

At the same time, the structure is itself a cultural symbol that mirrors the key values and assumptions of the organization. By shaping the mental maps of people, the culture influences the frame of reference that determines the structure. In this manner, structure and culture comprehensively explain and predict the causes and forms of the engagement of people in organizations.

These two attributes are not only closely interrelated, but are mutually symbiotic. The organizational culture dictates how the institution should be structured, while the structure becomes the vehicle through which the culture is implemented. The vice versa is also true—as indicated by the words of the famous British statesman, Winston Churchill, 'First we shape our buildings; thereafter they shape us'.

To build engagement, it is important to develop an intrinsically appreciative organizational culture. This constructive mode of functioning embodies respect for the uniqueness and inherent worth of each individual in the society. It enables the strengths of the employees to be affirmed and leveraged towards the efficient conduct of business. The inclusive character of the appreciative paradigm looks after the interests of all the stakeholders and thus provides a harmonizing work context for the people.

The other key enabler of engagement is a holistic organization structure that is characterized by a hierarchy of decision-making accountability of seven levels. These different strata represent specific functions that are critical for organizational vitality.

Why are there only seven strata or levels in a holistic structure? Scholars say that the number 7 denotes completeness and symbolizes perfect order. All the salient manifestations in the universe (such as colours, musical notes, directions and logic gates) are permeated with a seven-fold structure. As will become evident, seven levels of accountability also cover the operational, strategic and governance aspects of organizational vitality quite comprehensively.

As individuals move up the organization's hierarchy of authority and accountability, they integrate a greater range of competing priorities, ideas and values across continually expanding horizons of time and space, and thus solve increasingly more complex problems. When people move into more senior roles, their previous knowledge and expertise become less significant as compared to their ability to make judgements in the face of uncertainty and ambiguity.

The characteristics of an engaged organization may therefore be summarized as follows:

1. Role, authority and accountability in a hierarchical structure that is mapped with the organizational vitality functions

2. Clear assignment of roles, in the context of well-defined cross-functional relationships

3. Constructive cultural practices that help and encourage the employees to comprehensively deploy their capability, individually as well as collectively

4. A talent pool system that identifies meritorious employees for promotion and career development, and also supports effective succession planning

References

1. Engage for Success. What is employee engagement? *Engage for Success*. Available at: http://engageforsuccess.org/what-is-employee-engagement (accessed: 25 April 2018).

2. Janicijevic N. The mutual impact of organizational culture and structure. *Ekonomski Anali*. 2013; 58(198): 35–60.

3. Schein E. *Organizational Culture and Leadership*. San Francisco, CA: Jossey-Bass; 2004.

PATAGONIA

Every time I have made a decision that is best for the planet, I have made money.

—*Yvon Chouinard*

BACKGROUND

Patagonia Inc. is a family-owned American corporation that responsibly produces and promotes sustainable outdoor apparel of the highest quality. As a designated benefit corporation, it formally commits itself to the alleviation of public concerns alongside the creation of shareholder value. Patagonia's revenues shall cross the billion dollar mark in the year 2019.

Founded by the legendary climber and environmentalist Yvon Chouinard at Ventura, California, in 1973, Patagonia is one of the most environmentally responsible enterprises on the planet. The company's stated mission is to (a) build the best product, (b) cause no unnecessary harm and (c) use business to inspire and implement solutions to the environmental crisis.[1]

As an integral part of its environmental consciousness philosophy, the organization donates 1 per cent of its sales to around 650 grassroots environmental organizations through the '1% for the planet' programme. Since 1985 Patagonia has donated over $89 million in this manner. It has also persuaded 1,800 other organizations to join the initiative. In the company's judgement and experience, an investment into the well-being of the planet makes remarkable business sense.[2]

Patagonia champions eco-friendliness in the production as well as the use of its clothing. Its garments are made from responsibly sourced materials and are guaranteed for life. Further, the company nudges its customers to think twice before they purchase any of its products.

Extending the product life through due care and repair reduces the need to acquire more over time, thereby minimizing the CO_2 emissions, waste output as well as water usage. Patagonia therefore operates North America's largest apparel repair facility, which carries out more than 40,000 individual repairs annually. The company has also published over 40 repair guides for Patagonia products on its website in order to help the customers fix their gear themselves.

Patagonia also facilitates the recycling of garments upon the completion of their active life. It seeks to create a closed loop system, so that its products may never end up in a landfill.

Patagonia's mission, vision and values have all been directed towards a single end—the creative and synergistic amalgamation of 'profit' together with a sense of 'purpose' in order to drive a healthier bottom line for the 'planet'. On its ascent towards success and fulfilment, the company has made many bold and counterintuitive moves.

In November 2012, for instance, Patagonia introduced a full-page advertisement in the *New York Times* with the headline 'Don't Buy This Jacket'. Below a picture of the bestselling fleece jacket in question, the ad copy listed in detail how much water was wasted and carbon emitted in the course of its production. Contrary to conventional wisdom and expectations, the advertisement actually helped to boost the product's sales by 40 per cent over the next two years.

Patagonia's appeal stems largely from its deep commitment to the natural environment. The company enjoys an almost psychic bond with its customers, who in turn love to talk about its products.

A deeply reluctant businessperson, the company's 80-year-old iconoclastic founder Yvon Chouinard adopts a strictly hands-off approach to leading Patagonia. He describes his management style as MBA (management by absence).[2] Like a true entrepreneur, he often comes up with innovative ideas and new concepts. However, the translation of this ingenuity into action is left into the safe hands of the company's CEO Rose Marcario and her colleagues.

The quintessential environmentalist, Chouinard does not maintain a computer or a cell phone. He prefers to hand-write his letters and spends much time working on odd side projects and tinkering in his original blacksmith shop at the Patagonia campus. He also loves to test out the prototypes of new products in the outdoors. Thus, when Yvon Chouinard goes climbing in Europe, or kayaking with friends in South America, or fishing in Canada as he often does, he justifiably claims to be on a business trip!

THE CULTURAL PILLARS

Patagonia grew out of a small company that made climbing tools. Its founding values were reflective of a business that was initiated by a band of climbers and surfers, and the minimalist style they promoted.

Over the years, Patagonia has developed a constructive organization culture that supports the people within and without towards living a clean and examined life. The maintenance of lofty ethical and governance standards, while making functional and durable products of the highest quality with the least possible ecological impact, represents the core of the company's DNA.

The company continues to cherish (a) quality, (b) relational integrity, (c) environmental action and (d) an innovative outlook. These progressive values have spawned transformational business processes and practices that have been instrumental in the fulfilment of the company's charter.

Patagonia recruits capable, inspired and independent-thinking individuals in a very careful as well as methodical manner. Positions sometimes remain open for over a year, even at the senior levels, before the right person is found. Enormous effort is devoted towards the orientation of new employees. This includes a significant amount of time spent with the senior management team. The concept of an annual performance rating has been dispensed with, because it was found to change the role of the manager from being a coach to becoming a judge.

The organization allows its people ample flexibility and autonomy, in order that they may contribute to their highest potential. Patagonia's 2,200 employees are free to dress as they please. Their work hours are flexible. It is not uncommon to see employees walking barefoot across the grounds. People are encouraged to live the lives that they want to, regardless of whether that involves horseback riding, surfing or watching their kids play. The day's surf report is posted above the reception desk. Employees are free to take off during the day in order to go surfing or to play volleyball, so long as they fulfil their responsibilities and timelines.

The leadership team of Patagonia at the Board level frames the vision after wide-ranging internal consultation and debate, and then gets out of the way (so to say). The management team of the company keeps the attention of the organization directed at the vision. It also provides the employees with the necessary coaching, resources and autonomy in carrying out the actual work.

Patagonia is structured more like a network than a pyramid. There is a recognition that the best business ideas come from the people who dirty their hands with real work in the field or at the frontline. Thus, the communication within the company flows freely across organizational levels. There is an active disdain for the pecking order or the chain of command.

Interestingly, Patagonia's decentralized culture poses a challenge too. The decision-making process in such a democratic and transparent milieu suffers on account of the relative absence of hierarchy and the independent nature of the people that Patagonia hires.

Without a clear structure of accountability for decision-making, it often becomes difficult to determine which individual has the authority to make a particular decision or give a go-ahead for a certain course of action. And because the culture is consensus driven, people sometimes hesitate to make decisions for the fear of antagonizing one stakeholder or another.

Patagonia is very forthright in its approach. For instance, animal rights activists in Germany accused the firm of procuring goose feathers that were live-plucked. Promptly, the company sent two people to Hungary to check out the actual situation. They reported that the feathers were not being plucked while the bird was alive. However, the geese were being force-fed for foie gras. Patagonia did not invent a specious explanation, or cover up the issue. It simply reported the facts as they were and then moved on to source its down feathers from a different supplier.

In 1996, Patagonia switched to the exclusive use of organic cotton for producing its garments. This entailed a significant business risk on account of procurement constraints as well as sharply increased material costs. On the other hand, it was a concrete and bold demonstration of the company's stated resolve to protect the environment. By thus putting its money where its mouth was, Patagonia managed to evoke intense customer loyalty.[3]

The Patagonia headquarters look remarkably different from a traditional corporate office. Instead of a parking lot full of cars, bicycles and surfboards are seen lined up outside the building. The architectural arrangement does not allow for private offices. This helps to keep the communication lines open. The laughter of children playing in the yard, or having lunch with their parents in the cafeteria, lends a feeling of *joie de vivre* to the atmosphere. The presence of solar panels, Tibetan prayer flags and sheds full of rescued owls and hawks make this a unique corporate campus.

THE ORIGINS OF THE VENTURE

Yvon Chouinard and his wife Malinda established Patagonia over 45 years ago in order to share their love for nature and to create products that enable people to enjoy outdoor life. During high school, he discovered rock climbing.

Unfortunately, his passion was limited by a lack of appropriate climbing gear. Chouinard decided to make his own reusable hardware. He turned his parents' garage into a coal forge and began to manufacture robust chrome-molybdenum steel pitons. As the word of his invention spread, Yvon sold these from the back of his car for $1.50 each while he drifted across Yosemite and the California coast. The profits were slim and Chouinard often lived on a dollar a day.

However, the demand soon caught up. In 1965, Yvon partnered with fellow climber Tom Frost to create Chouinard Equipment. By 1970, Chouinard Equipment had become the largest supplier of climbing hardware in the United States.

However, the company had also become an environmental villain by this time. The use of its gear by the climbers was damaging the rocks. In 1972, the firm took its first eco-friendly step of replacing iron pitons with aluminium chocks.

Yvon once went on a climb wearing a colourful rugby shirt that he had purchased on an overseas trip. It was an interesting contrast to the dull shirts worn by the climbers back then. This shirt provided good protection from the natural elements and became an instant hit. More were imported in response to demand. The company slowly expanded into apparel in order to supplement the hardware trade.

By 1973, when Chouinard and Frost dissolved their partnership, the clothing line had become a profitable business in its own right. It was named as 'Patagonia' in order to reflect the romance and mystique associated with distant lands.[4]

ESTABLISHING THE ENTERPRISE

Patagonia was buoyed by the enthusiastic reception to coloured clothing. Thus, the company soon developed a line of climbing apparel that was colourful, rugged and attractive.

In 1980, Patagonia came out with insulating long underwear made of polypropylene. This was a synthetic fibre of very low specific gravity that did not absorb water. Using the capabilities of this new underwear as the basis, Patagonia became the first company to teach the concept of systematic layering to the outdoor community. This three-tier sartorial approach involved wearing an inner layer of clothing against the skin for moisture transport, a middle layer of the pile for heat insulation and an outer shell layer of apparel for wind and moisture protection.[5]

In 1985, the company made a risky shift of its entire line of polypropylene underwear to the newly developed Capilene® polyester and the Synchilla® fleece fabrics. The growing appeal of these technical fabrics, coupled with the dramatic colours, helped the label to become a fad.[5]

Sales soared and the company rapidly expanded into Europe and Japan. At one point, Patagonia was featured in Inc. Magazine's list of fast-growing privately held companies.[4]

Patagonia's rapid growth and expansion during the 1980s came to an abrupt halt in the summer of 1991. Patagonia was facing significant competition. Sales declined and profits plunged.

The bankers reduced Patagonia's line of credit twice in the space of a few months. They also called in their revolving loan. This forced the company to look for alternate sources of credit. The company also let go of 20 per cent of its workforce and dumped its inventory below cost in order to pay off the debt.[5]

Patagonia had perhaps tried to expand too quickly and nearly lost its independence as a result. At one stage, Yvon seriously considered selling out of the venture. Eventually, he chose to stay and lead the organization in a more sustainable direction.

Instead of abandoning his ideals, Chouinard decided to become truer to them. He invested in organic cotton and other sustainable materials. Yvon also decided to make Patagonia products more durable.

These were risky moves, considering that the growth of corporations is generally fuelled by consumers coming back to get replacement products. Greater durability would normally be expected to translate into lower product offtake. However, the exact opposite occurred. Consumers were found to develop greater loyalty to Patagonia on account of its environmental consciousness and the fact that they could trust the company's products to last for a long time.

Looking back, the crisis was a blessing in disguise. It led to a systemic transformation of the organization. Patagonia's performance rebounded in 1993. It has steadily improved since then.

In 2005, Patagonia launched its unique Common Threads Initiative as a partnership with its customers. The intent was to promote the sustainable purchase and use of apparel. The ultimate aim

17

was to close the loop on the lifecycle of its products and minimize the environmental cost through specific programmes that were directed towards reducing, repairing, reusing and the recycling of clothing.[6]

To minimize the incidence of repeat purchase, the company manufactured products of very high quality that lasted for a long time. Through the 'Buy Less' campaign, the customers were encouraged to refrain from buying Patagonia products that they did not really need.[7]

Patagonia, thus, built its success by encouraging its customers to think critically and not so much by persuading them to buy its products. Its enlightened initiatives helped to create numerous brand evangelists for the company. They facilitated its unabated growth.

THE ROSE MARCARIO ERA (2014 ONWARDS)

The life and career of Patagonia's current CEO Rose Marcario is indicative of the kind of inspiration and values that lie at the core of the organization. After pursuing a very successful career in finance for 15 years, Marcario faced a turning point. The trigger was the sense of frustration she felt when a homeless man crossing the street made her limousine wait at a street corner in New York.

Rose reflected deeply upon the source of her impatient behaviour. She began to search for a new definition of success in life. After taking two years off to visit India and Nepal in search of an answer, Rose returned home. She soon received a call from Yvon Chouinard and was impressed by his sincerity. Taking cognizance of the alignment between her personal values and those espoused by Patagonia, Rose joined the company in 2008 as its chief financial officer.

Upon joining the company, Marcario set out to streamline production and identify waste in order to save costs. She redesigned the process by which the company shipped its goods and cut back on leisure wear lines in order to refocus the company on its core products. Rose also facilitated a significant improvement in Patagonia's e-commerce capabilities.

Marcario was initially quite sceptical about the actual feasibility of living by Patagonia's values in a competitive business. However, she soon gained conviction about the Patagonia model—wherein a private enterprise cares deeply about each one of its varied stakeholders.

Rose was promoted as the President and CEO of Patagonia in February 2014. She was seen to have brought a full perspective to her role as a businessperson.

Marcario played a central part in helping the company strike the tenuous balance between sustained growth as a retailer and the promotion of environmentally conscious practices as a business with a significant footprint. She exemplified the conduct of an examined life that is so central to Patagonia's mission.

THE STRATEGIC PRINCIPLES

By its own example, Patagonia demonstrates how strong values and ethical leadership can create a successful organization that can act as a role model for those who genuinely desire to make a positive difference. Yvon Chouinard once stated that he never wanted to be in business. But he hung on to Patagonia—because it was his vehicle for demonstrating that corporations too are capable of leading examined lives and promoting social well-being. The company has been a pioneer in using the good offices of business towards the inspiration and implementation of solutions to the environmental crisis.

The following three key strategic principles come together to support the accomplishment of Patagonia's mission:

1. Family orientation

2. Environmental stewardship

3. Collaborative innovation

FAMILY ORIENTATION

Patagonia regards its employees as the most important stakeholders of the organization. It believes that a happier and more fulfilling workplace attracts and retains better workers, who in turn design superior products and develop smarter strategies. The company has thereby instituted many employee-centric policies, in order to look after the well-being of its people as well as their families.[2]

Patagonia offers flexible working hours to all. Mothers and fathers get equal two month-long paid parental leaves at the company. Job sharing is also offered, mostly for the benefit of working parents. Under the 'Travelling Baby' programme, parents get to travel with their babies while the company pays for a child development teacher to come along.

Patagonia serves healthy and subsidized organic lunch daily in its café. There is a yoga room available for employees at all times of the day. Health care is fully covered and everyone takes vacations. The employees are also permitted to take fully paid sabbaticals of up to two months in order to work on environmental projects about which they are individually passionate.

As far back as 1981, Patagonia recognized that the proper raising of a child actually required the contribution of a whole village full of people. Under the leadership of Malinda Chouinard, the company introduced an innovative, in-house childcare facility at its Ventura campus.

On-site childcare has some obvious benefits. Employees can see their kids during the day. They can thus have an engaging professional life, without compromising upon their parental responsibilities.

Further, when children cohabit with adults who love and care for them, they have the energy to participate in numerous developmental activities. The kids remain lively, curious and happy. They become more articulate and also develop greater self-esteem. Besides, the presence of children transforms the workplace into a community for all the people.

While around half the women in the industry either drop their careers or at least take an extended leave after having kids, nearly all the employees at Patagonia return to work after a standard parental leave. The company proudly claims that the children who come out of its on-site childcare programme are its best products. In fact, the organization actively hires many of the children who grew up with it.

Considered to be a radical initiative at that time, Patagonia's subsidized on-site childcare programme has now become a benchmark and role model for companies that genuinely endeavour to put their people first. In 2014, the then US President Barack Obama recognized and acknowledged Patagonia as a 'champion of change' in appreciation of its family-friendly policies.

ENVIRONMENTAL STEWARDSHIP

Patagonia was still a small organization when it began to devote time and money to the increasingly apparent environmental crisis.

Every 18 months, Patagonia sponsored a 'Tools for Activists' conference that was designed to educate and encourage activists towards becoming more effective advocates for the natural environment. The company also sponsored many other events over the years, ranging from promoting wildlife corridors to combating genetic engineering. 'Conservación Patagónia' is one such direct effort by the company's employees towards the creation of a 650,000 acres national park in South America.

In 2010, Patagonia assisted in the creation of the 'Sustainable Apparel Coalition'. This is a federation of companies that collectively produce more than a third of the clothing and footwear on the planet. It promotes the development of a more sustainable apparel industry. The forum has launched an index of social and environmental performance that designers (and eventually consumers) can use to make better decisions when developing products or choosing materials.[8]

In February 2014, Patagonia established an internal venture capital fund by the name of '$20 Million & Change'. This fund assists responsible start-up companies in bringing about positive benefits and make the world a better place via the clothing, food, water, energy, waste and other industries.

Patagonia advocates a simple lifestyle through its minimalist design and cutting-edge clothing technology. In its quest for ecological leadership, the company has engaged with specialized external agencies to help deliver continuous improvement in the areas of environmental impact, resource productivity, consumer safety, water emissions, air emissions and occupational health. Through its 'Worn Wear' campaign in 2013, Patagonia encouraged its customers to celebrate the clothes that they already owned before embarking upon the purchase of new ones.

The company has built deep bonds with a set of sophisticated consumers who identify deeply with the company's values. Somewhat paradoxically, these people support anti-consumerism by consuming Patagonia products![9]

COLLABORATIVE INNOVATION

Over the years, Patagonia teamed up with other corporations to develop initiatives that were aimed at reducing the environmental footprint of businesses. This helped to meet the company's environmental, social and animal welfare goals. Such collaborations also facilitated economies of scale that helped bring down the cost of new innovation to reasonable levels.

As an example, Patagonia researched plant-based options for wetsuits for four years. In 2013, it finally partnered with the biomaterial company Yulex in order to produce eco-friendly wetsuits. The Yulex wetsuit was made from rubber derived from guayule, a native Arizona plant.

Traditional rubber plants, as well as synthetic rubber production, required the use of environmentally harmful solvents that created non-biodegradable residual products. On the other hand, the Yulex rubber used water-based solvents that left only organic by-products.

Patagonia's sustainable Yulex wetsuit was made up of 60 per cent guayule and 40 per cent synthetic rubber. It performed as effectively as its petroleum and limestone-based counterparts in terms of warmth, flexibility and durability. And Yulex actually smelt better too!

Patagonia then engaged with the entire surf industry in order to help scale up the Yulex product at a reasonable price point. As soon as the product was ready for commercialization, it invited its peer companies to come and test the material. Many manufacturers initially balked at the high price of Yulex.

But when Patagonia's Yulex wetsuit was recognized at the 2015 Surf Industry Manufacturing Association Awards as the Wetsuit of The Year as well as the Environmental Product of the Year, the phone began to ring off the hook. Patagonia's entire wetsuit line is now based on Yulex rubber.[10]

In an earlier instance relating to cotton, Patagonia was successful in transiting its own product line to the use of organic cotton. However, the other industry players initially did not embrace this shift for reasons of high cost and decentralized farming. Eventually, no less a company than Walmart knocked upon Patagonia's doors for advice on the sourcing of organic cotton.

The company's sustained commitment to environmentally conscious practices is proof enough that its motives are at least partly altruistic. Using that stance as a means to continue to grow a sustainable retail brand through unorthodox means, Patagonia has reinvented the concept of retailing. Its relentless focus on making the best possible products has brought the company success in the marketplace too.

Most importantly, staying true to its principles over its four decades in business has helped Patagonia to create an organization that people are proud to engage with and work for!

REFERENCES

1. Patagonia. Patagonia's mission statement. *Patagonia.com*. Available at: www.patagonia.com/company-info.html (accessed: 16 May 2016).

2. Chouinard Y. *Let My People Go Surfing*. New York, NY: The Penguin Press; 2005.

3. Patagonia. 20 years of organic cotton. *Patagonia.com*. Available at: www.patagonia.com/20-years-of-organic-cotton.html (accessed: 26 May 2016).

4. Patagonia. Company info: Our history. *Patagonia.com*. Available at: www.patagonia.com/us/patagonia.go?assetid=3351 (accessed: 20 August 2016).

5. Patagonia. Company history. *Patagonia.com*. Available at: www.patagonia.com/company-history.html (accessed: 26 May 2016).

6. Patagonia. Introducing the common threads initiative—reduce, repair, reuse, recycle, reimagine. *Patagonia.com*. Available at: www.patagonia.com/blog/2011/09/introducing-the-common-threads-initiative/ (accessed: 16 May 2016).

7. Eric L. Patagonia's 'Buy Less' Campaign may lead to more revenue. *Harvard Business Review*. Available at: http://blogs.hbr.org/cs/2011/10/patagonias_buy_less_campai.html (accessed: 10 August 2016).

8. Patagonia. Sustainable apparel coalition. *Patagonia.com*. Available at: www.patagonia.com/sustainable-apparel-coalition.html (accessed: 26 May 2018).

9. Patagonia. Worn wear. *Patagonia.com*. Available at: www.patagonia.com/worn-wear.html (accessed: 26 May 2016).

10. O' Rourkea D & Strand R. (2016). *Patagonia: Driving Sustainable Innovation by Embracing Tensions: A Case Study*. Berkeley, CA: Haas School of Business.

VIDEO REFERENCE

Samatvam. (2016, August 31). *Patagonia: The Sustainability Champions*. YouTube. Available at: https://www.youtube.com/watch?v=bB8ZWOKoygY&feature=youtu.be (accessed: 26 November 2018).

2

THE ENGAGEMENT IMPERATIVE

To win in the marketplace, you must first win in the workplace.

— *Doug Conant*

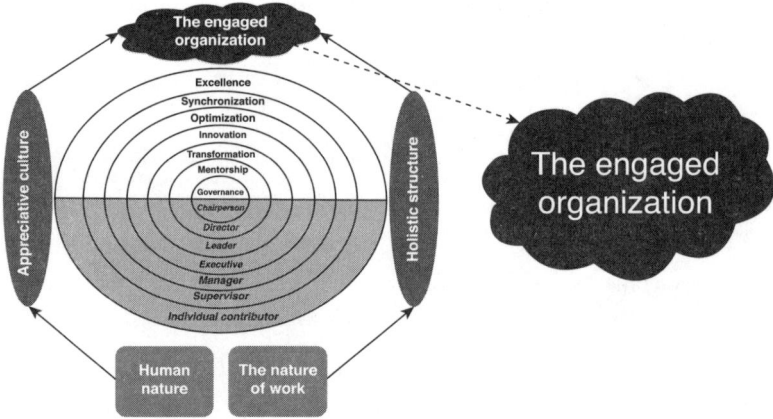

The Engagement Paradigm
Source: Samatvam Academy

Employee engagement refers to the strength of the mental and emotional connection that an employee feels towards his/her place of work. In 1990, Professor William Kahn of Boston University proposed the definition of engagement as 'the harnessing of organization members' selves to their work roles'.

Kahn looked upon personal engagement as the simultaneous employment and expression of a person's 'preferred' self in task behaviours that promote connections to the work and to other people, personal presence and active full role performances.[1] He reported that people employ and express themselves physically, cognitively and emotionally during role performances when they are 'engaged'.

According to Kahn, the domains of meaningfulness, safety and availability were important towards understanding the phenomenon of engagement.[1] Meaningfulness refers to the positive 'sense of return on investments of the self in role performance'. Safety is the ability to show one's self 'without fear or negative consequences to one's self-image, status or career'. Availability is construed as the 'sense of possessing the physical, emotional and psychological resources necessary' for completion of the work.[1]

Harter, Schmidt and Hayes built upon Kahn's ideas to define employee engagement as the individual's involvement and satisfaction with his/her work as well as enthusiasm for it. Through the meta-analysis of 7,939 business units across multiple fields, they were the first to study the linkage between employee engagement and business unit outcomes (profit).[2]

The Engage for Success Task force described employee engagement as 'a workplace approach which is designed to ensure that employees are committed to their organization's goals and values, motivated to contribute to organizational success and are able to enhance their own sense of well-being at the same time'.[3]

Work engagement is a modified construct that refers to a positive and fulfilling state of being. It is characterized by vigour, dedication and absorption. Vigour refers to a high level of energy and mental resilience at work. Dedication relates to strong involvement in one's work that yields the experience of a sense of significance, enthusiasm, inspiration and pride. Absorption is characterized by full concentration and happy engrossment in one's work.[4]

Engagement is thus a measure of an employee's emotional and intellectual commitment to the organization's success. It occurs when the organization respects the employee and the employee values the organization in turn. A state of engagement is characterized by the following attributes:

1. A belief in the organization

2. The desire to work towards making things better

3. A keen comprehension of the business context and the 'larger' picture

4. Expression of respect and helpfulness towards colleagues

5. Willingness to 'go the extra mile'

6. Keeping up-to-date with developments in the field

To summarize, employee engagement refers to the degree to which employees feel passionate about their jobs, display commitment, put discretionary effort into their work and feel a sense of flow while performing their tasks.

The Merits of Employee Engagement

Engagement is characterized by the integration of all the dimensions of the human personality. When deeply engaged, the individual gets fully immersed in a feeling of energized focus, complete involvement and enjoyment in the process or the activity. The work activity becomes intrinsically joyful and satisfying, and eventually yields an experience of flow.[5]

The expression of inherent individual strengths and talents, coupled with their productive utilization in the performance of work tasks, helps the person to accomplish professional objectives and attain personal satisfaction at the same time. The joy and satisfaction derived from accomplishment are revitalizing for the individual. The release of anxiety and the consequent relaxation contributes to the application of undistracted effort into the undertaking. The quality of output is greatly enhanced.

Owing to these merits, employee engagement has been found to influence a wide range of performance outcomes in business settings.

The Global Workforce Study conducted by Towers Watson in 2012 reported that companies with high employee engagement levels had an average operating margin that was nearly three times higher than that of companies with low engagement levels. The Hay Group reported that organizations in the top quartile of engagement scores demonstrated revenue growth 2.5 times greater than the organizations in the bottom quartile.

Based on their research in 158 organizations from a wide range of industries, the Kenexa High Performance Institute published evidence that three-year total shareholder returns were positively linked to employee engagement.[6] Another study of 39 organizations by Kenexa indicated that organizations with highly engaged employees achieved seven times greater five-year total shareholder return than organizations whose employees were relatively less engaged.[7]

Alfes et al. examined data from over 2,000 employees of a recycling and waste management company. They found that employee engagement was strongly linked to innovative work behaviour.[8] When different business units at the Royal Bank of Scotland were ranked in 2011 according to their employee engagement scores, a 7 percentage-point difference in customer service scores was found between the top 10 per cent and the bottom 10 per cent of the units.

Aon Hewitt found in 2012 that only 28 per cent of employees experienced a high level of job-related stress in high-engagement companies versus 39 per cent of employees in low-engagement companies. CIPD reported that people who were absorbed in their work were three times more likely to have key positive emotions at work (enthusiasm, optimism, contentment and calmness) as compared to the negative ones (feeling miserable, worried, depressed or gloomy).[9]

The Gallup Organization has shown a strong link between lower engagement scores and higher employee turnover. Its meta-analytic research based on 203 independent samples demonstrated that an increase in employee engagement is associated with reductions in unsafe behaviour, adverse events, accidents and injuries. An analysis of its Q12 engagement measure found that organizations with engagement in the bottom quartile averaged 62 per cent more accidents than those in the top quartile.[10] Their research data also shows that the earnings per share growth rates of those firms with engagement scores in the top quartile were 2.6 times that of enterprises with below-average engagement scores.[10]

Further, Gallup also uncovered a positive correlation between the physical health and the engagement levels at work. Employees who were engaged in their jobs were generally found to be in better health than the rest of the employees.[10] In another study during 2013, it was found that when employees felt engaged and productive at work, 31 per cent of them rated their lives as 'thriving', while 59 per cent considered themselves to be 'struggling' and 10 per cent were 'suffering'. Significantly, engaged employees were over three times as likely to rate their lives as thriving as compared to those who were actively disengaged.

This is a small sample of the available evidence that appears to confirm the existence of a synergistic feedback loop between employee engagement and organizational outcomes. Improved engagement has the power and potential to transform the modern workplace. Organizations must sincerely work to engage the employee, because the latter has a choice about the engagement level to offer.

An engaging work environment leads to increased productivity and improved business outcomes. This is because the way in which employers treat the employees has a direct effect upon how the latter treat their customers. And the customers vote with their feet and wallet, depending upon the quality of interaction that they experience.

The (Dis)Engagement Crisis

Despite the clarity of the benefits arising from engagement, its deficit in modern organizations remains surprisingly high. Managers and leaders in the digital era are so overwhelmingly preoccupied with the external environment that their capacity to constructively engage with their own people appears to have shrunk drastically. Employees are expected to offer loyalty to the employer, without a reciprocal commitment from the organization towards the protection of their work and pay cheque.

A 2013 Gallup study entitled 'The State of the Global Workplace' employed a meta-analysis of 263 research studies covering nearly 1.4 million employees across 140 countries. Overall, it found that actively disengaged employees outnumber their positively engaged colleagues by nearly two to one at the global level. This implies that work is widely regarded as a source of stress rather than of fulfilment.[11]

The analysis also showed that top quartile units reported 48 per cent fewer safety incidents and 37 per cent lesser absenteeism as compared to bottom quartile units. This means that countless workplaces across the world are less productive or safe than they could potentially be.

When it is reported that two-thirds of the workforce is not fully engaged with the work, it is akin to stating that only a third of an organization's computers work properly. The rest of them are either unreliable or spend their time infecting their fellow computer systems with viruses. Resource inefficiencies of this magnitude would usually be considered alarming.

Indeed, a disengaged workforce is very costly. In 2012, the Kenexa Institute measured employee engagement in 27 countries (that collectively accounted for 80% of global economic output) and also examined its relationship with GDP growth. They reported that across the world, a 1 per cent increase in employee engagement was linked to a 4.8 per cent increase in GDP growth.[12]

Ignoring the human engagement deficit is clearly no longer an option. Then, why is the issue not being adequately addressed? A part of the answer to this question, or perhaps at least a clue to it, lies in the developments that are taking place in the external socio-economic environment.

The New Engagement Context

Rapid technological development has had a far-reaching impact upon global economic activity. The instant and widespread availability of information broke down the partitions separating individuals, institutions and economies. Transportation and communication costs dropped, while global logistics and supply chains became more effective. Products became smaller, faster, cheaper and more resilient.

In the face of these upheavals, the way in which the human society conducts itself has undergone significant changes. The context in which employees are to be engaged has witnessed much change too.

First, the largest beneficiaries of technological innovation have been the innovators who provide the intellectual capital and the investors who contribute to the financial capital. The human workers, who commit their life energy to their jobs, are continuously being displaced by automatic machines. The demand for highly skilled workers has increased, while the larger mass of those with lesser education and skill are finding it difficult to get paid work. The benefits of economic growth have thus not really percolated down to the working class of people. This has worsened economic and social inequality.

Second, knowledge has become the principal factor of production in the present age while information is the basis of its economy. Many people now earn their living in an environment of 24×7 connectivity. Employees perform a large part of their work remotely on handheld technology-enabled devices. They work together with their colleagues around the world in virtual teams. As a result, the digital revolution is changing the human sense of identity. It is impacting the sense of privacy, notions of ownership, consumption patterns and the time that people devote to work and leisure.

Third, technology is unrelenting in substituting manual work in all sectors of the global economy. Of course, physical work still has its place. There is no doubt that manual labour shall continue to remain important, especially in areas such as agriculture, infrastructure, services and parts of manufacturing.

However, the trend of organized economic activity across the world is inexorably shifting towards mechanization and automation. This allows the firms to boost their productivity and competitiveness.

On the flip side, it also leads to progressively fewer opportunities for a human worker to express the creative and artistic elements of his personality. The deleterious effects upon mental health are obvious.

Fourth, business is becoming a unified global field. The boundaries between organizations as well as industries are turning more diffuse. Firms are beginning to actively utilize crowdsourcing in order to generate innovations and build markets.

Fifth, disruptive technologies are being evolved at breakneck speed. Novel platforms and business models are emerging rapidly. Centralized institutions are giving way to flexible work teams. Companies locate different parts of the organization wherever it makes most business sense. They learn to transcend the lines of time, culture and geography in order to thrive.

Sixth, consumer tastes are converging across the world—in everything from clothing to cellular phones. Everywhere, time-starved customers also welcome personalized attention. They expect new products to be rapidly developed and precisely customized, in order to meet their unique individual needs.

Seventh, the job market is now highly transparent. Attracting highly skilled workers has become a tremendously competitive activity. In the high-technology industry, two-thirds of all workers believe they could find a better job in less than 60 days if only they took the time to look. The bargaining power of highly skilled employees appears to have increased in the present era.[13]

Eighth, over two-thirds of the relatively young millennial workers expect their employers to focus on societal or mission-driven problems.[13]

Ninth, organizations have also become relatively flatter. This allows the employees a relatively lesser amount of time with their immediate managers. Regular performance feedback, job rotation and the identification of appropriate development opportunities for the people have therefore taken a hit.

Finally, individuals are now operating more as free agents as compared to the previous decades. They crave for work that permits them to leave a unique fingerprint on a finished product or outcome. Autonomy, mastery and sense of purpose are the driving forces of individual work in modern society.

Creating a New Engagement Paradigm

Enterprises and corporations have responded to these developments by increasing the use of modern technology in all aspects of their work. That may be useful, but is by no means enough.

The evolving scenario actually calls for a newer engagement paradigm that can facilitate quicker and keener collaboration, innovation and adaptation to the environment.

In the digital era, corporations need to reconfigure themselves around shared knowledge and value. Centralized command and control structures must make way for other organizational forms that can facilitate individualized and widely distributed value creation more effectively.

Engagement and empowerment of employees, accompanied by a focus on learning, is the recipe that would work well in the present epoch. Even in the midst of the global financial crisis, the Indian IT major HCL thrived like never before when its then CEO Vineet Nayar championed an 'employee-first' policy.

Innovators such as the Jaipur Foot, the Aravind Eye Care System and Narayana Health are striking examples of superior value creation at low cost. They have made it their business to cater to the health care needs of every person in society—regardless of creed, class or capacity to pay.

These organizations are driven by the inclusive and expansive vision of their founders. They do extraordinary social good, even as they score very well on operational parameters. These institutions have thus made world-class health care highly affordable as well as universally accessible.

Nevertheless, much more remains to be done. During the twentieth century, mainstream organizational conduct was guided by reductionist beliefs and a materialistic view of human existence. As a result, the value of human relationships and the sense of community have steadily lost ground in organizational life. The engagement of the employees with their work also continues to be abysmally low.

Regular surveys indicate that no more than one in seven corporate employees are engaged at work. The number of actively disengaged people is approximately twice that number.[11] The rest of the population works just enough to get by and protect their jobs.

This results in a colossal waste of value creation potential. It also yields social disharmony, as the aggrieved employees sometimes vent their dissatisfaction in unwholesome ways.

Lacking the human spirit, corporate organizations have been occasionally misled into creating ethical catastrophes too. In 2001, rogue executives at Enron and WorldCom destroyed public trust in business institutions. In 2008, the greed of some bankers nearly led to a meltdown of the global financial system. In 2018, Facebook allegedly compromised the private data of over 80 million users. It thereby possibly vitiated the outcome of the 2016 US Presidential elections as well as the Brexit referendum.

Such breaches of trust have led to a renewed search for a greater sense of meaning, purpose and spirit in the lives of corporate citizens. Business enterprises must provide space and challenge for individual employees to achieve, grow and enjoy their work.

The work environment should be designed to strengthen the bonds of mutual trust. Human dignity must be protected. A web of inclusive and satisfying relationships needs to be created, so that people may once again become excited about working together with others in an 'organized' setting.

The Drivers of Engagement

For sustained business success, the urgent need is to create a magnetically engaging organizational environment that facilitates a high level of performance and passion at the same time.

But what is the exact recipe for building greater engagement? Many credible answers are available, but none of these are able to crack the engagement puzzle in a structured and comprehensive manner.

For instance, the Engage for Success Task Force cites four broad engagement enablers that their research has identified as being critical towards employee engagement.[3] These are as follows:

1. A visible leadership that provides a strong strategic narrative, which includes a clearly articulated organizational vision and sense of purpose and also explains how the employees can contribute to its accomplishment

2. Line managers who facilitate and empower their colleagues, treat them with appreciation and respect, and also show a sincere commitment to developing and increasing their capabilities

3. An effective employee voice across the organization—whereby the ideas, views and experiences of the people are sought out as well as listened to and their opinions are made to count

4. A belief among the employees that the organization actually lives up to its espoused norms and values, resulting in trust and a sense of integrity

The Gallup Organization recommends that organizations should select the right employees, develop their strengths and continually promote their well-being, in order to facilitate engagement. The corollary is that employees must also be provided with the space to express themselves and their capabilities.

The consulting firm Deloitte has articulated five major factors that fit together into a system of engagement that helps create what they call as an 'irresistible' organization.[13] These are as follows:

1. Meaningful work

2. Hands-on management

3. Positive work environment

4. Growth opportunities

5. Trust in leadership

From his seminal research on organizational vitality, Elliott Jaques has concluded that a vast majority of employees are keen to get on with their work when provided with even half a chance. Even more, they crave for work that can adequately utilize their talents. However, what is needed is an adequate organizational framework within which they can collaborate and cooperate with one another in a constructive environment that is characterized by mutual trust.[14]

This requires a system of managerial layers, a framework of accountability and authority in lateral relationships, project teams with leaders who are fully accountable and the establishment of specific functions at given organization levels. It also requires a system of coaching and mentoring, merit recognition, talent pool analysis and career development. Jaques, thus, appears to convey that the path to employee engagement lies through the development of the organization.

The Engaged Organization

An engaged organization is a synergistic social system that comprehensively supports and delivers organizational vitality, alongside individual fulfilment.

The basic prerequisite for organization vitality is a clear articulation of the work that is needed for the achievement of strategic goals, combined with the ability to identify capable individuals who possess the ability as well as the willingness to match the work demands.

On the other hand, individual fulfilment arises when a person's level of cognitive capability matches the complexity of the assigned work so as to yield a state of flow. Decision-making comes naturally when the challenges of the role match the capability that the person brings to it.

Matching the role with the goals and the capability appears to be the key to engagement. However, this arrangement sustains over time when the overall cultural milieu respects and constructively engages the person's inherent nature, his/her core values, as well as the individual's basic sense of purpose.

Therefore, the art of the 'engaged' organization is to make provision for complex work, to be done by talented people within an appreciative ambience, in positions that appropriately fit the individual capability, as well as the institutional needs. Even as its work may be vertically structured into separate departments or functions that achieve particular kinds of outputs by carrying out specified processes, the organization strives for greater horizontal coordination of tasks and activities at the same time.

The concept of the 'engaged' organization builds upon the following two main disciplines:

1. The modified theory of bureaucracy that was propounded by Elliott Jaques

2. The appreciative approach to organization development that was evolved by David Cooperrider and Suresh Srivastava

Jaques proposed that organized work required seven qualitatively distinct levels or strata of abstraction, with progressively increasing time horizons.[15] As the required output became more complex, the demands for mental information processing also increased.

On the other hand, appreciative inquiry developed as a study of what gives life to human systems when they function at their best. It enables human systems to adapt effectively to their environment and also to innovate for greater success. Through inquiry and dialogue, people can shift their attention away from problem analysis and work towards the development of productive possibilities for the future.

Arising from these two paradigms, the basic organizational mandate for each of the seven roles in the accountability structure of an engaged organization is clearly defined and comprehensively described. This way, everyone in the organization knows what output, results or contribution they can expect from one another. Accordingly, they can provide the requisite support to their colleagues.

The appreciative process by which each of the respective role charters in an 'engaged' organization may be fulfilled is then crafted in exquite detail. Besides facilitating superior role performance, these process frameworks can facilitate capability building too. All across the organization, role holders then deliver upon the expectations that their colleagues hold from them—humanely as well as effectively.

That is how engaged organizations come into being!

References

1. Kahn W. Psychological conditions of personal engagement and disengagement at work. *Academy of Management Journal.* 1990; 33(4): 692–724.

2. Harter J, Schmidt F & Hayes T. Business-unit-level relationship between employee satisfaction, employee engagement, and business outcomes: A meta-analysis. *Journal of Applied Psychology.* 2002; 87(2): 268–279.

3. Engage for Success. What is employee engagement? *Engage for Success.* Available at: http://engageforsuccess.org/what-is-employee-engagement (accessed: 25 April 2018).

4. Schaufeli W, Salanova M, González-Romá V & Bakker A. The measurement of engagement and burnout: A two sample

confirmatory factor analytic approach. *Journal of Happiness Studies*. 2002; 3(1): 71–92.

5. Csikszentmihalyi M. *Flow*. New York, NY: Harper and Row; 2009.

6. Wiley J. *Driving Success Through Performance Excellence and Employee Engagement*. Wayne, PA: Kenexa Research Institute; 2009.

7. Wiley J. *Engaging the Employee*. Wayne, PA: Kenexa Research Institute; 2008.

8. Alfes K, Truss C, Soane E, Rees C & Gatenby M. The relationship between line manager behavior, perceived HRM practices, and individual performance: Examining the mediating role of engagement. *Human Resource Management*. 2013; 52(6): 839–859.

9. Alfes K, Truss C, Soane E & Rees C. *Creating an Engaged Workforce: Findings from the Kingston Employee Engagement Consortium Project*. London: CIPD; 2010.

10. Harter JK, Schmidt FL, Agrawal S & Plowman SK. *The Relationship between Engagement at Work and Organizational Outcomes 2012 Q12® Meta-Analysis*. Washington, DC: Gallup, Inc.; 2013.

11. Gallup. *State of the Global Workplace*. Washington, DC: Gallup, Inc.; 2013.

12. Kenexa Research Institute. *How Employee Engagement Can Help the Registers Ring. The World of Retail: A 2011 Work Trends Report*. Wayne, PA: Kenexa Research Institute; 2012.

13. Bersin J. Becoming irresistible: A new model for employee engagement. *Deloitte Review*. 2015; (16):146–163.

14. Jaques E. *Requisite Organization*. 2nd ed. Gloucester, MA: Cason Hall & Co; 1998.

15. Jaques E. *A General Theory of Bureaucracy*. London: Heinemann/Halsted Press; 1976.

ENGAGE!

PART II

THE FOUNDATIONS

THE INDIVIDUAL HUMAN BEING

3

A human being is only breath and shadow.

—*Sophocles*

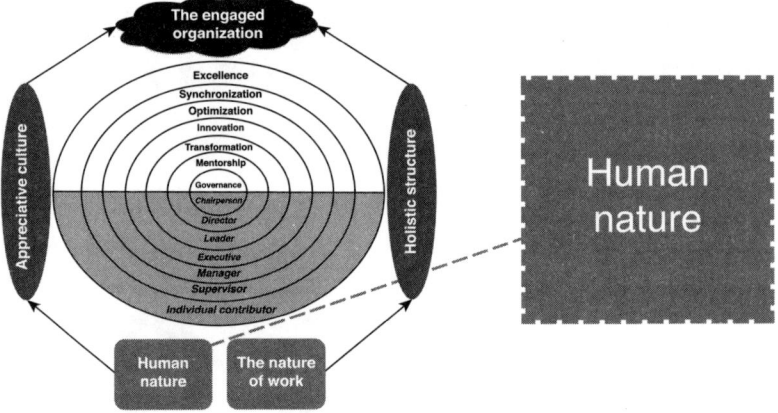

The Human Nature

Source: Samatvam Academy

Each one of us is proud to be born human. But what exactly is an individual human being? The human organism is a genetic, physiological, psychological and spiritually sentient being that is placed in a given familial, social, political, cultural and historical context.

And why does the human being exist? Across ages and cultures, the flowering of latent individual potential has been considered as the primary goal of life.

The 'individual' is considered as any unitary organism that is capable of an independent existence. The term is derived from the Latin word *individuum* (an indivisible thing), which is a sum of the roots *in* (not) and *dividuus* (divisible). Thus, the word 'individual' paradoxically refers to existence as 'a single, separate and indivisible entity' as well as that 'which is inseparable, or cannot be separated'.

In Buddhism, the individual human being is conceived to exist as a series of interconnected processes that work in close cooperation with one another in a way that provides the appearance of being or forming a single and distinct whole. Instead of an atomic, indivisible self that is distinct from reality, Buddhists regard the individual as an interrelated part of an ever-changing, impermanent universe.

Thus, Buddhism considers individual existence to be indivisible from total cosmic manifestation.

At the other end of the spectrum, objectivist philosophy regards every individual human being as an independent and sovereign entity with a natural and inalienable right to his/her own life. An individual is considered to be a specific person, while individuality is considered as the state or quality of being a distinct entity that possesses uniquely particular needs or goals.

Thus, individuality appears to be a condition of autonomy (the self as separate from others) as well as dependence (the self as a part of others). In practice, it represents a state of mutual interdependence.

The individual human being may finally be conceived as the child of interrelated patterns of cosmic or universal forces that progressively gains the appearance of being a socially distinct living entity, with an apparent ability to function wilfully and relatively independently.

The universe consists of space, time, various energy forms (including electromagnetic radiation and matter), and also the natural laws that relate these together into a complex but orderly pattern. The term 'universe' itself signifies an orderly arrangement of things, whereby the particulars are characterized by external connections as well as internal relationships.

The ancient sages conceived the universe as being constituted of numerous planes or levels of manifestation. Physical objects represent the universe at just one plane or density. Manifest reality is hierarchically composed of several different (but continuous) dimensions through which the universe reveals itself to experience. These reach from the lowest, densest and least conscious to the highest, subtlest and most conscious. Each senior level not only transcends but also envelopes its junior dimensions.

This is akin to a series of nests within nests of existence. The phenomenon is often referred to as the Great Chain of Being.[1]

In the natural order, earth (rock) is at the bottom of the chain. This element possesses only the attribute of existence. The next higher level is that of the vegetable kingdom, whose inhabitants possess life and growth too. The plane of the vital animal body adds motion and sensations. While the human mind includes bodily emotions in its makeup, it also adds cognitive faculties such as reason. The soul adds higher cognitions such as illuminating insight and vision that are not found in the rational mind.

The ancient seers visualized these planes of existence as the degrees of experience through which each sentient being has to pass, in the course of its own evolution.

The Individual Human Personality

The human being is an expansive entity that exists at multiple levels of being and knowing. The term 'personality' is derived from the Greek word 'persona', which originally referred to an actor's mask. This suggests that the human personality is merely an outward cloak that is overlaid upon a transcendent, inner self.

The different dimensions or levels that constitute the individual human personality may be (somewhat simplistically) summarized as follows.

ENGAGE!

44

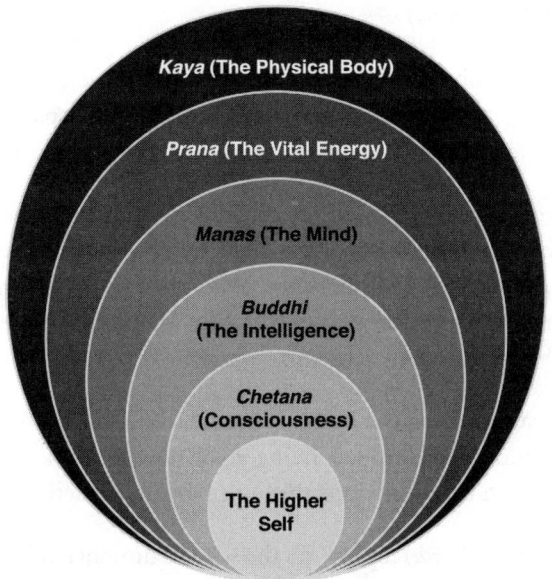

The Dimensions of Human Personality

Source: Samatvam Academy

Kaya (The Physical Body)

The physical body represents the outermost sheath of the human personality. It is composed of many different types of cells that coalesce together to create tissues and organ systems. A strong skeleton made of bone and cartilage, surrounded by fat, muscle, connective tissue, organs and other structures, determines the shape of the human body.

At a gross level, the body is merely a lump of solid matter. It is a physical object that needs nourishment in order to survive. Food is the source of chemical energy, which is ingested into the system so as to provide glucose and other chemicals that are needed for nourishing the vital tissues and organs.

The human body is said to be created from food and is sustained by it too.

Prana (The Vital Energy)

Every material object appears to be a distinct piece of matter that is divided from other objects by the boundaries of space and time. However, the apparent solidity of matter is actually an illusion.

When investigated through more sensitive means, the physical matter is discerned as a configuration of waveforms ($E = mc^2$). When material objects interact with one another, they are found to continuously change their external forms and patterns. This flux is experienced as energy, which manifests as moving activity.

At a more subtle level, the body is thus a bundle of bioenergy or vital force. The individual human being may now be conceived of as a living organism that functions through purposeful activity.

This vital force (*Prana*) represents the second dimension of the human personality. It denotes the very basic principle that distinguishes between living and dead matter. *Prana* is constituted of the subtle patterns of living energy that people experience in their lives.

Manas (The Mind)

The external world of matter and energy appear to be a random flux, without any predictability or regularity in its patterns of interaction. However, a careful examination of these patterns reveals the presence of several natural laws and other useful data about the world we inhabit. At a deeper level of experience, these energy patterns represent 'information' that illuminates our existence.

The vital human being is equipped with five instruments in the forms of sense organs that import stimuli from the external world. These are delivered to a mechanism known as the mind. The mind constitutes the third dimension of the human personality.

Filling and pervading the vital sheath, the mind makes up the subtle body that is the field of our impressions. It comprises the faculties of sensation, emotion and thought as well as instinctual consciousness.

ENGAGE!

Through the mind, we are conscious of ourselves as beings in the world.

Objectively, the sensory impressions give rise to thoughts that are subsequently organized together. This enables the recognition of objects in the external world. Subjectively, the sensory data is correlated with the reservoir of our past impressions. This gives rise to an active and immediate response in the form of emotion. Further, all sensory perception is retained in the memory through imagination—which is the projection of a future possibility or action.

These mental processes form the basis on which the human knowledge of the world is gradually developed.

Buddhi (Intelligence)

The dynamic stream of sensations that arise from the mind is delivered to the faculty of human intelligence, which has two components: (a) intellect and (b) intuition.

Intelligence constitutes the fourth dimension of the human personality. It represents a kind of central processing unit (CPU) that connects the outer world of senses with the inner world of consciousness.

The ambient weather of a place at any given point in time is conditioned by its general climate. Similarly, sensory information is conditioned by the values and perspectives held by the person.

Likewise, the elements of information obtained by means of the senses yield meaning and significance only after they are related, contrasted and juxtaposed with the fundamental beliefs of the person. The latter act as the frame of reference through which the world is perceived. They also guide the processing of selected stimuli from among the thousands that one is bombarded with at every moment. It is the function of the intellect to assimilate the fleeting sensory impressions by the application of reasoning methods so as to arrive at the truth of phenomenon.

On the other hand, intuition is the discriminative power that is capable of directing inner perception. Its operation transcends the medium of the senses. This latter sensibility of intuitive judgement embodies the imprints of wisdom.

Chetana (Consciousness)

The elements of perception are seen to continuously appear and disappear in what we refer to as our 'experience'. However, when the mind comes to rest (as in deep sleep), it seems that there is no experience at all.[2]

Yet we remember deep sleep as a refreshing experience. How do we know the changes and variations in our experience?

In order to detect change, an element of continuity must extend through all the variations that have taken place. For example, a common thread must run through the many individual beads in order to make a rosary. In the natural world, it is the *motionless* pivot that enables the wheel to spin. In the cinema hall, it is the *stationary* screen that makes film projection possible.

The continuity that enables an individual to discern the qualitative conditioning of the world is provided by consciousness, which is the fifth and final dimension of the human personality. Consciousness is the final ground of all our perceptions and of reality itself.

As objects come and go at the changing surface of our minds, they are illuminated by the consciousness that continues at the underlying background of experience. When the object comes into appearance, its properties are comprehended through a reflection back into consciousness. From underlying consciousness, understanding is then expressed as feelings, thoughts and actions.[3]

The singular principle of consciousness is the stable core of the human personality. It is the stationary screen upon which the cinematic images of the world are witnessed.

Hence, the entire human personality arises from consciousness itself. The expression of consciousness in our being is limited only by our own capacity for awareness.

Every human being is born with these five dimensions or coverings. These may be considered as individual repositories of capacity, aptitude and potential. In other words, every person carries exclusive gifts and endowments as he/she makes his/her way into this world. In Sanskrit, these source potentials are referred to as *vasanas*.

These *vasanas* crave for expression in the course of human life. When these intrinsic possibilities get channelized through appropriate kinds of external activity, they manifest as a person's strengths. When an individual's strengths are mutually aligned together and deployed in the service of a higher purpose, we arrive at the attainment of excellence in (and through) action.

The Higher Self

Within these five coverings, there is the pure awareness of the Higher Self. This is the innermost centre of each person, as well as the supporting ground of all that is perceived externally.

There was once an argument among the gods over where to hide the secret of life, so that men and women would not find it. One god said, 'Bury it under a mountain; they will never look there'. 'No', the others said, 'one day they will find ways to dig up mountains and will uncover it'. Another said, 'Sink it in the depths of the ocean; it will be safe there'. The others objected, 'No, the humans will one day find a way to plumb the ocean's depths and find it easily'.

Finally, the wisest among the gods said, 'Put it inside them; men and women will never think of looking for it there'. All the gods readily agreed. That is how the secret of life came to be hidden within the individual.

The foregoing description of the human personality posits that men and women are multidimensional beings. Along with an outer life, individuals possess a rich and extensive inner life.

However, people usually do not have ready access to their interior reality. The inner dimension of the human personality is like the butter that is present in curd; it comes to the fore only after a process of intense churning in the form of discipline, introspection and meditation.

The Perennial Philosophy

Aldous Huxley has succinctly captured the essence of this pheno-menon in a set of three statements that are collectively referred to as the Perennial Philosophy. They sum up the goal of human life as follows[4]:

1. There is an infinite, changeless reality beneath the world of change.

2. This same reality lies at the core of every human personality.

3. The purpose of life is to discover this reality experientially.

The metaphysical assumptions that underlie The Perennial Philosophy imply that consciousness is the basic stuff of the universe and that matter is derived from it. To paraphrase the great Indian mystic *Nisargadatta Maharaj*, 'Matter and consciousness are not separate; they are the twin aspects of one and the same energy. Look at con-sciousness as a function of matter and you have science. Alternatively, look at the matter as the product of consciousness and you have spirituality'.

Engagement, Health and Individual Well-Being

A mounting body of research evidence indicates that engaged employees remain in better health as compared to their disengaged counterparts, as evidenced by lower incidences of hypertension, high cholesterol, obesity, diabetes, diagnosed depression, heart attacks and other chronic health problems. They eat healthier and exercise more frequently. This leads to improved physical and psychological presence at work, and lower absenteeism, attrition as well as accident rates.

People who are healthy as well as engaged are thereby found to be the happiest and most productive of all individuals.[5]

A healthy workforce is characterized by high productivity and commitment, enhanced resilience, improved retention, reduced sickness and fewer accidents. Healthy individuals are also found to learn more effectively, work more productively, have better social relationships and are more likely to contribute to their community.[6] Employee health and wholeness has become a 'hard' economic factor for contemporary organizations, independent of its relation to workforce engagement.

However, personal health and wholeness is the primary responsibility of the respective individual. Much of the organizational effort to create an engaged work context can go waste if the people persist in an unhealthy and unwholesome approach to their life. Therefore, it is critically important for the individual employee to learn how to remain healthy and whole.

The Whole Individual

It was observed in Chapter 2 that engaged individuals bring about an integration of the head, the hand and the heart with their work. True engagement occurs only when the individual harmonizes all the numerous outer and inner dimensions of the being into a seamless whole. How exactly may one bring about such wholeness and consequently, engagement?

The term 'wholeness' refers to being in harmonious alignment—complete, perfect, unbroken, uncut and free of any defect, deformity, mistake or impairment among the constituent parts and components. It is a state of undivided oneness or total unity, and represents the most natural state of being possible.

Wholeness is characterized by the integration of the various dimensions of the human personality. Conflicts and divisions are transcended so as to achieve a totally 'resolved' state of being. This enables the holistic perception and accurate evaluation of situations. It also facilitates the basic survival as well as the social adaptability of the human being.

In all states other than wholeness, there arises a scope for confusion and strife. The question then arises, 'How does an individual maintain wholeness in his/her being? How can the person resolve the sense of multiplicity and disjunction that impedes creativity, alignment and effectiveness?'

It is observed that the words 'heal', 'whole', 'health' and 'holy' share a very close etymological relationship; they all arise from the old English word 'hale' that translates, 'wholeness, and being whole, sound or well'. In turn, hale comes from the Proto-Indo-European root *kailo*, meaning 'whole, uninjured, of good omen'.

The art of maintaining wholeness thus appears to be closely related to the science of preserving health.

Health As a State of Balance

ENGAGE!

Health is a positive concept that indicates the extent to which the individual is able to satisfy needs and realize aspirations. It also refers to the person's capacity to change and cope successfully in the face of significant adversity or risk.

Health is a notion that is applicable to the human being as a unitary whole. It is characterized by anatomical, physiological and psychological integrity.

Thus, the phenomenon of health has connotations at all the different planes of human existence—physical, vital, emotional, mental, intellectual, moral, social and spiritual. This is because the body, the mind and the spirit are deeply intertwined and mutually interdependent entities. A phenomenon that affects any one of these dimensions usually has a discernible impact upon the others too.

For instance, a scary dream is primarily a mental phenomenon. However, its effects on the body (such as sweating or palpitation) are quite tangible in nature. Conversely, a tranquilizer tablet ingested into the body is observed to produce a definitely calming impact upon the mind.

The World Health Organization (WHO) defines health as 'a state of complete physical, mental and social well-being, and not merely the absence of disease or infirmity'. Health represents the harmonious functioning of all the different faculties possessed by an individual, within a given cultural context.

Hippocrates, the father of modern medicine, stated that health is a state wherein the primary properties (wet, dry, cold, hot etc.) of the body balance each other. All the different systems of medicine across the world also agree that a healthy body enjoys a general state of equilibrium, wherein every organ of the body functions in harmony with all the other organs.

The internal environment of the human body constantly reacts to changes in the external environment. In order to maintain an overall state of balance, the different physiological functions of the body interact and interlock with one another through feedback loops. They regulate each other in order to maintain overall homeo-stasis.[7] This kind of integral performance helps the organism to preserve itself.

When this homeostatic state is disrupted (as when hunger, sleep or cold is felt), the body involuntarily attempts to regulate itself. It signals the need for corrective action—such as eating food, or lying down for rest or wearing a sweater. When the body's needs are thus satisfied, it returns to a balanced state.

The Holistic Approach to Health

Individual health is best preserved and maintained by preventing any disease from occurring in the first place.

Yoga and Ayurveda are two sacred sciences that together facilitate human health and wholeness. Both the disciplines are grounded

THE INDIVIDUAL HUMAN BEING

in ancient Vedic tradition, and thereby complement each other in practice.

The concept of physical and mental equilibrium is Ayurveda's first principle. It declares that there are three basic humours (or *doshas*) acting in the body—the breath (*vata*), the bile (*pitta*) and phlegm (*kapha*).

Ayurveda defines good health as *Sama Dosha, Sama Agni, Sama Dhatu, Mala Kriya, Prasanna Atma, Indriya Mala Swastha iti abhidhiyate*. This translates, 'A state of health exists when a person's digestive fire is in a balanced condition, the bodily *doshas* are in equilibrium, the body's tissues are well-nourished, the waste products are produced at normal levels and are properly excreted, the senses are functioning actively and the body, mind and consciousness are harmoniously working as one'.[8]

On the other hand, Yoga is an exact science of wholesome living. It advocates that the absence of physical disease or mental disharmony is just one aspect of health. Positive health is marked by vigour and vitality. An individual is regarded as truly healthy only when he/she is strong, sturdy and muscular with proportionate body parts, and remains free of any pain or disease.

The Four Pillars of Health

The presence of even warmth all over the body, lightness of feeling, keen hunger, sound and restful sleep with the person feeling cheerful and bright upon waking, clarity and perfect coordination of mind, ability of the body for physical exertion, freedom from laziness and timely elimination of the waste products are the symptoms of true health.[9] Good health is also characterized by a feeling of lightness; the presence of the body and its weight are not experienced as burdensome.

Such an exalted degree of health is achieved through the adoption of certain values, attitudes and lifestyle practices that are conducive to optimal human functioning. These are encapsulated as the four pillars of good health—*aahaar, vihaar, aachaar* and *vichaar*.

They may be represented as shown below.

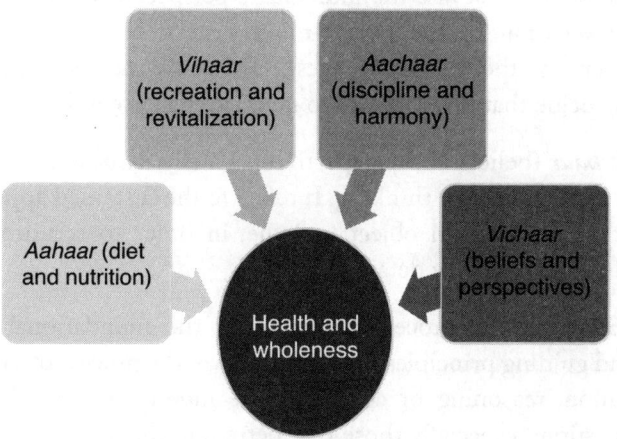

The Four Pillars of Health
Source: Samatvam Academy

1. **Aahaar** (diet and nutrition): The term *aahaar* refers to food, which plays a major role in human existence. An ancient saying declares, 'As is the food, so is the mind. As is the mind, so is the man'.

2. **Vihaar** (recreation and revitalization): The Sanskrit term *vihaar* originally stood for a monastery or sacred shrine that comprised of gardens as well as a resting place for use by hermits. The modern connotation of *vihaar* relates to a pattern and style of life that leads to the relaxation, recreation, rejuvenation and revitalization of the body and the mind.

   The regular practice of Yogic techniques such as *asanas, kriyas* and *pranayama* enable people to build up a strong body and a balanced frame of mind. Physical and mental health also depends on the cues that people observe about themselves—such as sleep patterns, exercise behaviour and nutritional intake.

3. **Aachaar** (discipline and harmony): *Aachaar* refers to good conduct and a positive demeanour. It implies moral and ethical rectitude, as well as the inculcation of benevolence in one's behaviour.

A disciplined adherence to the norms of moral conduct in daily life helps to elevate the individual's perspective. It brings about rejuvenation in the body—mind system, and also assists in reversing the disease process. Thus, *aachaar* is behavioural medicine that helps people to maintain balance in life.

4. **Vichaar** (beliefs and perspectives): Finally, *vichaar* is translated as discernment or thinking. It refers to the sustained application of mind upon an object or issue, in order to scrutinize and discern its specific details.

   Vichaar is the process of exploring the foundational beliefs and guiding principles in life. It involves the process of discrimination, reasoning or contemplative inquiry into fundamental questions, especially those that pertain to the nature of the Self.

Assimilation of the practices of *ahaar, vihaar, aachaar* and *vichaar* into daily life gradually leads to the development of wholeness of the human personality.

The human longing to satisfy the existential needs of the human being becomes stronger when one's material existence has become affluent. Attainment of physical health clears the ground for the exploration of higher-order needs such as affiliation, affirmation, dignity and respect. Organizations must imbibe these values—if they wish to attract and engage scarce, high-quality human talent.

References

1. Wilber K. *The Marriage of Sense and Soul: Integrating Science and Religion.* New York, NY: Random House; 1998. p. 9.

2. James M. *Happiness and the Art of Being: An Introduction to the Philosophy and Practice of the Spiritual Teachings Of Bhagavan Sri Ramana.* 2nd ed. California, USA: Createspace Independent Pub; 2012.

3. Wood A. *Ways to Truth: A View of Hindu Tradition.* New Delhi: D.K. Printworld; 2008. p. 77.

ENGAGE!

4. Huxley A. *The Perennial Philosophy: An Interpretation of the Great Mystics, East and West.* UK: Harper & Bros.; 1960.

5. Brunetto Y, Teo S, Shacklock K & Farr-Wharton R. Emotional intelligence, job satisfaction, well-being and engagement: explaining organisational commitment and turnover intentions in policing. *Human Resource Management Journal.* 2012; 22(4): 428–441.

6. Coats D & Lekhi R. *Good Work.* London: Work Foundation; 2008.

7. Yogendra S. *Yoga Simplified.* Bombay: Yoga Institute; 1975.

8. Lad V. *Textbook of Ayurveda: Fundamental Principles of Ayurveda,* Vol. 1. Albuquerque, NM: The Ayurvedic Press; 2008. p. 8.

9. Lakshmana Sarma K. *Practical Nature Cure.* Tamil Nadu: Nature-Cure Publishing House; 1939.

THE INDIVIDUAL HUMAN BEING

THE NATURE OF WORK

4

*If you cannot work with love but only with distaste, it is better
that you should leave your work and sit at the gate of the temple
and take alms of those who work with joy.*

—*Khalil Gibran, in 'The Prophet'*

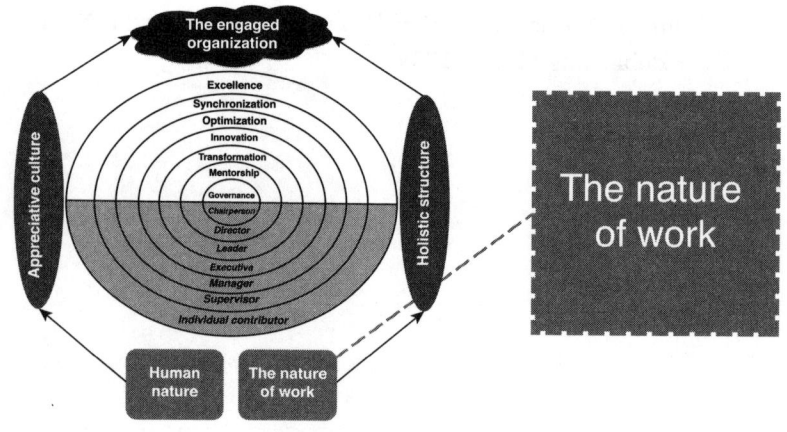

The Nature of Work
Source: Samatvam Academy

What is work? The term refers to all kinds of deliberate effort and activity that promote human sustenance and growth.

Work may be considered as the social and psychological activity of intending, planning and acting as well as a social obligation to produce some real-world output. Psychologically, it involves a combination of continuous intuitive mental activity and action within a framework set by conscious perceptions and ideas or plans.[1] Socially, work involves carrying out some definite project within a specific time frame.

At the core of the concept of work lies the desire of the individual human being as well as the collective humankind to survive and evolve. It is important to note that the notion of work takes concrete shape only in the context of the various problems and questions that human beings deem important.

The Evolution of Work

In the earliest stages of civilization, work was confined to simple tasks that involved the most basic of human needs: food, shelter and childcare. When crop cultivation began to replace hunting and gathering, the men commonly bore responsibility for seasonal tasks such as ploughing, sowing, tilling and harvesting, while the women cared for children, prepared food and made clothing.[2]

The development of irrigation increased the food supply and allowed larger numbers of people to agglomerate into towns and cities. Some individuals began to pursue crafts such as pottery making, textiles and metallurgy.

As town life grew more vigorous during the Middle Ages, craft guilds were formed in order to regulate production. These guilds also served to limit the supply of labour in any particular profession. Early factories gradually emerged out of these craft workshops. They divided the work carried out by a single craftsman into a number of distinct tasks that were now performed by semi-skilled workers, with the assistance of rudimentary machinery. However, the workers balked at the discipline that such factories demanded of them. Thus, it became necessary to install a supervisory hierarchy. This represented the start of the modern factory system.

The machines introduced during the eighteenth century demanded a rational organization of job functions that differed greatly from the old handicraft tradition. The development of machine tools in the nineteenth century made it possible to manufacture large quantities of goods at relatively low unit costs, through the use of standardized parts and precise division of labour. This phenomenon was referred to as mass production.

The growing size of the manufacturing concerns and the increasing complexity of their operations encouraged the employment of managerial personnel. They specialized in service areas such as accounting, engineering, research and development, human resources, information technology, distribution, marketing and sales.

The American automobile manufacturer Henry Ford designed an assembly line that commenced operations in 1913. As the assembly line spread through American industry, it brought about dramatic productivity gains. Skilled workers increasingly began to be replaced by low-cost unskilled labour.[2]

The next technological development was the automation of work. Automated machinery allowed small numbers of highly skilled workers to operate sophisticated, computer-controlled equipment. The process of manufacturing gained unprecedented flexibility with the advent of computer-enabled automation.

The next step was robotized production. Robotic machines could perform unpleasant or dangerous jobs such as painting, quite easily and without complaint. Moreover, they handled loads of up to a ton or more. Robots have also been making impressive gains in sensitivity, mobility and autonomy. Going forward, they shall serve in a larger variety of roles—from the design and prototyping stages through production and shipping.

Services have now come to represent the growth engine of the world economy. Personal services had hitherto been considered relatively difficult to deliver via robots because they require greater flexibility, adaptability and common sense that these devices could ordinarily deliver. But again, the situation is changing fast.

Future developments in machine intelligence and cognitive computing are likely to facilitate the next round of overwhelming productivity increases. With the help of 3D printing, fast automation, artificial intelligence and advanced IT systems, the manufacturing and service operations of tomorrow are likely to be able to independently coordinate along the entire supply chain and actually run themselves.[3]

Hopefully, they would still work under human oversight!

The Essence of Work

Work may be defined as an organism's use of judgement in making the decisions that are necessary to reach a goal. Human work fundamentally caters to solving problems that come in the way of survival and growth. When a person does not have any problem, she has no obligation to work. This occurs when the basic human needs have been satisfied and psychological conflict has been fully resolved. This actually signifies the state of human fulfilment, of which the sages have spoken since time immemorial.

However, most individuals are still some distance away from complete fulfilment. Problems start with the unavailability of something valuable that a person needs or wants. They may arise either from an individual's personal and intrinsic desires, or from the necessity to accomplish a task towards meeting an organizational requirement. Either way, the person must sort through all the situational elements in order to specify exactly what would satisfy the identified need. A goal is, thus, formulated.

Elliott Jaques provided a brilliant conception of organizational work through outstanding research that spans across half a century. He stated that the specification of a goal comprises two elements[1]:

1. The result that is required, in quantity and quality (what)

2. The target completion date (by when)

Once the goal has been specified, the person must then work to formulate the task for attaining the goal. The task comprises the following:

1. The goal itself—the what and by when

2. The method to be used

3. The resources required

4. The prescribed limits within which the work must be done—policies, rules and regulations

Work may, thus, be regarded as an undertaking to find the means for traversing through the field (as in hockey or football) in order to get to the goal.

Since a field has to be traversed in order to reach the goal, a pathway has to be created. When a person moves across a pathway, she encounters repeated problems and obstacles. To surmount each such problem, the individual is required to muster the available knowledge resources along with the details of the situational context. All this data is processed by means of a range of mental processes that include taking in information, playing with it, analysing and reorganizing it, and judging as well as reasoning with it. An appropriate conclusion or decision is then arrived at. The traversing of an uncertain pathway, thus, requires the continued exercise of discretion, judgement and decision-making.

Mental Processing

Elliott Jaques employs the concept of 'mental processing' to describe a combination of discretion, judgement and decision-making. The complexity of such processing refers to the maximum scale and intricacy of the world that a person is able to pattern, construe and function in. This includes the amount and the complexity of information that must be processed in doing so.[1]

The most elementary aspect of mental processing is that which goes on in words. This is intimately connected with the knowledge that is possessed by the person. Knowledge is accumulated through formal learning and experience. Knowledge is held in memory and is verbally articulated.

The true source of difficulty in any problem lies in its complexity, which may be defined in terms of (a) the number of variables that have to be dealt with in a given time in a situation, (b) the clarity and precision with which they can be identified and (c) their rate of change. The human faculty of *Buddhi* comes into play when the person seeks solutions to increasingly more complex problems.

The Role of *Buddhi* in Mental Processing

Buddhi is the human faculty that enables people to discriminate and comprehend the factual nature of things, as distinguished from mere appearances or speculations. *Buddhi* possesses a dual capacity of being sensory as well as intuitive in nature, depending upon whether it is directed outward or inward.

When *Buddhi* functions externally, it manifests as the human intellect that connects the outer world of the senses with the inner world of consciousness (refer to Chapter 3). The concrete side of the intellect allows people to grasp external objects. This includes the capacity to understand and reason about verbal information and also to recognize, compare and fathom perceptual patterns. On the other hand, the abstract side of the intellect enables people to comprehend ideas.

The acme of this cognitive process is achieved when the operation of the externally oriented intellect is complemented by the use of internally directed intuition. The latter represents the power of direct perception, without the mediation of the human mind and the five senses.

Gary Klein defines intuition as the way individuals translate experience into action.[4] His research concludes that intuition is an important subconscious decision-making tool that originates from an ability to recognize patterns and interpret cues. Klein has demonstrated that intuition is a natural outgrowth of experience and preparation.[4]

When the intellect works in conjunction with intuition, *Buddhi* becomes the mainspring of human creativity. It also acts as the executive part of the human personality that decides what the individual must do or pursue. The functioning of the *Buddhi* involves a continual interplay between overt knowledge and the underlying consciousness. This interchange enables the whispers of consciousness to inform the operations of the *Buddhi* in real time. As a result, the mental effort remains squarely oriented towards the servicing of human needs— which is what the phenomenon of work is all about in the first place.

Work Equals the Use of *Buddhi*

The application of *Buddhi* (inclusive of its intellectual as well as intuitive facets) is central to the process of decision-making, wherein the person makes a choice from among an unlimited number of options just at the moment of truth.

If an individual can completely enumerate all the reasons why she made a decision, she would have merely carried out a calculation. It does not constitute true decision-making. This may be regarded as a particular kind of learned knowledge that comprises learned psychomotor patterns and calculating routines. These help to simplify work by enabling a person to carry out parts of a problem-solving activity, without having to think about them. Skilled knowledge can be improved with practice.[1]

The knowledge of procedures that people learn to use at work without having to think about can be described as 'skilled' knowledge. It is possible to develop skilled knowledge to support literally anything that a person does. When a particular type of task or routine is carried out often enough, the individual might begin to perform the activity without the active use of the intellect. For instance, the famous cardiac surgeon Dr Devi Shetty is known to listen to an assistant's narration of office documents that require his urgent attention, even when he is engaged in stitching up a patient's heart in the operation theatre (OT) after a successful surgery.

However, skilled knowledge is not equivalent to work. This is because when all non-verbal judgement is taken out of a decision, it becomes a mere calculation. The possible outcomes are predictably limited and the process may, thus, be mechanized or computerized. Computers and robots are unable to even approach human choice processes, because they cannot deal with ideas, perceptions, feelings and emotions that have not yet been verbalized.

Even though modern computers increasingly appear to be intelligent, they cannot authentically serve human needs without the guidance of human consciousness that the *Buddhi* provides.

Thus, the core effort in making judgements and decisions involves the processing of knowledge elements by human intelligence in order to arrive at accurate conclusions. These outputs subsequently emerge into verbalized mental awareness and become available for use in problem-solving. That is work!

References

1. Jaques E. *A General Theory of Bureaucracy*. London: Heinemann; 1976. pp. 18, 25, 99, 117.

2. Kranzberg M & Hannan MT. History of the organization of work. *Encyclopedia Britannica*. Available at: www.britannica.com/topic/history-of-work-organization-648000 (accessed: 5 May 1999).

3. Kilpi E. *Perspectives on New Work: Exploring Emerging Conceptualizations*. 2nd ed. Sitra Studies; 2016. p. 114. Available at: www.oph.fi/download/188379_Esko_Kilpi_on_New_Work.pdf (accessed: 5 May 2018).

4. Klein G. *Intuition at Work*. New York, NY: Currency/Doubleday; 2003.

PART III

THE APPROACH

THE APPRECIATIVE CULTURE

5

No man is an island; every man is a piece of the continent, a part of the main. Any man's death diminishes me, because I am involved in mankind.

—*John Donne*

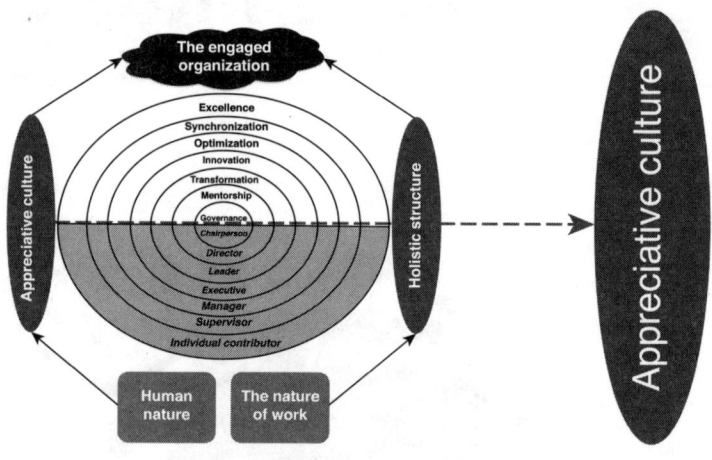

Appreciative Culture
Source: Samatvam Academy

The twenty-first century is witnessing the re-emergence of a timeless perspective that is fundamentally reorienting the institutional approach towards building a healthy organizational culture. The focus of institutional effort is progressively shifting away from the correction of deficits and weaknesses towards the affirmation of strengths and capabilities that reside within individuals, teams and organizations.[1]

This is referred to as the appreciative paradigm or the strengths-centric approach.

The notion of appreciation possesses many of the cognitive and emotional elements that are important for the experience of satisfaction and happiness in life. While the construct was initially equated with being positive, it now includes all kinds of linguistic constructions that are considered as life enhancing.[2]

The appreciative approach embodies respect for the uniqueness and inherent worth of each individual in the society. Drawing upon humanistic psychology as well as contemporary scientific research, it emphasizes the discovery of the positive features in every human system. The latent potential that resides within the people may then be harnessed towards individual benefit as well as collective gain.

The basic necessities of harmonious social existence are preservation of human dignity (unconditional respect for every human being) and empowerment (the freedom to make informed choices at work). The salient attributes of the appreciative paradigm are precisely these. They contribute mightily towards the development of a constructive and humane organizational culture.

The Characteristics of Appreciation

Appreciation is the process of placing a value upon something and bestowing love and attention upon it. Mitchel Adler[3] defines appreciation as 'acknowledging the value and meaning of something (an event, person, behavior or object), and feeling a positive emotional connection to it'.

The phenomenon of appreciation is characterized by a focus on what the person has (as opposed to what one lacks) as well as a keen experiential awareness from moment to moment. It involves being one with the perceived object and feeling deeply connected with it.

Empirical experience indicates that people can locate positive worth in any given situation when they firmly make up their mind to do so.

For instance, the Viennese psychotherapist Viktor Frankl managed to find a tremendous sense of personal strength and meaning even during his incarceration as a prisoner at a concentration camp of the Third Reich. He was therefore successful at helping many of his distraught mates in doing so too. Frankl was thereby instrumental in saving many lives during that most deplorable of episodes in human history.[4]

The capacity for genuine appreciation is tremendously valuable in facilitating individual as well as institutional vitality. Every individual is inherently capable of locating the positive facets of a situation and of making constructive judgements thereupon. However, it is to be borne in mind that he/she may legitimately approach the circumstance in an evaluative vein and look out for defects—without necessarily being non-appreciative.

For instance, an appreciative stance is easily seen as fundamental to the practices of teaching and mentoring that involve the articulation and development of the interests and talents of the learner. On the other hand, a medical consultant is expected to critically evaluate the patient's situation and symptoms prior to making a diagnosis and prescribing treatment.

If the medico is able to expertly carry out this work with genuine empathy and compassion, and refrain from exploiting the situation for narrow or unworthy ends, this approach too shall count as being appreciative. This is because an appreciative stance values all the numerous different ways of knowing and being. Each one of these is potentially assumed to have some contextual validity.

This leads to a capacity for openness, which is very useful in the modern workplace that is characterized by an array of distinctive values, beliefs and aspirations as well as racial, religious, gender and diversity.

The integrative nature of the appreciative approach helps people to creatively transcend discord. It nips any potential tendency towards majority dominance or social conformity in the bud.

However, appreciation ceases to remain significant as a positive sentiment when it is employed as a manipulative tool to exploit or secure profit. Pseudo-appreciation is a counterproductive strategy that is not able to deceive anyone for too long and eventually spells a cultural disaster.

Connectedness—The Soul of Appreciation

Human beings are observed to readily 'connect' with that which they consider as a part of their core self—or its extension in any form and manner. For instance, a mother effortlessly locates beauty, strength, character and other positive or desirable attributes in her own child. She may not find it as easy to spot these qualities in a neighbour's child who has been acting as a bully, or in the case of another who has emerged ahead of her own offspring in the classroom or in a sports competition.

On the other hand, the poet or sage who has meditatively experienced all manner of division and differentiation to be illusory in nature is able to locate beauty, wonder and awe in all of creation.

The Bhagavad Gita (chapter 2, verse 47) enjoins that every person has the right to perform one's prescribed duties, but the fruits of those actions are not under the control or the purview of the individual. Thus, nobody should consider oneself to be the cause of the results of one's activities. Yet none should slide into inaction. This is a succinct statement of *Karma Yoga* or the Yoga of Action. It offers a deep insight into the way human work may be performed in a world or universe whose constituent elements (so to speak) are inextricably 'connected' together.

Individuals who accept wholeness as the essential characteristic of human existence rest secure in the knowledge that there are innumerable cross-linkages and forces larger than one's individual desire, will or effort that eventually determine the occurrence (or otherwise) of external events. However, does that mean that such people are unwilling to achieve results, or are incapable of doing so?

The truth is perhaps the opposite. When the anxiety for achievement drops away, the person's vitality does not get leaked or dissipated in stress and worry. It is now devoted to the actual pursuit of the outcomes. The chances of accomplishment, thus, improve significantly. Such people are also better positioned to locate the true, the good, the beautiful and the valuable elements in the world outside without feeling intrinsically threatened by these in any manner.

Conversely, a reluctance to accept the 'connected' nature of life stunts the person's capacity for genuine appreciation. To ascribe a sense of limitation to that which is limitless has traditionally been looked upon as a form of nescience. The sage Patanjali (*Yoga Sutras, Sadhana Pada*, sutra 5) regards it as a primary human affliction that is the substantive source and root cause of human misery.[5]

The acknowledgement of 'connectedness' helps to expand one's self-identity to include all of life and even beyond. This leads to the development of a sense of positivity and an intrinsic faith in the larger process of life. People then engage in action from the positive belief and understanding that all of what happens in one's life is eventually for one's own good.

Positivity—The Effect of Appreciation

Positivity represents the visible expression of appreciation in human life.

A longitudinal study of college students coping with ordinary life problems found that positive emotions correlated with the use of creative and broad-minded coping strategies.[6] In another longitudinal assessment of college students before and after the 9/11 attacks at New York's World Trade Centre, positive emotions were found to be associated with psychological resilience.[7]

Positive emotions help to break down the sense of 'us versus them'.[8] They have also been found to help bring about satisfaction at work, physical health, effective problem-solving and other outcomes.[9]

ENGAGE!

Appreciation in Action: The Strengths-Centric Approach

The phenomenon of appreciation forms the bedrock of the contemporary strengths-based approach to human and organization development. This paradigm places a deep value upon the capacity, skills, knowledge and abilities that lie dormant within individuals as well as institutions.

The strengths-centric approach revolves around the integration of personal talents into one's action repertoire. Its focus is upon the careful discovery and utilization of human abilities that drive exceptional performance, without ignoring situational challenges or naively portraying struggles and gaps as strengths. As Steve Jobs advised the graduating students at Stanford University in 2004, 'The only way to do great work is to love what you do. If you haven't found it yet, keep looking!'[10]

When one's inherent talents are deployed, it feels effective, easy and natural. Before the activity, one has a feeling of anticipation. The conduct of the activity is characterized by focus and inquisitiveness. After the activity, authenticity and fulfilment are experienced.

Nevertheless, strengths may not be directly correlated with the performance that may result from their deployment. There are many activities that people may do well, but nevertheless find these as a drain upon their energy. Such activities are more properly called as weaknesses.

For instance, the initial career choices of the youth are usually dictated more by job prospects and peer pressure than by intrinsic interests of the individual. Youngsters even manage to excel at their adopted profession for a while, by the force of sheer willpower or external support. Eventually, such people get burnt out in due course of time because the work leaves them drained. This is a weakness in action.

Irrespective of personal competence, 'strength' is an attribute that *strengthens* the person when it is deployed while a 'weakness' is anything that appears to *weaken* the individual when engaged with it.[11]

THE APPRECIATIVE CULTURE

Just as different individuals possess diverse strengths, they are unique in their weak attributes too. The strategies for managing the weakness range from a minimum acceptable performance in the weak area to maximizing a strength area so that it can compensate for or even overshadow the deficit.

For instance, the deaf and blind girl Helen Keller became one of the most remarkable women in history despite her physical disabilities. This became possible on the strength of her determination and courage.

Every individual must therefore closely examine her personal needs, desires and capabilities. These are key to value creation by the individual for society. Work tasks should be chosen according to personal strengths as well as abilities. Each person must professionally engage only with those activities that she wants to do and also possesses the capability of doing them well.

The Appreciative Individual

A verse from the ancient Indian text *Subhashita Ratna Bhandagara* (chapter 3, verse 162) states, 'There is no alphabet without power; no root without medicinal property; no person without ability; but rare is the [appreciative] person who can connect, organize and utilize the myriad words, things and people of the world'.[12]

This suggests that genuinely appreciative people are precious, but relatively uncommon commodities. While that holds broadly true in contemporary organizational life, it is equally correct that an appreciative individual is hard to miss on account of the vivacity and zest that characterizes such a being.

The appreciative individual possesses a seemingly enigmatic capacity to infuse collective action with a deeper sense of meaning and purpose. He/she becomes a sculptor of elevating conversations and inspires her colleagues to act upon exalted values that transcend the material plane and conditions of the world.

ENGAGE!

Appreciative individuals operate from the belief that human life is not so much a *problem-to-be-solved*, as it is a *mystery-to-be-embraced*. They possess an uncanny ability to see deeply into persons and circumstances, perhaps because their perception is infused with insight and imagination. These people engage in a rational as well as an emotional assessment of the situation, before formulating a response.[13]

Appreciative individuals create organizational contexts that are supportive of constructive creativity. They encourage people to engage in serious play with ideas and concepts, juggle impossible juxtapositions, consider wild hypothesis, express the ridiculous and take spontaneous hunches as serious prospects. Such individuals also provide direction and exercise control when necessary, but do so in ways that liberate (rather than constrain) the capacity for innovation.

Appreciative personalities create a climate of psychological safety that is characterized by a spirit of openness to experience and tolerance for ambiguity. Instead of punishing the negatives or encouraging complaints about shortcomings, they build a culture of praise, encouragement and empowerment. In the firm belief that every individual has inherent worth and boundless potential, these people guide, facilitate and enable their colleagues to deliver their personal best—time after time.

Appreciative individuals also encourage people to broaden their perspective, so that they may learn to spot the proverbial 'woods' together with the 'trees'. This facilitates the ingenious integration of opposing values or conflicting priorities. Such an inclusive approach forms the very basis of a synergistic way of organizing and yields individual effectiveness alongside institutional benefit.

As an example, Sir Richard Branson is the well-known founder of the United Kingdom's Virgin Group. He features in the list of the world's top 500 billionaires. Being dyslexic, Sir Richard had a difficult childhood. He left studies without finishing high school on account of poor academic performance.

The secret of Sir Richard's phenomenal business success lies in his ability to remain calm and relaxed in the face of contradiction and ambiguity. This has enabled him to develop innovative new businesses within the context of uncertainty. The organizational culture at Virgin tolerates and even celebrates failure, because it is virtually impossible to innovate and grow without trying something new.

Virgin is also characterized by an employee-first mindset. Branson says, 'If you take care of your employees, your employees will take care of your customers and your customers will take care of your shareholders'.[14] He emphasizes that it is very important to look out *for* the best in people all the time, so that you can eventually draw out the best *in* them.

ENGAGE!

Sir Richard Branson perennially remains on the lookout for people who can complement his own abilities. He has thereby mastered the art of delegation that many so-called 'intelligent' people struggle with. An appreciative outlook, thus, enabled Sir Richard to rapidly establish several businesses, such that the Virgin Group is now a highly successful conglomerate—comprising of over 400 different companies.

The Appreciative Culture

The culture of any organization refers to a system of shared assumptions, values and beliefs that govern how people behave in organizations.[15] It represents a set of shared norms that guide what happens in a collective setting, by defining appropriate behaviour for various situations. Accordingly, culture may also be regarded as the self-sustaining pattern of behaviour that determines how things are done.

Incidentally, Elliott Jaques was the first management researcher to employ the term 'culture' in the organizational context. In his book *The Changing Culture of a Factory* (1951), he described 'organizational culture' as the customary and traditional way of thinking and doing things that is shared to a greater or lesser degree by all its members.[16]

Every organization develops and maintains a unique culture, which provides guidelines and boundaries for the behaviour of its members. An appreciative approach to organizational functioning helps to create an engaging institutional culture that evokes inspired action.

Since the appreciative mindset is a holistic one, it minimizes boundaries across the larger ecosystem of the organization. People are aware of the entire picture, how everything fits together and how the various parts of the organization interact with each other and with the external environment. Ideas bubble up from across the system in order to help the organization seize opportunities and manage crises. The organization thereby manages to create a sense of delight for all its stakeholders.

An appreciative culture is based upon equality. Every person is encouraged to be oneself. People use their natural style, which permits the full and free expression of their innate self. Individuals earnestly try to do their best. Trust and collaboration prevail. Chronic conflicts and tensions are conspicuous by their absence. The attrition is low.

The appreciative culture represents an attempt to return to the agile conditions of a classic entrepreneurial firm. There is widespread sharing of information across the institution so that people can act quickly. Formal systems are implemented in order to manage large amounts of complex information and to detect deviations from established standards. The accumulated actions of an informed and empowered workforce contribute to strategy development. Newer channels of communication are opened with customers, suppliers and even competitors. Ideas flow in all directions.

Patagonia Inc. (Case Study: Patagonia) provides a good example of an appreciative organizational culture. Whole Foods Market (Case Study: Whole Foods Market) presents another fine instance of a constructive cultural paradigm. Both of these organizations are highly inclusive by design. They look upon their employees and associates as 'sources' rather than resources and place them at the heart of their activities.

These two institutions actively involve their people in all aspects of organizational functioning and look after their well-being too. Promoting the vitality of the community or the planet is also central to their charter and forms an integral part of the higher purpose for which they exist.

The leaders of Patagonia and Whole Foods Market are remarkable visionaries. They look beyond the limited human self and organize their activities around the Higher Self. In the mould of JRD Tata, they concentrate on 'the ounce of gold' in their colleagues and overlook the mounds of earth that must be mined in order to reach it. These pragmatic idealists infuse their people with a missionary zeal to serve the community/society in a manner that leads to organizational prosperity at the same time.

In their own unique way, both the enterprises strive for synergy between (a) the employees/people, (b) profit and (c) the humanity/ planet. That is the reason why they are characterized by a constructive organizational culture. The structure of the organizations is also organic in nature. This allows for an easy flow of communication across organizational levels and facilitates collaboration across boundaries.

The culture and the structure come together to create a highly engaging workplace in both these instances. As a result, Patagonia and Whole Foods Market manage to evoke intense loyalty from their people—who work for the enterprise with all their heart and soul.

Appreciative Capacity

The following four competencies are critical for nurturing the human capacity for appreciation[17]:

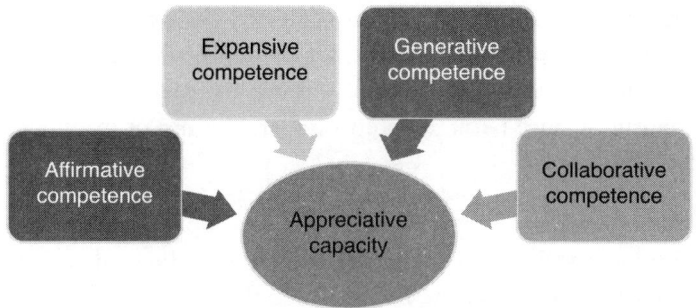

The Development of Appreciative Capacity
Source: Samatvam Academy

1. **Affirmative competence:** The ability to identify positive possibilities by focusing upon successes and strengths, without being dismissive of existing imperfections

2. **Expansive competence:** The ability to challenge the existing organizational thinking and practices in order to stretch the capability of its people

3. **Generative competence:** The ability to create integrative systems that allow people to see the consequences of their actions and to recognize them when they make meaningful contributions

4. **Collaborative competence:** The ability to create spaces and forums, wherein people can freely engage in dialogue and exchange diverse perspectives

Developing Appreciative Capacity

The scientific world view that dominated the minds and intellects of the twentieth century effectively discouraged people from taking cognizance of all those deep inner experiences from which human societies had historically obtained their ultimate sense of purpose and guiding values.

The traditional scientific paradigm neglected the exploration of the higher human aspirations and ideologies that could help people to navigate the course of their lives. As a result, the cosmos described by materialistic science became bereft of a larger sense of meaning and nobility of purpose.

On the other hand, any endeavour to develop one's appreciative capacity inevitably awakens the desire to inquire beyond superficial appearances into the deeper, life-enhancing essentials.[18] The phenomenon of appreciation is then found to be a function of how people identify their own self in the first place, and thereafter how they look upon the external object in relation to themselves.

Appreciative individuals possess an expansive consciousness. They look beyond narrow 'personal' concerns and see all as one as well as oneself in all.

Jamsetji Tata, the founder of the venerable Tata Group, was one such personality. The enterprise started by him was nurtured and expanded by his successors over a period of 150 years. It remains as India's largest business house to this day. The next case study tells the incomparable story of this remarkable conglomerate that 'also' does business!

ENGAGE!

References

1. Cederbaum J & Klusaritz HA. Clinical instruction: Using the strengths-based approach with nursing students. *Journal of Nursing Education*. 2009; 48(8): 422–428.

2. Barge JK & Oliver C. Working with appreciation in managerial practice. *Academy of Management Review*. 2003; 28(1): 124–142.

3. Adler M. Conceptualizing and measuring appreciation: The development of a positive psychology construct [Doctoral dissertation]. New Brunswick, NJ: Rutgers University; 2002.

4. Frankl V. *Man's Search for Meaning*. Boston, MA: Beacon Press; 2006.

5. Hariharananda Aranya S. *Yoga Philosophy of Patanjali with Bhasvati*. 4th ed. Calcutta: University of Calcutta; 2000.

6. Fredrickson BL & Joiner T. Positive emotions trigger upward spirals towards emotional well-being. *Psychological Science*. 2002; 13(2): 172–175.

7. Fredrickson BL, Tugade MM, Waugh CE & Larkin G. What good are positive emotions in crisis a prospective study of resilience and emotions following the terrorist attacks on the United States on September 11th, 2001. *Journal of Personality and Social Psychology*. 2003; 84(2): 365–376.

8. Dovidio JF, Gaertner SL, Isen AM & Lowrance R. Group representations and intergroup bias: Positive affect, similarity, and group size. *Personality and Social Psychology Bulletin*. 1995; 21(8): 856–865.

9. Lyubomirsky S, King L & Diener E. The benefits of frequent positive affect does happiness lead to success. *Psychological Bulletin*. 2005; 131: 803–855.

10. Jobs S. *Stay Hungry, Stay Foolish*. Stanford: Speech presented at Stanford University; 2004.

11. Buckingham M & Clifton D. *Now, Discover Your Strengths*. London: Pocket Books; 2001.

12. Paraba K & Acharya N. *Subhashita Ratna Bhandagara*. Bombay: Nirnaya Sagar Press; 1886.

13. Srivastva S & Cooperrider D. *Appreciative Management and Leadership*. Euclid, OH: Williams Custom Publishing; 1999.

14. Schawbel D. Richard Branson: His views on entrepreneurship, well-being and work friendships. *Forbes.com*. 2017. Available at: https://www.forbes.com/sites/danschawbel/2017/10/23/richard-branson-his-views-on-entrepreneurship-well-being-and-work-friendships/#708ff83755d2 (accessed: 31 May 2018).

15. Watkins MD. What is organizational culture? And why should we care? *Harvard Business Review*. Available at: https://hbr.

org/2013/05/what-is-organizational-culture (accessed: 20 August 2018).

16. Jaques E. *The Changing Culture of a Factory*. West Devon: Tavistock Publication Limited; 1951.

17. Barrett FJ. Creating appreciative learning cultures. *Organizational Dynamics*. 1995; 24(2): 36–49.

18. Adler MG & Fagley NS. Appreciation: Individual differences in finding value and meaning as a unique predictor of subjective well-being. *Journal of Personality*. 2005; 73(1): 79–113.

ENGAGE!

THE TATA GROUP

In a free enterprise, the community is not just another stakeholder in business—but is in fact the very purpose of its existence.

—*Jamsetji Tata*

BACKGROUND

Founded by the legendary pioneer Jamsetji Tata in 1868, the Tata Group is one of India's oldest private sector business entities. A global enterprise that operates in over 100 countries across six continents, the Tata Group has been India's largest business house almost uninterruptedly for over a century now. Its companies collectively clocked revenues of ₹673,347 crore during FY 2016–2017; on the other hand, the 29 publicly listed entities among these together possessed a market capitalization of ₹944,057 crore (as on 28 March 2018).

With its deeply entrepreneurial and patriotic spirit, the Tata Group established several industries of national importance. It started India's steel industry at Jamshedpur in 1907, and also set up the nation's first major hydroelectric power project (at Khopoli) in 1910. Meanwhile, Jamsetji Tata had constructed the country's first luxury hotel in 1903. The Taj Mahal Hotel was Mumbai's first building to use electricity and was equipped with American fans, German elevators, Turkish baths and English butlers.

The India Cement Company was set up in 1912, while the Tata Industrial Bank took shape in 1917. The Group also brought civil aviation to India in 1932, when the Tata Aviation Service took to the skies. In fact, Jehangir Ratanji Dadabhoy Tata (hereafter JRD) held the Indian Pilot License Number 001.

The Tata Group proactively introduced several labour welfare benefits at their facilities, including an eight-hour working day, free medical aid, leave with pay, provident fund scheme, workmen's accident compensation scheme, maternity benefits, profit sharing bonus and retirement gratuity. Most of these welfare initiatives were incorporated into national statutory legislation, several years after they were first introduced at the Tata Group.

Headquartered in Mumbai, the Tata Group is highly decentralized in nature. It presently comprises nearly 100 operating companies that collectively employ around 700,000 people. Each company is relatively independent and operates autonomously under the guidance and supervision of its own board of directors. The Group manages the relationship with its member companies through its representatives on their Boards.

The Tata Group is governed by a complex, interwoven federal structure. Tata Sons is its principal investment holding company.

Tata Sons is the promoter of the various Tata companies and maintains an equity stake in nearly all of them. It sets the overall strategy for the Group and provides investment capital to its affiliate companies as required.

The Tata corporate brand serves to unify the Group. It embodies the cherished values of integrity, excellence, understanding, responsibility and unity. However, different group entities use the Tata brand in different ways. While Tata Steel, Tata Motors and several others explicitly use the corporate name and logo, many others such as Trent and Taj Hotels refrain from doing so.[1]

A business excellence and brand promotion (BEBP) agreement governs the manner and extent of the use of the Tata brand by the respective Group companies. These companies pay Tata Sons a nominal fee that is used to run centralized services for the benefit of all the Group companies.

The pattern of corporate behaviour of the House of Tata was established by the business ideas, strategies and ethics of Jamsetji Tata. Over nearly 150 years of existence, the Tata Group has been led by visionaries who stayed true to the values of its founder. Dorabji Tata, the elder son of Jamsetji, succeeded the latter as the group chairperson in 1904. After Dorabji's death in 1932, Jamsetji's nephew Nowroji Saklatwala took over as the Tata chairman.

Bharat Ratna JRD, the son of Jamsetji's cousin and business partner R. D. Tata, came next. Remaining as chairman for 53 years, JRD guided the Group from the pre-Independence era right until the economic liberalization of 1991. Ratan N. Tata (hereafter RNT), the great grandson of the founder, held the forte thereafter till 2012. Cyrus Mistry became the next chairman of the Tata Group. He held the position for the next four years, before being unceremoniously ejected in 2016.

Natarajan Chandrasekaran is the current chairman of the Tata Group.

THE SOCIAL MANDATE

The Tata Group was originally founded for the purpose of creating and spreading wealth in order to strengthen the Indian nation. Its present mission is to improve the quality of life among the communities that it serves globally.

Tata Sons remains a closely held firm. Two-thirds of its equity share capital is held by philanthropic trusts that have endowed institutions for science and technology, medical research, social studies and the performing arts. The Tata Trusts also provide aid and assistance to non-governmental organizations working in the areas of education, health care and livelihoods.[2] In addition, a wide range of social welfare activities are independently undertaken by the individual Group companies at their locations.

Jamsetji Tata placed the greater good of society at par with business growth. His belief in returning to society manifold of what the business earns from the people continues to form the bedrock of the Tata culture. Few other corporations of comparable size and visibility across the world have been known to place their charitable arm at the controlling nexus of the business. This evokes deep trust and respect among its customers, employees and the community.

The commitment of the House of Tata to protect its heritage of trusteeship was poignantly on display after the 2008 terrorist attack in Mumbai. This assault had badly damaged the Group's flagship hotel—the Taj Mahal Palace and Tower.

The Tata Group directly oversaw the medical treatment of injured staff members, and paid generous health and school tuition benefits to the families of all slain individuals. This included railway employees, police officers and even the passers-by who had had no direct connection with the hotel before the attack. The hotel itself was repaired and re-opened within a year of the tragic event.

The Tata Group operates on the premise that a business thrives on social capital (the value created by investing in the greater good to community and human relationships) as much as it does on hard assets.

THE DORABJI TATA ERA: THE ERA OF DISCIPLINED GROWTH

Jamsetji's idea of philanthropy found true and ample expression in the work of his sons Dorab and Ratan, both of who donated a major chunk of their personal wealth for public good. Sir Dorab Tata was the quintessential entrepreneur who worked tirelessly to make his father's visionary ideas a reality. He roamed the jungles of Jharkhand in a bullock cart to set up Tata Steel, and also pioneered the generation of hydroelectric power in the wilderness of the Western Ghats. On the other hand, Sir Ratan Tata was a connoisseur of the arts and a passionate votary of social development.

Following Jamsetji's death in 1904, the chairmanship of the Tata Group passed on to Dorabji Tata. At that time, the fledgling Tata Group owned three textile mills and the Taj Mahal Hotel in Mumbai. Dorabji guided all the three unfulfilled passions of his father's life to fruition—the steel mill, the hydroelectric plant and the Indian Institute of Science at Bengaluru.[3]

Under Dorabji's stewardship, the Tata Group also added two other electric power companies, an edible oil and soap company, two cement companies, a leading insurance company and an aviation unit. The other industrial companies established during Dorabji's tenure were those that manufactured and supplied commercial goods such as tinplate, steel tubes and transport vehicles—which India did not have at that time.

Dorabji Tata expanded Jamsetji's commitment to economic development and community welfare to include the workplace. In 1917, he invited the famous British social scientists Beatrice and Sidney Webb to recommend a medical services policy for his employees The Tata Iron and Steel Company was the worldwide pioneer in instituting modern pension systems, workers' compensation, maternity benefits and profit-sharing plans.

Dorabji Tata's business sense and audacity saw the steel company undertaking a five-fold expansion programme in the post-World War I period.[3] However, spiralling costs combined with transport and labour difficulties in the West and an earthquake in Japan upset his calculations. Steel prices tumbled, and the venture slipped into trouble in 1924. It got to a point when there was not enough money in its coffers to pay wages to the steelworkers. However, Dorabji's commitment to his father's vision and values was so strong that he staked his entire fortune (including his wife's personal jewellery) to save the steel company.

Like his father, Dorabji too believed that wealth ought to be put to constructive use. Among his most valuable legacies was the establishment of the Sir Dorabji Tata Trust. The mandate of this Trust is to advance learning and research and relieve human distress, without any distinction of place, nationality or creed. Its trustees were empowered to sell all of Dorabji's lands, securities and jewellery. However, they were not permitted to withdraw the shares of Tata Sons that he had to his credit. In this manner, Dorabji sought to ensure the integrity of the parent firm.

Sir Dorabji gave the credit for his achievements to Jamsetji's pioneering spirit. It was his belief that 'kind' fate had enabled him to advance his father's inestimable legacy of service to the country.

NOWROJI SAKLATWALA: THE ERA OF SKILFUL NAVIGATION

Nowroji Saklatvala, the son of Jamsetji's sister, became the third chairman of the Tata Group in 1932. Confronted with the task of consolidation during the global depression of those years, Sir Nowroji steered the Group admirably through a difficult period during his six-year tenure.

Nowroji saw consolidation and cost control as his most urgent task. He focused upon Tata's iron and steel, textile, banking and power sectors. Doing 'more with less' became his mantra.

Then, he turned his attention to integrating the several cement businesses in India for the sake of their continued survival. Blessed by an ability to listen to all the sides and to bring rationality to the table, Nowroji was successful in helping find a common ground among the conflicting interests of the several players in the cement industry. Thanks to his diplomacy, the various businesses were saved and merged to form the Associated Cement Companies (ACC).

Within the Group, Nowroji was seen as a valuable team member who put his Tata colleagues and employees before himself. Although comfortable working behind the scenes, Nowroji was not afraid to accept responsibilities or to speak his mind. Blessed with the traits of respect, leadership and flexibility, he worked closely beside Dorabji as a Tata inner circle member.[4]

Sir Nowroji was a visionary who placed a tremendous premium on staff welfare. As the Tata chairman, he provided the labour force with unprecedented benefits and privileges that included an innovative profit-sharing scheme. In September 1937, he raised the wages of the lowest paid workers and improved the service conditions of temporary employees at Tata Steel in Jamshedpur.

The well-being of the people was always at the heart of whatever Sir Nowroji did. No work, especially that which benefited people, was too small for the big man.

JRD TATA: THE ERA OF EXPANSION

JRD was the chairman of the Tata Group for an extraordinary 53 years after Sir Nowroji passed away. He nurtured the Tata Group's reputation for integrity and innovation and is credited with expanding its activities in India after the country gained independence.

JRD had joined the Tata Group as an unpaid apprentice in December 1925 under the tutelage of John Peterson, a retired Indian Civil Service officer. The following year, JRD's father R. D. Tata passed away.

The 22-year-old JRD was then appointed as a director on the Board of Tata Sons. When he was elevated as the chairman in 1938, JRD was the youngest member of the Tata Sons Board.

With the Group having passed through several years of financial struggle, JRD's mandate was expansion. Over his five decades of stewardship, the Tata business grew from 14 companies to 95. Simultaneously, its assets ballooned from $100 million to over $5 billion. The Group entered into chemicals, automobiles, beverages and information technology.

JRD's unflinching and unwavering commitment to the highest principles and standards was the light that forever illuminated his path and guided his actions.

JRD was an unusually warm and caring person. He is considered a meritorious leader as he got on with individuals according to their ways and characteristics. This sometimes involved self-suppression, which he considered as painful but necessary. He held that a true leader was one who could lead human beings with 'affection'.

JRD was a deeply appreciative soul. He concentrated on 'the ounce of gold' in his colleagues, and overlooked the mounds of earth that must be mined to reach it. JRD inspired performance and never needed to command it. He touched power, but personally remained untouched by it.

JRD detested pomposity and avoided the public eye. He fit perfectly into Bob Galvin's mould of humility, which 'does not mean that one thinks less of oneself; it means that one thinks of oneself less'. For instance, upon being informed that the Indian government was bestowing the Bharat Ratna (the country's highest civilian award) upon him, JRD is reported to have said, 'Why me? I don't deserve it'.

Most of all, JRD came to represent an exalted idea of Indian-ness—progressive, benevolent, ethical and compassionate. To JRD, the term 'national interest' meant advancing the country's scientific and economic capacities. He had strong views on what would help India in its gigantic struggle to eradicate poverty. Other people did not necessarily agree with his views on issues such as the country's economic model, its growing population, or even its business practices. However, nobody ever doubted the nobility of JRD's intent. He will always remain as a symbol of integrity and righteousness.

RATAN TATA: THE ERA OF INTERNATIONALIZATION

RNT assumed the chairmanship of the Tata Group when JRD passed on the baton to him in 1991. RNT was the son of Naval Tata, who had been adopted by Jamsetji's younger daughter-in-law Navjibai Tata. Naval Tata was closely involved with the Tata Group for over five decades and was elected to the governing body of the International Labour Organization (ILO) 13 times.

Appreciating that the organizational culture created by JRD made it impossible to rule by fiat, RNT decided to invest financially in each company. This helped to increase Tata Sons' direct control of key Group entities. As the chairman of the Tata Trusts that held majority stakes in several Tata companies, RNT utilized this additional indirect leverage upon these firms. These moves helped to re-establish productive ties with the companies, and helped to catalyse their mutual cooperation with one another.

In addition to acquiring a strategic financial stake in key companies, RNT promulgated the Tata Code of Conduct (TCoC) in 1998. This served to unite the (then) contentious individual companies in their adherence to a common purpose and set of values. It also helped to build a uniform ethical identity for the Tata Group and all its constituents.[5]

In order to seal the task of integrating the Group, RNT instituted a corporate branding initiative. This was designed to reposition the Tata Group as a progressive Business House. It also served to clarify which companies constituted the Tata core.

Under this novel scheme, each company was required to earn the right to use the Tata name through a BEBP agreement with Tata Sons. The BEBP document outlined the business principles that a Group company had to sign up for before it was permitted to use the Tata brand or logo. Instead of the Tata name being imposed on the affiliated companies, this brand was leveraged to bring the divergent companies back into the Tata fold.

These measures to assimilate the Group companies together, and to create a common set of business expectations and practices, were admirable. These were tremendously effective too, as they led to the House of Tata becoming whole once again!

RNT had taken over as the group chairman just prior to the liberalization of India's economy. While the Indian businesses were protected from external competition at that time, they were also limited by very tight government controls. RNT surmised that liberalization was both an opportunity and a threat for the Tatas. While growth became relatively easier under the new regime, the Group was deeply vulnerable on account of several of its companies being overmanned and undermanaged.

Further, the Tata Group's brand identity as well as business interest were strongly rooted in the Indian national culture and history.

However, when the markets gradually opened up as a result of the economic reforms, the Group swiftly moved to internationalize itself.[1]

In the new millennium, Tata's international acquisitions transformed the Group from a primarily Indian corporate into one of the world's most visible conglomerates. The first major acquisition was that of Tetley Tea (one of Britain's leading tea brands) in the year 2000. This move went almost unnoticed. In 2007, Tata Steel acquired the Anglo-Dutch steel giant Corus for an excessive $12.1 billion. That same year, the Indian Hotels Company renamed Boston's venerable Ritz-Carlton Hotel as the Taj Boston after acquiring it for $134 million. In 2008, Tata Motors acquired Jaguar Land Rover (JLR) for $2.3 billion.

The changes were dramatic. From being identified with secure employment ('for shoes there's Bata, and for jobs there's Tata'), the Group now became obsessed with customer service of international standards. Over two-thirds of the Tata revenues were earned abroad during RNT's time.

In December 2012, RNT assumed the title of chairman emeritus after relinquishing his position as the head of the Tata Group in favour of Cyrus Mistry. This was the first instance in history when the Group Chairman was drawn from outside the Tata family. This was a remarkable feat, which spoke volumes about the level of openness that the Tata Group had embraced during RNT's tenure.

CYRUS MISTRY: THE ERA OF CONSOLIDATION

Cyrus P. Mistry was appointed as the Chairman of Tata Sons in December 2012, at a relatively young age of 44 years. As the successor to RNT, Cyrus Mistry was the sixth chairman in the relatively long history of the Tata Group. He was only the second one from outside the immediate Tata family.

Innovation was one of Cyrus Mistry's pet themes. A group technology and innovation office was created to lead research and deliver innovative products and services across the Tata Group. The domains of energy, food and wellness, digital consumer products and services, and digital factory and fleets were identified as its focus areas.

After the remarkable expansion that took place under his predecessor, Cyrus Mistry undertook some steely measures in the interest of consolidating the operations of the Group. However, there was no sign of the emergence of an expansive vision that had been the hallmark of the Tata leadership in the past.

In October 2016, in a relatively sudden and highly controversial move, Cyrus Mistry was 'replaced' as the chairman of Tata Sons—the parent company of the Tata Group.

While no cogent reasons were provided for the move, it was alleged that Cyrus Mistry had eroded the values and the ethos of the Tata Group. He was also accused of dismantling its governance structure in order to centralize the power in his own hands. There were counter-allegations of corruption, constant interference in operational functioning, poor corporate governance and the lack of empowerment towards taking tough business decisions that appeared to be the need of the hour for the Group.

NATARAJAN CHANDRASEKARAN: THE ERA OF AGGRESSION

Upon Cyrus Mistry's untimely dismissal, RNT became the interim chairman of the Group for a period of four months. The erstwhile chief of Tata Consultancy Services (TCS) Natarajan Chandrasekaran 'Chandra' was thereafter appointed as the new chairman of Tata Sons on 21 February 2017.

A computer engineer who joined TCS from campus in 1987 and became its CEO in 2009, Chandra brought with him an unparalleled track record of value creation and visionary leadership that was the need of the hour for the Group. Under the watchful eye of the chairman emeritus, he is energetically attempting to transform the Tata Group into an agile business that is intensely focused upon profitability.[6]

It is still premature to assess how the House of Tata shall shape up under Chandrasekaran's watch. The prognosis appears to be quite positive though.

The Tata Group has done business across the world for a century and a half in a spectacularly unique way. Its combination of developing-country experience and socially progressive business values has given it a distinctive edge. If the Tata business model continues to be financially sustainable, the Group shall remain a beacon for other corporations that seek to maintain growth, build a reputation as true global citizens, and above all fulfil their own sense of purpose.

The Tata culture of probity has helped to insulate it from India's endemic corruption in the past and guided its behaviour when standards have slipped. For instance, when the Group discovered widespread irregularities in Tata Finance in 2001–2002, it blew the whistle on itself.[7]

However, the Group has not escaped unharmed from the 2G spectrum allocation scandal in 2008. RNT chose to personally move the Supreme Court in 2010 against the publication of his taped conversations with the corporate lobbyist Niira Radia, on the grounds that it was a violation of his right to privacy.[8] Also, the ruthlessness with which Cyrus Mistry was divested of his Board positions within the Tata Group despite unclear reasons reflected poorly upon the corporate governance within the conglomerate.

Nevertheless, these are mere aberrations in an otherwise remarkable record of excellent corporate citizenship. The Tata leadership sticks to the familiar argument that 'doing well by doing good' makes immense business sense. While the Group does not have clear evidence of success for its philosophy, it really knows of no other way of conducting itself.

As JRD once said, 'If we had done some of the things that some other (business houses) have done, we would have been twice as big as we are today. But we didn't, and I would not have it any other way'.[9]

REFERENCES

1. Financial Times. Case study: TATA. *FT.com*. Available at: www.ft.com/content/8e553742-136c-11e0-a367-00144feabdc0 (accessed: 1 May 2016).

2. MacNeice B & Bowen J. *Powerhouse: Insider Accounts into the World's Top High-performance Organizations*. London: Kogan Page; 2016.

3. Lala R & Miranda M. *The Creation of Wealth*. 1st ed. New Delhi: Penguin Books India; 2004.

4. Casey P. *The Greatest Company in the World?* London: Penguin; 2014.

5. Tata. Tata code of conduct. *Tata.com*. Available at: www.tata.com/aboutus/articlesinside/Tata-Code-of-Conduct (accessed: 5 May 2017).

6. Vijayraghavan K & Kalesh B. How N Chandrasekaran is transforming Tata Group into a business intensely focused on profitability. *The Economic Times*. Available at: https://economictimes.indiatimes.com/news/company/corporate-trends/how-n-chandrasekaran-is-transforming-tata-group-into-a-business-intensely-focussed-on-profitability/articleshow/63435532.cms (accessed: 26 April 2018).

7. The Economist. The Tata group out of India. *The Economist*. Available at: www.economist.com/node/18285497 (accessed: 16 May 2016).

8. NDTV. Ratan Tata to move Supreme Court on Radia tapes. *NDTV.com*. Available at: www.ndtv.com/india-news/ratan-tata-to-move-supreme-court-on-radia-tapes-440458 (accessed: 12 November 2018).

9. Lala RM. Opinion/News Analysis: The business ethics of J.R.D. Tata. *The Hindu*. Available at: www.thehindu.com/2005/07/29/stories/2005072905991100.html (accessed: 20 May 2016).

VIDEO REFERENCE

Samatvam. (2018, August 23). *The Tata Group*. YouTube. Available at: https://www.youtube.com/watch?v=B8bSErrPHuE&feature=youtu.be (accessed: 26 November 2018).

6

THE HOLISTIC STRUCTURE

Life is like a cobweb, not an organization chart.

—*Ross Perot*

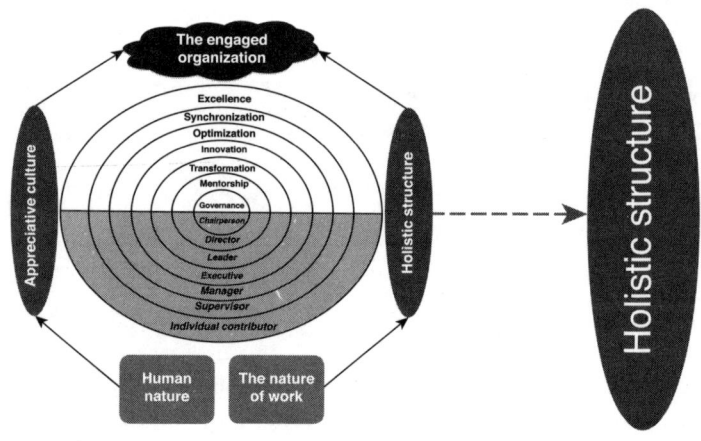

The Holistic Structure
Source: Samatvam Academy

The organization is a structured social entity. It is characterized by a coordinated activity system that remains in close and continuous interaction with its external environment.

As a social unit every organization is presumed to have a special and limited purpose (such as providing education or generating profits). Further, its creators intend it to last beyond the accomplishment of a single action. Regardless of whether it is configured as a firm, corporation, trust, partnership or trade union, all organizations begin life by constituting or electing a governing body for themselves.

An organization actually comes into being when a governing body decides to get its work done by employing people. Each employee assumes a specific position within the institution. Work is done through the specialization of different functions. The output is generated by means of process movement across vertical functions.

A system of organizational layers is gradually formed. Work cascades down its successive levels. People at higher levels of decision-making authority and accountability provide directional inputs to their colleagues at the lower strata towards the meeting of articulated goals and the performance of tasks.

The core function of the organization, and also its chief merit, lies in its capacity to judiciously manage the uncertainties that are inherent in complex work.[1]

Organization Structure

The term 'structure' refers to the mutual relationships that exist between the components of any organized whole. For instance, a building is a structure that represents the relationship between the foundation, skeleton, ceiling and the walls. Similarly, the human body is a structure that comprises the relationships between the bones, organs, blood and the tissues. Likewise, every organization has a structure that represents the framework of mutual relationships between jobs, roles, systems, processes and the people who work to achieve goals.

The structure of the organization is a method of dividing and coordinating its activities. It is designed to clarify who is to do what and which person is responsible for what results and outcomes.

In the simplest of organizations, people share an informal relationship with one another. Task allocation is decided on the basis of mutual agreement amongst the team members.

The functional structure divides the organization by means of a logical grouping of people who share common tasks or goals. Within each function, members are grouped according to the process, the product, the customer type or the geographical region where the activity takes place.

When the functional structure becomes too cumbersome for agile decision-making, the organization typically takes on a multidivisional form. It is divided into several relatively independent divisions or business units. Each of these units is provided with considerable autonomy in making operational decisions. The corporate headquarter formulates the enterprise strategy and monitors unit performance.

The matrix organization exists as a combination of the functional and multidivisional structures. It employs functional as well as project managers. The functional manager is responsible for assigning specialists to projects and facilitating the acquisition of skills that are necessary for project completion. On the other hand, the project manager supervises each project in terms of the budgets and timelines.

In the matrix structure, group members are assigned to project teams based on an agreement between the functional and project managers. They report to both of these positions. These dual lines of authority and accountability often create conflict.

The network organizational structure is formed when several enterprises come together to form a partnership, usually with the help of modern technology in order to produce valued goods and services. Technology-mediated coordination of activities lowers the administrative costs and enhances efficiency.

A virtual organization is a temporary or fleeting network of otherwise independent entities that are linked together through electronic communication and technology in order to provide skills, costs and accessibility to different markets. All the task activities of such an entity are generally outsourced.

These are some of the ways in which organizations structure themselves, with varying degrees of effectiveness.

Role, Authority and Accountability

Interpersonal interactions in all kinds of organizational forms and structures take place within established role relationships.

A role represents a position in a dynamic social system that allows the person to use her discretion and ability in order to achieve an outcome. A role, thus, defines the nature of responsibility for a distinct area of work.

Authority and accountability are the two primary attributes attached to every role. They determine who can say what to whom, who must say what to whom and establish who can get whom to do what.

Accountability refers to a statement of promise to oneself as well as one's colleagues with respect to the delivery of specific results. It occurs when a person is answerable to a higher authority for work, resources and outcomes. Accountability requires room for personal judgement and decision-making. The terms 'accountability' and 'responsibility' are virtually synonymous with each other.

Accountability assumes a proactive and conscious commitment to the purpose of an organization. It applies to individuals. It is neither shared nor conditional.[2]

On the other hand, authority refers to the aspects of a role that enables the role holder to act appropriately with respect to other colleagues. A person with the requisite authority may legitimately direct his or her colleagues towards the accomplishment of tasks and activities assigned to them.

Authority, thus, makes it reasonably possible to do what needs to be done, in order to carry out the responsibility or accountability with which the person has been charged.

Wholeness in Structure

Empirical observation indicates that reality is characterized by a nested structure. Everything in the universe is whole and complete by itself, but is simultaneously a part of a greater whole. Each element becomes significant only in the context of its peer elements as well as the supra-structure to which it belongs.

Arthur Koestler coined the term 'holon' in order to describe universal reality from a holistic perspective. He defined a holon as a self-reliant unit that is simultaneously a whole as well as a part. Every holon is considered to possess a certain degree of autonomy that enables it to handle contingencies without seeking instructions from its senior authorities. At the same time, it is subject to regulation and control from these higher agencies.[3]

A 'holarchy' is construed as an upwardly evolving hierarchy of self-regulating holons. It is characterized by differentiation, followed by the integration of differences at successive levels. Each level of integration provides the next level of difference, and thus helps to tackle a higher level of complexity.

The physical world shows this ordering, as we move from subatomic particles to atoms to molecules to complex molecules to compounds of complex molecules which are the stuff of planets, solar systems, galaxies and finally to the cosmos itself. Human beings extend this patterning of differentiation and integration into abstractions such as the nuclear family, the extended family, the tribe, the nation state, unions of states and ultimately the United Nations.[4]

Corporate institutions too are organized on holarchic lines. Each stratum of management represents a Holon that addresses complexity by being the integrator of its reporting management levels. For instance, a shop floor employee is part of the assembly department, which is integrated into the manufacturing function, which in turn is integrated with additional functions (such as marketing or finance) in order to make up a business.

Suppose X represents the manufacturing function while Y is the marketing function and Z is the overall business unit. While X is very different from Y, both of them have their respective functional purpose as well as a higher business purpose. These two functions come together to create the business Z that is different from either of them. This is akin to hydrogen and oxygen combining together to form water.

The business is differentiated from competitors, but is integrated into a domestic industry structure. This in turn is integrated into a worldwide industry structure.

Ongoing differentiation and integration are seen. Each level contains and respects all its lower levels. The sense of purpose becomes progressively broader as the hierarchical levels are ascended.

The Holistic Organization Structure

Research shows that the job roles in any organization vary from less to more complex, in a series of distinct steps of complexity. Each step represents a discrete level that is referred to as a stratum (or 'strata' in plural).

The work at each stratum has some distinctive characteristics. These are derived from the particular quality and complexity of tasks, goals and objectives of work that needs to be accomplished.

All organized work is seen to fall into a natural hierarchy that comprises seven strata. A holistic organizational structure therefore comprises seven strata or perspectives that are organized into a ladder of accountability. In a stratified system of this nature, people at various levels are accountable for the work of others who are placed at a relatively lower stratum. Each senior level demands a more comprehensive response to the world and its many situations as well as possibilities.

The logic underlying a holistic organization structure is a conceptually integrated one. The roles at ascending levels of the hierarchy are accountable for solving problems of growing intricacy. People at a senior level take decisions that cannot be taken at a lower level because the subordinates lack the relevant knowledge, experience or capability.

The range of objectives to be achieved and the environmental circumstances to be taken into account progressively broaden with each upward progression and the nature of work becomes more complex. Work at higher strata of the organization is therefore experienced as being relatively more responsible. This is how the decision-making process is enriched along the organization's spine of accountability.

A holistic structure takes advantage of the judgement and decision-making capabilities of people at all levels. Job holders are held accountable for the results that are obtained by all those subordinates who work under their guidance.

An individual's ability to handle complexity is referred to as his/her 'cognitive' capacity. It reflects the person's mental horsepower, so to say. Cognitive capacity is a measure of the person's ability to organize, extrapolate and apply judgement in the making of decisions and solving of problems. When selecting a candidate for a role, it is important to find a person who is willing to do the work, possesses the necessary skills and is also equipped with the cognitive capacity needed for the role.

Employees generally wish to be guided by a person who is at least one stratum of cognitive capability above them. This is because a manager at the same level of capability as the employee breathes down the latter's neck. On the other hand, a boss who is two or more strata above the subordinate feels too distant. He also does not want to slow down to coach the employee.

Such micromanagement (in the first instance) and aloofness (in the second instance) are not personality problems. These are merely the symptoms of a poorly designed organization structure.

In the absence of a holistic structure, subordinates are often manipulated into doing things—in the name of 'people' skills. This occurs due to the lack of clear and correct assignment of authority and accountability.

Teamwork and Network Are Complementary to Hierarchy

The notion of hierarchy has naturally evolved with society, throughout its post-tribal history. All attempts over the millennia to establish a sustainable alternative have failed.

This is probably because the hierarchy is the only structure that truly fits human nature. As indicated in Chapter 3, the human personality itself is constituted of numerous hierarchical levels.

Yet some of the newer approaches to organization design maintain that the notion of hierarchy is now outmoded. They advocate open and egalitarian organizations, wherein the differences in the levels of allocated work as well as the authority are systematically abolished. The need to respond to distinctions in the levels of cognitive complexity that is required for solving various kinds of problems is also done away with.

An especially popular concept in modern times is that of the cross-functional team. This is considered to be a self-organizing work group that draws its members from different functional areas. Within such a team, roles are broadly defined and members are trained in multiple skills.

Cross-functional teams are generally mandated to look after a complete business process. They are, thus, expected to help eliminate any silos or other dysfunctional boundaries that may exist between the different organizational functions.[5]

The presence of teams is often confused with the absence of hierarchy. The general impression about teamwork is that it demands interaction between equals without any exercise of authority whatsoever. However, most teams do have an internal structure that is different and separate from the management styles adopted during its functioning. The individual who takes personal accountability for results is seen to be the team leader, for example. This is especially visible in times of crisis.

The modern 'team' gurus Katzenbach and Smith say,

> Contrary to popular opinion, teams do not imply the destruction of hierarchy. Indeed, quite the reverse. Teams and hierarchy make each other perform better, because structure and hierarchy generate performance within well-defined boundaries. Teams, in turn, productively bridge these boundaries in order to deliver yet greater and higher performance.[6]

The network form of organization is another design that has lately emerged as a tool to cope with the uncertainty and turbulence of modern environments. Without a doubt, the network is a brilliant way of tapping into the talents of a dispersed community through the use of modern technology.

Networks can help to build inclusive organizational communities that are characterized by mutual respect, support and encouragement.[7] However, network-based organizations also struggle with the assumption of accountability by its diverse membership.

Traditionally, people looked to an individual leader upon whom to place the buck. But in a quasi-autonomous and self-organizing network how does anyone assert control or accept responsibility? Ensuring decision-making accountability in a networked environment remains very tricky.

On the other hand, natural hierarchies are seen to assert themselves wherever human beings organize themselves to work. Regardless of the flat or stratified nature of the organization, there is no substitute for the assignment of decision-making responsibility at various levels of complexity to different role holders. The more complexity that a job holder can deal with, the bigger the problems that he/she can solve and greater the number that this person can potentially manage or lead.

ENGAGE!

The Seven Accountability Levels in a Holistic Structure

In any organization, the people at different strata within the structure hold the accountability for unique aspects of institutional work. As one moves up the organizational pyramid, the complexity involved in making decisions and judgements increases at each successive stratum.

The presence of role holders at different strata who can handle different levels of complexity helps the organization to adequately fulfil its mandate. The art of organization development lies in maintaining a dynamic equilibrium between each person's potential capability and the level of complexity involved in her work.

The basic building block of every organization is the 'individual contributor'. This is a non-management role that contributes to the accomplishment of the larger organizational goals by completing the assigned tasks within the given time frame and other parameters.

The next higher level in the organization is referred to as the team, project, department or section. It represents a collection of individual contributors that work harmoniously together under the guidance of a supervisor or team leader.

The third stratum generally represents the functional area or a geographical region. Its work operations are handled and coordinated by a job holder who is quintessentially referred to as the 'manager'.

The fourth organizational rung is the business unit or division. It comprises several functions or geographical regions that work in tandem with one another to produce and deliver goods and services.

The division is an operationally distinct entity that is allowed considerable autonomy and independence in the way it conducts its business. It works under the tutelage of an 'executive'.

At the fifth level of analysis is the organization itself. This is often a coalescence of divisions or business units that come together to make an integrated whole. The overall mandate for this entity is usually entrusted to a chief executive officer or the organizational leader.

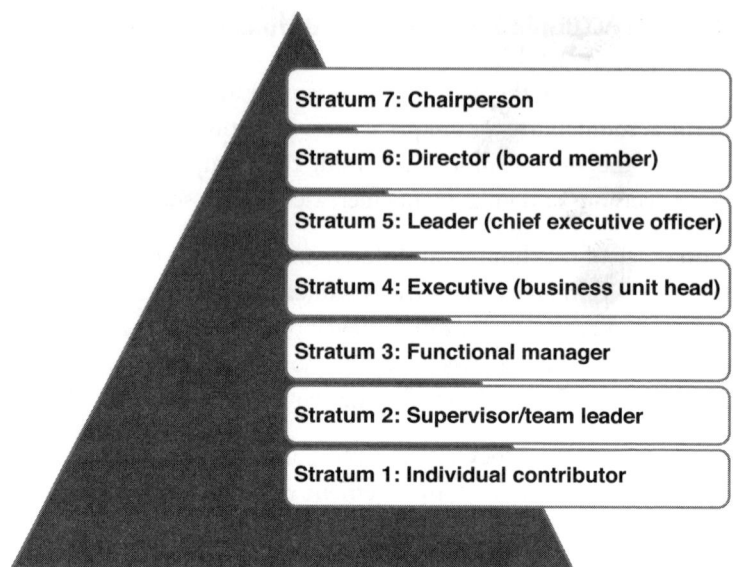

The Seven Accountability Levels
Source: Samatvam Academy

Several enterprises are often grouped together into a business conglomerate that works under the guidance of a supervisory board or governing council. Alternatively, a transnational corporation comprises country-wise subsidiary organizational units that work under an executive committee whose members are group business heads in charge of different geographies. Its members constitute the sixth stratum in organizations.

Finally, there is a chairperson at the helm—who occupies the apex or the seventh level.

In consonance with these institutional levels, there are a set of seven organizational roles that make up a whole organization: (a) the worker, (b) the supervisor, (c) the manager, (d) the executive, (e) the leader, (f) the director and (g) the chairperson. The nomenclature may vary according to the legal, geographical or cultural context. But the essence of each role remains the same.

The Challenges at Each Accountability Level

The work challenges at each of the seven strata in the hierarchy of accountability are as follows.

Stratum I (Individual Contributor: Worker)

People who hold direct responsibility for task achievement are referred to as individual contributors.

The tasks to be accomplished by them are essentially demands or requirements such as a product to be made, a service to be rendered, some specific information to be collected or a prescribed test to be carried out. These demands must be met within the prescribed parameters of time, cost, safety and quality etc. The output or service that is expected of an individual contributor is prescribed in detail. The objectives as well as the circumstances of the work are well defined.

Individual contributors are expected to respond swiftly by way of concrete action. If there is any doubt about whether the task is to be pursued in the first place, the matter can be referred to a higher authority.

The problems that usually present themselves in the work of an individual contributor have discrete solutions that are provided by the supervisor. When the appropriate response to a problem is not clear, guidelines exist for an expert referral. If emergency situations occur, the procedures for coping with these are laid out.

Individual contributors manage themselves and their resources to optimal effect. While they are not accountable for making changes to a given schedule, they may seek improvement within that schedule.

Individual contributors continuously use judgement by way of practical watchfulness in relation to immediate tasks. Their performance ideal is to accomplish their mandate with excellence.

Excellence is the art of doing ordinary things extraordinarily well. Noble intention, sincere effort, intelligent direction, skilful execution and the vision to see obstacles as opportunities yield excellence by way of efficacy, mastery, as well as a sense of fulfilment that arises during task performance.

Stratum II (Supervisor: Team Leader, Department Head or Project Incharge)

Supervision is the process wherein one person sets the purpose or direction for some of the other colleagues and gets them to move together in that direction with competence and commitment.[8] The tasks to be accomplished by the supervisor are concrete in nature. However, many of these must be handled simultaneously.

Supervisors synchronize the efforts of numerous individual contributors. The skills expected of them include the planning and assignment of work, facilitating the engagement of people and an accurate measurement of the work done. The supervisor provides expert input when a system is down and installs checks and balances to prevent the recurrence of mistakes.

Supervisory work requires fact gathering and diagnosis of a given situation often making use of specialist knowledge and expertise. Situational demands must not be taken at face value; there is an implicit requirement to explore and find out the 'real' needs of the people or situation being handled.

Supervisors are therefore expected to gather information step by step, in order to reveal the underlying complexities of each particular circumstance. Whereas the individual contributor gives the customer or stakeholder what she asks for, the supervisor always seeks to find out what it is that he/she really wants.

The resources available to supervisors are restricted to the existing products, geography, customers, suppliers, technology and systems. The required output can only be partially specified beforehand.

The job holder is permitted to flex the schedule, that is, make short-term changes to the work plan.

Supervisory work is carried out in emergent circumstances. The mettle of the supervisor is tested particularly when workplace complaints, conflicts and performance problems need to be addressed. Facilitating the kind of symphony witnessed in a musical orchestra is the primary supervisory mandate.

Stratum III (Functional Manager: Regional Head or Practice Leader)

The third level of accountability is that of the quintessential manager. The manager has to meet plans that are specified by volume, quality and time.

The problems faced by managers are operational in nature, but are quite challenging. Finding solutions to these problems involves the identification of patterns in the actual performance of existing products, systems and services. Managers analyse the situation, evaluate the linkages between the different variables, develop a new system, negotiate its introduction and iron out the teething problems.

Managers are responsible for the effectiveness of current operations. Work from different departments or sections needs to be harmonized. This requires the integration of a number of teams and disciplines. The resources to be managed comprise of a mini organization, which includes a set of people, technology, equipment and premises.

Managers handle diverse situations. They judiciously manage the interaction between situational variables in order to achieve the planned outcomes. Managers typically choose or select new methods and procedures from what is given and generally accepted in the light of local conditions. Best practices are gradually established.

The core managerial mandate is to harness the maximum output from the deployment of minimal resources. Managers are held accountable for the improved performance or productivity of existing assets, products, systems and processes, but not for their reconfiguration. They are expected to develop concrete mental models towards dealing with the future, in the light of past experience.

Managers typically know personally all the employees in their region, practice or function. They make the most of people as well as technology in order to realize the chosen purpose or goals. Managerial interaction with the external environment involves customers or suppliers in different locations.

Stratum IV (Executive: Business Head, Divisional Head)

Executive work involves the management of divisions or business units. The executive mandate is to deal with the imbalances and delinquencies in meeting the needs of a given operation or territory. The gaps in the availability and performance of resources and systems are analysed. New linkages among the existing body of ideas, practices and policies are established. Potentially innovative solutions are conceptualized, assessed and implemented. Constancy is integrated with change by means of skilful navigation between the current certainty and the preferred future.

Executives are required to engage in abstract modelling. This requires the capacity to discard past experience and engage in the breakthrough, outside-of-the-box thinking. While creativity may exist at all levels in the organization, the accountability for the discovery, conceptualization and invention of new solutions resides squarely in the executive domain.

In a dynamic business environment wherein interactions are rife with conflict and contrasts, the business executive is required to promote stability and growth, tradition and innovation, collaboration and competition, order and freedom—all at the same time. The primary executive challenge is to pull together these apparently incompatible priorities that are simultaneously critical in delivering value.

The executive genius lies in recognizing that extraordinary synergy may be obtained by the transcendence of dichotomy through the creative integration of opposing perspectives. The synergistic approach to management has a logic that reconciles differences. It enables people who hold contrasting value systems to sit down and break bread together, so to say.

Business executives need to respect and value different people as well as divergent perspectives. They must systematically leverage these, in order to create 'win-win' outcomes. Perceptual flexibility helps the executives to recognize complementarity, in situations where others see only conflict.

Executives evolve innovative solutions through an integrative approach. Intrepid entrepreneurs across the ages have been doing just that in order to generate disruptive innovation. This is now the mandate of contemporary entrepreneurs and organizational executives alike.

Stratum V (Organizational Leader or Chief Executive Officer)

Leaders are responsible for the integrated functioning of a fully resourced, self-sufficient operating enterprise. They weave together and integrate all of the value creation work that occurs at the subordinate levels in the organization's hierarchy of accountability.

Leaders translate the vision and mission of the institution into meaningful objectives for the people. They are expected to guide the organization towards continued viability as well as sustainability.

Leaders assess the business and cultural model of the enterprise and facilitate the necessary adjustments such that the vitality of the organization may be preserved. Their goal is to generate sufficient returns on capital. Leaders also ensure that a budgetary structure and financial regulations are developed for the organization as a whole.

The mandate of leadership is to stage revolutions in organizational systems. At its best, this involves the reinvention of the institutional identity through the realization of a shared vision. Even in times of stability, leaders awaken the organization to new possibilities.

Leaders act as the chief representative of the organization in the larger society. They continually monitor trends in the external environment and highlight the developments that are happening there.

Leaders assess what is socially, politically and environmentally feasible. They spell out what the organization must do in order to adapt to the external changes. Leaders usually communicate the direction and intent and then step back to allow their executive colleagues to do the actual work.

Leaders welcome uncertainty. In fact, they employ it as a resource. Leaders draw upon an innate sense of interconnectedness in order to relate together apparently diverse issues, events or matters. They leave situations open and fluid rather than prematurely narrowing the field or the flow of information.

The judgement patterns of leaders are relatively free of preconceptions. A long-term strategic direction is the focus of their problem-solving efforts.

Finally, leaders look after the well-being of the people. They continually shape the interconnections within the organization so as to maintain congeniality in the working atmosphere.

Stratum VI (Business Group Head: Director, Governing Board Member)

At the sixth stratum of the organization, business group heads or directors are accountable for the performance of a cohesive network of independent enterprises or self-sufficient organizational units.

The mandate at this level becomes more holistic. It covers a cluster of discrete operating entities either in the same territory or in multiple geographies. The challenge moves beyond the responsibility for a single domain towards the membership of supervisory or governing boards. The response primarily involves the development of principles and frameworks for general application. Coordination and boundary issues affecting the different operating entities are suitably dealt with. The concern is to help the organization in becoming and remaining a good corporate citizen.

The work of directors demands a deep understanding of the political, economic, social, religious, technological and educational trends across the globe. These role holders gather data and intelligence about what is happening in these various spheres.

Directors are expected to continually probe for any unexpected sources of opportunity or instability that can impact the organization. They alert as well as protect the enterprise against excessive turbulence. Any external issues that present themselves are viewed from all the possible perspectives.

Directors help to establish the acceptable central as well as local degrees of freedom that can facilitate appropriate decision-making. For instance, joint ventures in a new geography or culture require a balance to be struck between the espoused values of the parent organization and the norms that arise from the local culture. Since these value sets are often quite different from each other, one set is bound to challenge the other. Thus, tolerance towards diversity is the key to success at the director level.

The work of group business heads or supervisory board members calls for the transcendence of their own limitations, as well as the provision of guidance to other people. Mentoring business executives towards the flowering of their individual career potential is, thus, a key mandate for these job holders.

Mentorship is a supportive relationship between a caring individual who is ready to share knowledge, experience and wisdom with another who is willing to benefit from this exchange. It helps to unlock the courage to think and act beyond existing paradigms.

Founded upon a spirit of openness, empathy and mutual respect, mentorship entails a series of supportive conversations and interventions that facilitate personal growth as well as capability development. It helps to build confidence and conviction in the mentee, towards the realization of professional aspirations in a personally fulfilling manner.

Stratum VII (Chairperson: Corporate Governor)

The chairperson exists and functions at the seventh or the apex level of the organization. In many cases, this is a very large institution that is the microcosm of the society itself. The central mandate of this role is to help sustain the viability of the enterprise for future generations.

Chairpersons are accountable for corporate governance. This entails legal and fiduciary responsibilities to the society. Central to the art of governance is the ability to define and disseminate detailed institutional values. These are not only necessary for the business but also set the limits within which everyone is expected to behave. Consonant values are the unifying force of any organization. To the extent that people can share common beliefs, desires and aspirations, they can commit themselves to work together.

Chairpersons are also responsible for determining how value can be established across all the activities of the corporation in line with the overall corporate purpose. Of course, this is to be done in a way that satisfies a wide range of stakeholders. This part of the work includes setting the resource limits that govern the work at the operational and strategic levels of the organization. Chairpersons also seed and incubate many apparently peripheral initiatives that can offer a strategic advantage in the very long run.

The quest for good governance is first and foremost a journey of self-discovery, into the depths of one's identity. In order to do justice to their role, chairpersons must reinvent their self-concept. Inner shifts in motives and values must be combined with an outer change in attitudes as well as behaviour.

Chairpersons are expected to motivate and inspire the entire stakeholder population through a variety of communication tools. The role requires an ability to proactively sense any significant shifts in the socio-economic context, and respond with tremendous sensitivity.

In other words, chairpersons must develop foresight and act with insight, based upon hindsight!

Building holistic organizations is an applied art. Every case is unique and requires specific comprehension for the creation of innovative solutions.

The next case study details the case story of how the American Fortune 500 enterprise Whole Foods Market was built as a remarkably whole organization in ways more than just its structure and culture.

References

1. March J & Simon H. *Organizations.* New York, NY: Wiley; 1958.

2. Klatt B, Irvine D & Murphy S. *Accountability: Getting a Grip on Results.* Calgary: Bow River Publishing; 1999.

3. Koestler A. *The Ghost in the Machine.* London: Hutchinson & Co.; 1967.

4. Fairfield J. Profit by raising a key function to the next level: Tools to build a work levels shifting strategy. In: Shepard K, Gray J, Hunt J & McArthur S. (Eds.) *Organization Design, Levels of Work and Human Capability: Executive Guide.* Toronto: Global Organization Design Society; 2018.

5. Smart K & Barnum C. Communication in cross-functional teams: An introduction to this special issue. *IEEE Transactions on Professional Communication.* 2000; 43(1): 19–21.

6. Katzenbach J & Smith D. *The Wisdom of Teams: Creating the High-Performance Organization.* New York, NY: HarperCollins Publishers; 1994.

7. Podolny J & Page K. Network forms of organization. *Annual Review of Sociology.* 1998; 24(1): 57–76.

8. Jaques E & Clement S. *Executive Leadership: A Practical Guide to Managing Complexity.* Oxford: Blackwell; 1991.

WHOLE FOODS MARKET

There is no inherent reason why business cannot be socially responsible, ethical and profitable. It must view people not as resources, but as sources.

—*John Mackey*

BACKGROUND

Whole Foods Market Inc. is a mission-driven, socially conscious retail enterprise that makes natural foods and environmentally friendly products available to consumers in a relaxed and pleasing ambience. Its motto is 'Whole Foods, Whole People, Whole Planet'.

The company presently ranks 176 on the Fortune 500 list. Its revenues of $16 billion are generated from 470 expansive stores located across the United States, Canada and the UK. In August 2017, the company became a part of Amazon Inc.

Whole Foods Market is a moderately profitable company. Its net income of $245 million amounts to 1.5 per cent of its FY 2017 revenues. However, profit is not the company's primary goal. Among its eight core beliefs, only one is tied to creating wealth through profits and growth.

John Mackey founded Whole Foods Market in September 1980 in association with three other entrepreneurs. The idea was to create a 'health' food store that featured wholesome food instead of pills and potions. John remains as the CEO of the organization from inception till the present day.

An avid reader and a straight-talking maverick, Mackey is a strong supporter of the free market economy. He advocates love, joy and happiness at the work place, and sponsors a unique environment that is characterized by fun, friendliness and acceptance.

THE ORGANIZATIONAL ARCHITECTURE

The organizational architecture at Whole Foods has been shaped by the humanistic and counter-cultural values of its founder. Rather than simply being a food provider, Whole Foods Market positions itself as the leader of a food movement. The fulfilment of its vision is measured on five parameters: (a) customer satisfaction, (b) team member happiness and excellence, (c) return on capital investment, (d) improvement in the state of the environment and (e) local and larger community support.

Whole Foods Market is governed by a cellular architecture. Each store is divided into teams in a manner that is similar to how people band together within a tribe. Team leaders at a store, the store leaders within a region and even the company's 12 regional presidents collectively represent a cell, each. Every cell represents an autonomous profit centre that is fully authorized to take key operating decisions, for example, hiring, food placement, pricing, ordering and in-store promotion. The cells closest to the customer have the maximum power for execution.

The Whole Foods organization is more of a social system and less a rigid hierarchy. Innovation and experimentation are allowed to occur at the store level. Energy and ideas work their way up rather than the other way around. Peer pressure substitutes for bureaucracy.

Whole Foods Market is unparalleled with regard to its inspired and entrepreneurial employees. The leadership at the company is decentralized. Employee inputs are regularly sought on operational matters. Team members are encouraged to act with alacrity in order to accomplish whatever needs to get done and not waste time waiting for orders from above.

A strong culture of empowerment permeates the company. With respect to rules, the belief is that less is more. Employees are encouraged to ask for forgiveness rather than prior permission. All these features help to elicit tremendous associate loyalty at every level of the organization.

Whole Foods Market's open book policy provides every team member with complete access to the company's financial records. These include the salary and remuneration information for all of the company's associates right up to the CEO. A salary cap at the company limits the maximum cash compensation (wages plus profit, incentive, bonuses) payable to any executive at the company in a calendar year to 19 times the company-wide annual average salary of all full-time team members. Since 2007, John Mackey himself earns only a symbolic $1 per year.[1]

A unique gain-sharing plan at Whole Foods helps to provide additional wages to the tune of around 6 per cent to its employees. Further, a whopping 94 per cent of the company's stock options are distributed to non-executives. These measures help to enforce a shared identity under which everyone feels equal and valued. This keeps the 89,000 employees of Whole Foods Market's happy and engaged. The company has been featured on the Fortune '100 Best Companies to Work For' list every year since its publication in 1998. In 2017, it was placed at the 58th rank.[2]

The governing principles of Whole Foods Market are oriented towards making a positive difference in the world at large. This Austin-based company has, thus, turned the (often vacuous) slogans of inspiration, autonomy and teamwork into a powerful business model. It represents a remarkable corporate experiment in democratic capitalism.

STAKEHOLDER-CENTRIC APPROACH

Whole Foods Market espouses the notion that all of its stakeholders are involved in the business together. It defines the term 'stakeholder' to mean any person or agency that has an investment in what the organization does or sells. This includes the investors, the customers, its employees, its suppliers and the social communities within which the company operates.

The management's job is considered to be that of looking after the employees, who in turn serve the customers with all their heart. Happy customers take care of the shareholders, who in turn support the management. It is a virtuous circle. Paying attention to a broad swathe of stakeholders and making decisions mindful of their collective interest is a win-win exercise.

Whole Foods Market undertakes a number of measures to give back to the communities in which it operates. Each individual store has a lot of latitude in deciding the best way to meet the needs of the local community. Several times a year, stores hold community-giving days whereby 5 per cent of that day's net sales are donated to a local non-profit or educational organization. Further, team members are paid for up to 20 hours of community service yearly.

The company features local products in the farmers' markets that are held in the parking lots of its stores. It also helps independent farmers and local food artisans to flourish by providing up to $25 million in low-interest loans through its Local Producer Loan Programme. The Whole Foods Foundation supports projects that relate directly to organics and environment-friendly production methods, animal welfare, sustainable seafood and healthy families and nutrition.

THE DECLARATION OF INTERDEPENDENCE

The core vision and the stakeholder-centric values of Whole Foods Market are enshrined in its 'Declaration of Interdependence'. This unique document was originally created in 1985. It has been periodically revised thereafter. Its eight constituent themes are summarized as follows:

1. **Selling the highest quality products available:** Whole Foods Market celebrates the fact that good food and cooking improves the lives of all of its stakeholders. It offers high-quality natural and organic products at a competitive price.

2. **Satisfaction, delight and nourishment of customers:** Customers are recognized as the most important stakeholders in Whole Foods Market's business. The organization goes to extraordinary lengths in order to satisfy and delight its customers within an inviting, informal, comfortable, nurturing and educational store environment.

3. **Supporting team member happiness and excellence:** Whole Foods Market designs and promotes a safe work environment wherein motivated team members can flourish and reach their highest potential. It strives to achieve a unity of vision and build trust amongst team members, while respecting diversity and individual differences.

4. **Creating wealth through profits and growth:** Profits are essential towards the creation of capital for growth, job security and overall success. The management team is the steward of the financial investments that facilitate value creation activities and is committed to increasing the shareholder value in the long term.

5. **Serving and supporting the local and global community:** The business of Whole Foods Market is intimately tied to the

neighbourhood and the larger communities that it serves. Besides donating 5 per cent of its after-tax profits every year to not-for-profit organizations, the company also responds readily in times of community need.

6. **Practising and advancing environmental stewardship:** Whole Foods Market practices active environmental stewardship through (a) the provision of support to sustainable agriculture, (b) reduction of waste and minimizing the consumption of non-renewable resources and (c) environmentally robust programmes for store cleaning and maintenance.

7. **Allying with business associates:** Whole Foods Market depends upon hundreds of other businesses in creating an outstanding retail shopping experience. It regards these trade partners as indispensable allies in the service of its stakeholders, and treats them with mutual respect, fairness and integrity.

8. **Balance and integration:** Whole Foods Market seeks to dynamically balance the needs and interests of the numerous stakeholders of the organization. Accordingly, people at all levels are encouraged to listen compassionately, think carefully and act with integrity.

THE GENESIS OF THE ENTERPRISE

In the 1970s, a barely detectable trickle of consumer concern had begun regarding chemicals, hormones and artificial ingredients that had percolated into the food chain. In 1978, John Mackey and his girlfriend Renee Lawson raised seed capital of $45,000 from their family and friends in order to establish a health food store-cum-restaurant called Safer Way Natural Foods at Austin, Texas.

Originally, the duo insisted on making everything from scratch. This inefficient method of production, coupled with parking shortages, led to Safer Way losing half of its capital during the first year.

However, the venture encountered greater success in its second year. This led John Mackey's father as well as one of the store's customers to invest $25,000 each towards the establishment of a larger store. Mackey also persuaded two other local organic grocery owners to collaborate with him and Renee in this endeavour.

With this business background, the first Whole Foods Market was opened in 1980. Built over 10,500 square feet of area and employing 19 staff members, the store became an instant success. It carried a very large selection of natural and organic items. When a flood nearly destroyed the store in early 1981, it was saved by fierce customer loyalty. Dozens of people pitched in to help get it up and running again. And the company never looked back thereafter.[3]

THE CULTURAL PILLARS

The holistic culture of Whole Foods promotes a strong sense of community, along with a fierce commitment towards productivity. Employee participation reinforces individual attention to performance and profits. In turn, the robust financial results provide people with more freedom to innovate.[4]

Combining democracy with discipline, the company's operational strategy rests upon four cultural pillars: (a) teamwork, (b) measurement, (c) internal competition and (d) employee centricity.

TEAMWORK

The organizational culture of Whole Foods is premised on decentralized teamwork. The 'team' is the defining unit of its activities. Each store is an autonomous profit centre that is composed of 10 or more self-managed teams. Each such team has a designated leader and clear performance targets.[4]

Team members have the exclusive power to approve the selection and appointment of any new candidates on their team. After a 30-day probation period, it takes a two-thirds vote of the respective team for a candidate to get confirmed as a full-time employee of the company.

The team members collectively assume psychological ownership for their own performance standards. They routinely reject prospective candidates who are not perceived to be good enough. Another reason for the intense scrutiny of potential recruits to the team is that the company's 'gain-sharing' programme ties bonuses directly to team performance.

Whole Foods Market supports teamwork with a radically open and transparent financial system. The company collects and distributes information to an extent that would be almost unimaginable elsewhere. Sensitive data on team/store sales revenues and profit margins are available to every person across the organization. So much information is shared so widely, that the US Securities Exchange Commission has designated all of the organization's 89,000 employees as 'insiders' for stock-trading purposes.

Trust is the primary prerequisite for effective teamwork. The building of trust starts with the hiring vote, and is reaffirmed by the company's open-salary policy. Whole Foods considers that it can afford to keep only a very few secrets if the organization wishes to create a high-trust organization where people are 'all-for-one' and 'one-for-all'.

However, there is also a competitive angle to teamwork at Whole Foods. Teams, stores and regions compete vigorously with one another on quality, service and profitability. Superior relative performance translates into enhanced remuneration, recognition and promotions.

MEASUREMENT

'What gets measured, gets done' is one of the most popular aphorisms in business. Whole Foods Market has taken it deeply to heart. The organization zealously measures its work results. It then disseminates this data all across the company. When the information is shared with people, they stay aligned with the vision of a collective fate.

Any curious team member has access to nearly as much operational and financial data as anyone at the company headquarters. A sheet posted next to the time clock in every store lists the previous day's sales, broken down team wise. Another sheet lists the sales numbers for the same day last year.[4]

Once a week, each store posts a report that lists the sales of every store in its region broken down team wise, with comparisons to the same week last year as well as 'year-to-date' totals. Another weekly report gives sales information for every store in the company.

Once every month, stores get detailed information on profitability. This report analyses sales, product costs, wages and salaries and operating profits for all the 470 stores. Since individual teams make decisions about labour spending, ordering, pricing and all the other factors that determine profitability, these reports are indispensable for the team members.[5]

The company conducts an annual morale survey to probe employee attitudes. It asks questions about the confidence that people have in their own team leaders, store leaders and regional leaders. It enquires about the fears and frustrations of the people. Further, it also seeks the opinion of the associates on where the company seems to be straying from its values.

The results of this survey become public information, and are even included in the company's annual report to its shareholders.

INTERNAL COMPETITION

At Whole Foods Market, the pressure for performance comes not so much from the bosses as it does from one's own peers. All the teams are expected to set ambitious targets and are held accountable for their achievement. They are encouraged to not only compete against their own goals for growth and productivity but also to vie against different teams in their store, and even against their counterpart teams in different stores across the various regions.

Productivity is evaluated monthly. The teams that manage to deliver with less-than-budgeted labour costs become eligible for a so-called 'gain-sharing' payout. Store team leaders are also eligible for an economic value-added bonus. This is based on the extent to which the store delivers a return that is higher than the corporate cost of capital.

The main vehicle for competition at Whole Foods is an elaborate system of peer reviews through which the different teams benchmark each other. The 'Store Tour' is the most intense of these measures. On a periodic schedule, each Whole Foods store is toured by a group of as many as 40 visitors from another region.[6] It is a two-day mix of social interaction, reviews, performance audits and structured feedback sessions. The visiting troupe includes regional leaders, store team leaders, associate store team leaders and leaders from two operating teams (for instance, grocery and nutrition) who work intensively with their colleagues in the host store.

The Customer Snapshot is another key exercise. Ten times every year, each store is toured by a headquarter official or regional leader and is rated on 300 different items. Unlike store tours, The Customer Snapshot is a surprise inspection that lasts for a full day. Once a month, The Customer Snapshot results of every store go to every other store. These ratings carry great weight within the Whole Foods organization. They constitute yet another avenue for the stores and teams to contend with each other. This has helped to build a culture of incremental progress in the company.[4]

EMPLOYEE CENTRICITY

Whole Foods is successful because its gutsy founder has largely handed over the operation to his employees. And they have responded with remarkable commitment and dedication.

The company has a uniquely pleasant and helpful workforce that is committed to healthy food, service of the customer and the promotion of a healthy environment. The covenant that exists between the organization and its employees is that the people shall be treated as fully informed partners in the business, in return for the assumption of full responsibility for ace performance.

Each Whole Foods store employs 40 to 650 individuals. They are organized into self-directed teams. Eighty-seven per cent of the team members are full-time employees. The employee attrition stands at a relatively low rate of 26 per cent.

When a new store is opened, at least 30 per cent of the staff comprises company veterans who have accepted a transfer to the new location. The organization actively discourages the formation of worker unions at its facilities.

The individuals who succeed at Whole Foods are the ones who have a knack for pleasing customers and enjoy the candid style of give and take. However, the organization's appeal for its prospective employees lies beyond its social mission and its deep commitment to natural and organic foods.

In urban areas, many employees are recent immigrants who are attracted to the company because it offers full-time jobs with health insurance and other benefits that are particularly generous in comparison with conventional supermarket positions. In suburban areas, employees include high school students or graduates who want a steady job close to home.

While the guiding values at Whole Foods Market appear to be soft, a hard-core competitive spirit pervades the organization. The company does not see any conflict between wearing its heart on its sleeve and running an organization that cares about profits. In fact, these two orientations are viewed as complementary and profoundly synergistic with one another.

THE PURSUIT OF ETHICS

Whole Foods Market is something of an ethical conundrum. It simultaneously pursues apparently conflicting values or qualities and straddles both the ends of the ethical equation. In fact, John Mackey himself has popularly been labelled as (a) spiritual and calculating, (b) forthright and aloof, (c) humble and arrogant as well as (d) good natured and prickly.

While Mackey advocates the pursuit of a deeper purpose beyond profits and also acknowledges the interdependencies among all the stakeholders, Whole Foods Market continuously strives to rout small-scale competition. Even as the company believes that business should be ethical and socially responsible, Mackey personally spread misinformation about wild oats for a number of years prior to Whole Foods acquiring that company.

Further, Whole Foods believes that its primary objective is to provide consumers with healthy and natural food of the highest quality. At the same time, the company is savvy enough to position itself as a trendy shopping place. This enables its customers to make a statement about their perceived status.

Also, while the organization professes to deeply care about its employees and seeks to build a happy workplace, it actively promotes competition among its various teams, store and regions that invariably leads to friction. The list of such dichotomies is quite long.

Ethics often demand standards of behaviour that follow popularly established norms. Like a parent demonstrating 'tough love' to a recalcitrant child, the methodology followed by Whole Foods may sometimes be questionable. Some of its actions might even appear to be bizarre. However, the company's intent has always been unquestionably noble. It has relentlessly pursued the larger good and also the well-being of all its stakeholders.

Whole Foods Market has long been admired as an innovative company with quality standards, responsiveness to the community and the environment, a healthy growth model and highly regarded employment practices.[7] The company has remained faithful to its core mission by and large, even as it bent a few norms in order to accommodate customer needs and stay competitive. This may appear hypocritical to some people, but sound progressive to others.

To revitalize the company from historical lows, Amazon Inc. acquired the company in August 2018. It has introduced many changes at Whole Foods Market after the takeover. The prices of food items in several categories have been cut, some by as much as 40 per cent. Whole Foods is now selling its products on Amazon.com, and its erstwhile loyalty programme has been replaced with Amazon Prime.

The freedom of the local stores to sell regional items is being curtailed as the company stocks up on more national brands. The brand representatives are now banned from visiting the Whole Foods Market stores. These moves are intended to cut costs and modernize the company's back-end operations.[8]

Under the new ownership and in a tough market, it shall be interesting to watch how Whole Foods Market manages to maintain its wholesome spirit as well as the authenticity of its social mission.

REFERENCES

1. Martin E. 10 top CEOs who earn salaries of less than $50,000. *CNBC.* 2017. Available at: www.cnbc.com/2017/05/18/10-top-ceos-who-earn-salaries-of-less-than-50000.html (accessed: 26 May 2018).

2. Fortune. Whole Foods Market. *Fortune.* Available at: http://fortune.com/best-companies/2017/whole-foods-market/ (accessed: 26 May 2018).

3. Whole Foods UK. Available at: www.wholefoodsmarket.com/company-info/whole-foods-market-history (accessed: 26 May 2016).

4. Fishman C. Whole foods is all teams. *Fast Company.* Available at: www.fastcompany.com/26671/whole-foods-all-teams (accessed: 10 June 2016).

5. Freiberg K & Freiberg J. *Guts!* New York, NY: Currency Doubleday; 2005.

6. Lewis R. Whole Foods Market. *Encyclopedia Britannica.* Available at: www.britannica.com/topic/Whole-Foods-Market (accessed: 26 May 2017).

7. Hamel G. The why, what, and how of management innovation. *Harvard Business Review.* Available at: https://hbr.org/2006/02/the-why-what-and-how-of-management-innovation (accessed: 21 August 2016).

8. Taylor K. Here are all the changes Amazon is making to Whole Foods. *Business Insider.* Available at: www.businessinsider.in/Here-are-all-the-changes-Amazon-is-making-to-Whole-Foods/articleshow/60784053.cms (accessed: 11 May 2018).

VIDEO REFERENCE

Samatvam. (2016, December 26). *The Whole Foods Market*. YouTube. Available at: https://youtu.be/Y026oEzdd0Y (accessed: 26 November 2018).

PART IV

THE ARCHITECTURE

7

INDIVIDUAL EXCELLENCE

Excellence is to do a common thing in an uncommon way.

—*Booker T. Washington*

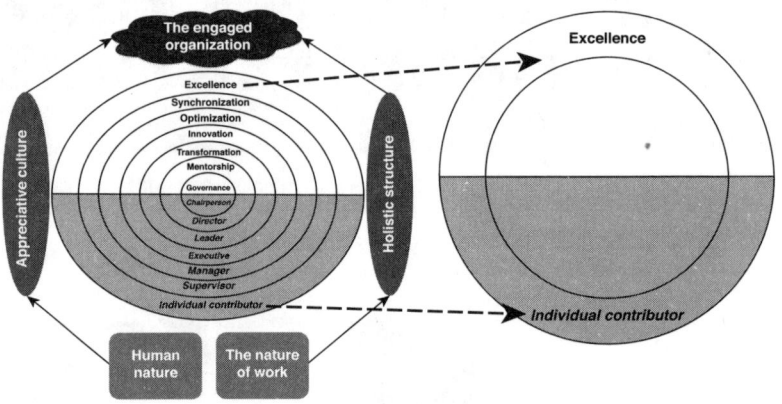

Individual Contributor's Mandate of Excellence
Source: Samatvam Academy

By their very nature, human beings seek to gainfully employ their intrinsic abilities—whether in employment, professional service, entrepreneurial work or even running a home. People yearn for the opportunity to perform challenging work that employs their capability and also helps to yield useful output at the same time.

Individual workers are expected to achieve the assigned tasks through the diligent use of their personal skills in different functional areas. These people are referred to as 'individual contributors'. They leverage technology, bring skilled knowledge into play, apply personal judgement and make decisions such that the impediments to task accomplishment are suitably overcome.

Individual contributors work towards the accomplishment of specified tasks, such as the selling of a product, delivery of a certain service, or the repair of a system. Their external interactions typically involve a fixed number of customers or suppliers, within a framework of regular contact. For instance, salespeople working within a territory are likely to have a regular routine, a call pattern and an indicative price list to work with.

The first few years in a career are usually spent in making individual contributions. However, there is at least a small component of individual contribution vested in every organizational role—regardless of its position in the accountability hierarchy.

In an organizational setting, individual contributors typically work in conjunction with the other members in a workgroup. They usually have access to large amounts of information as well as ample freedom to deploy their intrinsic capabilities towards the delivery of results.

The quest of individual contributors is to make the job resemble 'play', which is marked by flexibility, variety and challenge. Their performance ideal is to accomplish their assignments with *excellence*.

The Phenomenon of Excellence

Excellence is the act of doing ordinary things extraordinarily well. It represents a way of life in which the individual strives for accomplishing the very best in everything.

The term 'excellence' is derived from the Latin word *excellentia* that translates as 'primacy'. It is defined as a state of exalted virtue or the possession of good qualities to an eminent degree. Excellence is characterized by flawlessness and impeccability.

However, excellence is the very opposite of perfectionism. The latter involves an attempt to satisfy social demands while losing one's true self in the process. Perfectionism is about spending 90 per cent of the time on achieving the final 10 per cent improvement in a project. On the other hand, excellence is about creatively and mindfully identifying how to accomplish 80 per cent of the outcome exceedingly well in 20 per cent of the time without any loss in quality.

The gaze of excellence is usually directed inwards. Current attainment levels are benchmarked with the results obtained in the immediate past. Excellence does not involve making very many external or competitive comparisons, except for the purpose of learning and development. Driven by an inner sense of purpose, the endeavour to excel is an attempt to do things differently—and thus create a game-changing impact.

Excellence is a win-win endeavour. It is rewarding for the organization as well as the individual.

When people work at a task with their head, hand as well as the heart, the parameters of quality, cost, time and responsiveness are often transcended. This serves the organizational interest.

At the same time excellence requires the involvement of one's complete being in whatever the person is engaged with. This is individually fulfilling.

The achievement of excellence requires the conquest of physical and mental distractions. These are enumerated by the sage Patanjali (*Yoga Sutras, Samadhi Pada*, sutra 30) as (a) illness, (b) dullness, (c) doubt, (d) negligence, (e) laziness, (f) cravings, (g) misperceptions and (h) failure.

The phenomenon of excellence is aptly illustrated in the manner that the ancient Indian treatise *Natya Shastra* characterizes the performance of the dancing arts: 'Where the hand goes, there the eyes should follow; where the eyes go, the mind should follow; where the mind goes, the feelings are generated; where the feelings are, the sentiment of [excellence] will be experienced there'.

The Pursuit of Excellence

Individual excellence requires all the intrinsic elements of the human personality to be synchronously brought to bear upon the task as per a defined process. In the pursuit of excellence, people transform the limitations and constraints of their environment into opportunities for expressing their creativity.

The following anecdote is illustrative of excellence as striving to operate at peak potential.

A visitor to a temple that was under construction saw a sculptor making an idol of God. Casually looking around, he noticed a similar idol lying nearby. Surprised, he asked the sculptor, 'Do you really need two statues of the same idol?' 'No', said the sculptor—without looking up. He then continued, 'We need only one, but the original statue got damaged at the last stage'.

The visitor examined the discarded idol and found no apparent fault with it. 'Where is the damage?', he asked. Still busy with his work, the sculptor replied, 'There is a scratch on the nose of the idol'. The visitor then asked, 'Where are you going to install the idol?' The sculptor indicated that it would be installed on a pillar that was 20 feet high.

'If the idol shall be placed that high, who is going to know that there is a scratch on the nose?" the gentleman asked. The sculptor stopped his work, smiled sweetly, and said, 'I will know it.'

The Attainment of Individual Excellence

The technology of excellence entails a natural, three-step process that helps to arrive at a specific solution to any problem or to obtain a desired result as the output. The three stages are simultaneous and synchronous (and not sequential) in nature. These may be described as follows:

1. **Frame:** Organize or gather together the input resources

2. **Focus:** Align the input resources so as to direct these towards a focal point

3. **Flow:** Carefully synchronize the resources in order to initiate the result

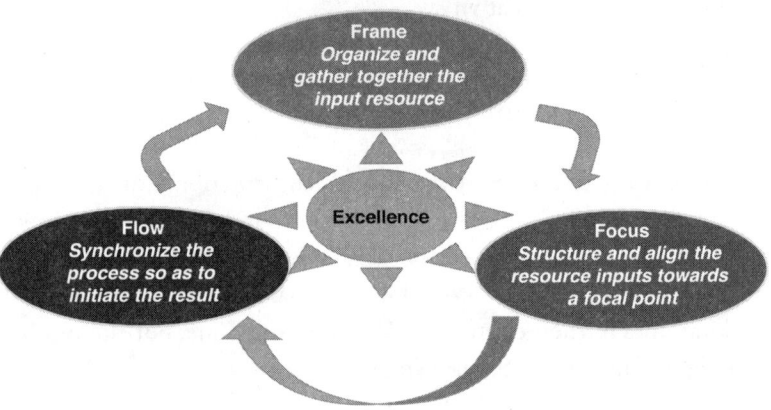

Technology of Individual Excellence
Source: Samatvam Academy

At the operational level, the technology of excellence may be grasped by examining how an ordinary sheet of paper is naturally ignited through the use of solar energy—with the help of a magnifying glass.

As a first step, the input resource is organized through the gathering of sunbeams upon the sheet of paper. This is achieved by turning its face to the sun.

Next, environmental influence is applied upon the input resource so as to bend it to a focal point. This is accomplished by the introduction of the magnifying glass between the sun and the paper. The energy of the sun is thereby transmitted on to the paper through the phenomenon of resonance.

Finally, the process is continued for a sufficient duration of time so that the temperature of the paper progressively increases to combustion point. Lo and behold, the paper catches fire!

ENGAGE!

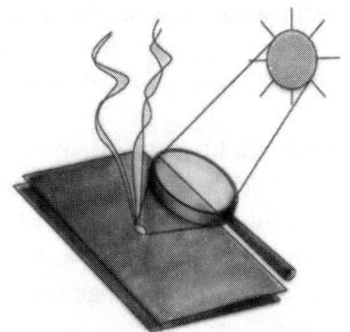

Ignition of Paper by Focusing Solar Energy
with the Help of Magnifying Glass
Source: Samatvam Academy

At the conceptual level, this elegant process of excellence may be comprehended by examining how a judge delivers an accurate judgement in the courtroom. Suppose two vehicles collide at a street corner. This results in an accident. The police register a case and bring it to the courtroom. The judge needs to pin down the cause of the event and deliver justice.

The judge is able to accomplish this par excellence by means of the following processes:

1. As the first step, the judge divides the horizontal field of vision around the accident into a number of equal segments. She calls for a number of eyewitnesses (one from each sector) to relate their observations with respect to the accident. The judge notes down their statements.

2. Once the recording of witnesses is complete, the judge starts to rationalize the different statements. She finds similar and complementary statements emanating from the witnesses located in adjacent segments.

    However, the facts appear to differ slightly from one eyewitness account to the next one. This is due to the slight relative difference in the physical location and perspective of each witness.

3. In the third step, the judge matches the opposing accounts of the event as well as the varying perspectives of the different witnesses until the specific cause of every deviation is accounted for.

4. When all the facts are fitted precisely and unambiguously in her mind, the judge finds that she is actually able to witness the accident in her mind's eye. In that instant she comes to an unequivocal conclusion regarding the cause of the accident. Now, the judge is ready to pass judgement on the matter with complete confidence.

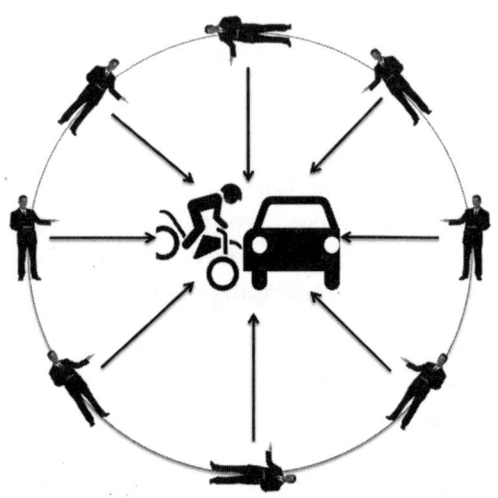

Process Used by a Judge to Deliver Accurate Judgement
Source: Samatvam Academy

The judge thus followed the three-step process of collecting the information (frame), mutually aligning the different elements of information (focus) and analysing the permutations and combinations so as to unambiguously fit all the facts together (flow) in order to arrive at a unique and accurate solution.

The beauty and elegance of this process arises from the fact that the view of the accident arrived at by the judge is more accurate than that of the witnesses actually present at the site. Each eyewitness was erroneously committed to the belief that his observation was totally correct. He was surprisingly unaware that a 'bird's eye view' of the accident could give a more holistic and accurate view of the accident.

Despite not being physically present on site at the time of the accident, the judge comes across as the only expert witness of the event. She could accurately recount the happenings on account of a diligent adherence to this simple, natural and elegant process that yields excellence.

The Individual Excellence Framework

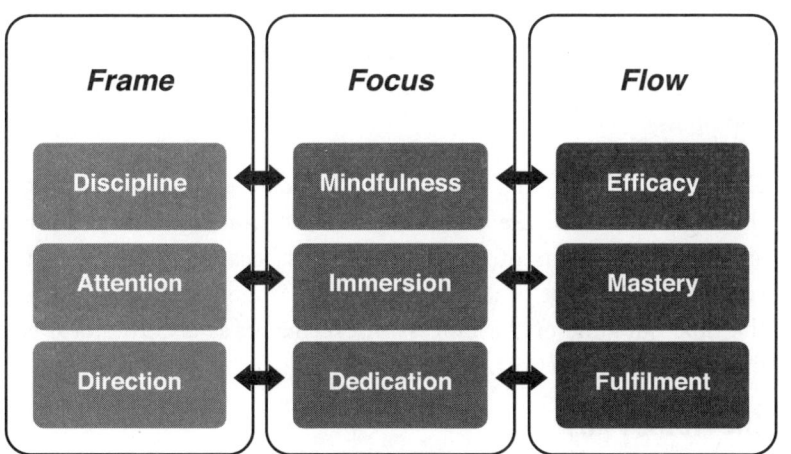

The Individual Excellence Framework
Source: Samatvam Academy

Excellence emerges from an active progression through the stages of frame, focus and flow. Each stage operates concurrently across the affective, cognitive and behavioural dimensions of the personality. This model draws upon ancient *Sankhya* philosophy.

At the behavioural level, the process of excellence progresses through *discipline* (the capacity to exercise self-direction and inner control over one's personality) that facilitates *mindfulness* (the maintenance of a moment-by-moment awareness of one's subjective conscious, experience) and culminates into *efficacy* (the capacity to produce the defined amount of a desired effect).

With respect to the cognitive dimension, excellence arises from paying *attention* (the conscious application of the mind to any thought or sense object) followed by *immersion* (the complete submergence into something, or the deep mental engagement with some activity), leading to the capacity for *mastery* (the possession of comprehensive knowledge or consummate skill).

On the affective plane, the phenomenon of *direction* (a clear line of thought or action) naturally facilitates *dedication* (a strong physical connection or adherence towards something) that eventually leads to a state of *fulfilment* (a feeling of intense satisfaction and happiness).

ENGAGE!

Discipline is the starting point of the excellence endeavour. It signifies the organization of the relevant resources. Immersion is the pivot, as also the very crux of excellence. This is because it represents the complete alignment of all the personality dimensions. Fulfilment is the final outcome of the process of excellence, as also the ideal end product of human effort.

The Frame Phase

At the behavioural level, 'frame' refers to the capacity for discipline that is denoted by orderliness in bearing and conduct. In the mental domain, 'frame' connotes the capacity to devote mental energy and attention exclusively upon a chosen object or endeavour. On the affective plane, 'frame' implies a sense of personal direction through the discovery or gathering together of the cognitive, affective and conative capabilities that are potentially resident within the individual.

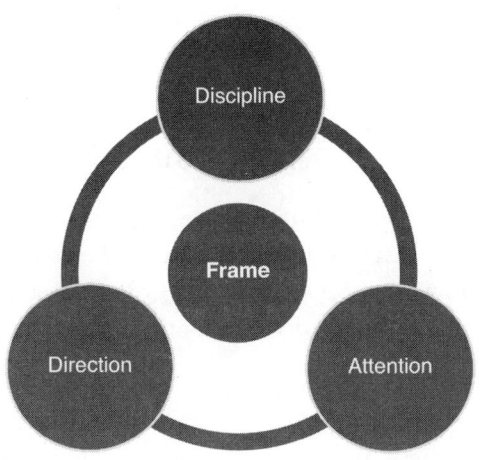

The Frame Phase
Source: Samatvam Academy

Discipline

Discipline is the capacity to exercise self-direction and inner control over one's personality. It refers to the process of the learning or training of an individual's physical, mental or moral faculties.

Discipline builds the person's capacity to proceed in an organized manner according to a given plan of action. It is an opportunity to free oneself from weakness and distraction.

Biological research has identified over 100 internal clocks that govern our heartbeat, breathing, metabolism, body temperature, sense of time, memory and other parameters.[1] When the biorhythms created by these tickers operate in mutual alignment with one another, the human being naturally experiences a sense of order and discipline in one's life.

Discipline reflects an individual's capacity to break dysfunctional habit patterns, restrain impulses, regulate desires and accept internal authority. External behaviour and attitudes are aligned with one's basic motives and deeper values. Discipline is, thus, a vehicle for personal transformation.

Attention

Attention is the state or act of applying the mind to any object of sense or thought. It is the cognitive process of deliberate concentration upon a discrete aspect of information to the exclusion of other events.

Attention is the act of directing one's awareness upon a single entity, or a limited sphere that is selected from among the multitude. It involves a selective narrowing of consciousness in order to deal effectively with some things while momentarily withdrawing from others.[2]

A governing process deep within the human psyche selects a particular sensory input (to the exclusion of numerous others) and provides its entry into awareness. The faculty of attention then allows the person to engage with the selected stimulus. Attention, thus, refers to the human ability to:

1. Take cognizance of all the stimuli being bombarded upon the senses.

2. Immediately categorize and organize the information as significant or irrelevant.

3. Direct the conscious resources upon the object that has been chosen as salient.

Direction

The term 'direction' generally refers to a line of thought, action, inclination or path along which a person or thing begins to move or develop. A direction may also be referred to as one's *swadharma*, which is a mode of life and action that arises out of an intrinsic sense of duty and responsibility in accordance with one's inherent nature.

A sense of direction determines the behaviour patterns and rhythms of a person's daily life. Direction finds expression in the goals and objectives that people create, the effort devoted towards these aims and decisions with respect to the time, energy and attention to be expended towards goal achievement.

The direction is crystallized when a person finds a way to productively use one's key strengths, talents and values towards the economic, social as well as moral good.[3] It involves incessant reflection and exploration of one's inner world.

The Focus Phase

On the behavioural plane, focus takes the form of *mindfulness*—the openness and receptivity to the whole field of awareness so that it can be directed to the currently experienced sensations, thoughts, emotions and memories. On the mental plane, focus may be achieved by the practice of deep *immersion* over an extended period of time. The intent is to expand our habitually limited capabilities through the careful channelization of psychosomatic power. In the emotional domain, focus reflects a sense of *dedication* to the ideal.

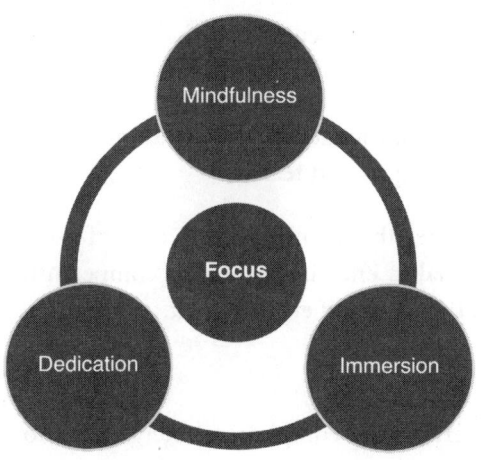

The Focus Phase
Source: Samatvam Academy

Mindfulness

Mindfulness refers to the maintenance of moment-by-moment awareness of one's subjective and conscious experience from a first-person perspective.[4] It is a flexible state of existence, an attitude of open acceptance and the witnessing of one's own perceptions and sensibilities. Mindfulness helps the person to experience a calm, relaxed and alert state of being.

Mindfulness is characterized by an attentive awareness of the reality of things in the current instant, coupled with a clear comprehension of whatever is taking place. It involves the following five factors:

1. Perceiving stimuli, emotions and the elements of inner experience without being reactive

2. Observing and noticing sensations or perceptions, even when they appear unpleasant or painful

3. Acting with awareness, and without distraction

4. Easy and nuanced articulation of beliefs, opinions and expectations in words

5. Abstaining from judgement or criticism of oneself for having irrational thoughts and feelings

Mindfulness shapes the learning experiences of human beings. It is particularly crucial in enabling people to competently deal with the uncertainty in their life and environment.

Immersion

Immersion refers to the complete submergence into something or deep mental engagement with some activity or interest. It is the state of being wholly engrossed or absorbed.

Immersion is a state of dynamic equilibrium. A fragile sense of balance is established between the availability of action opportunities and the individual's capacity to capitalize upon these. If the challenges exceed the level of skill, the person becomes anxious. On the other hand, when the abilities exceed the challenges one gets bored.

An immersed person enters a subjective state that is marked by an intuitive state of knowing in the present moment. Action and awareness are merged. The activity is experienced as intrinsically rewarding, and leads to enhanced confidence and self-assurance.

The finest creative or intellectual work usually occurs only when a state of complete immersion is attained. For instance, the inventor solves the most daunting riddles when she is not conscious of any deliberate effort to solve a problem. The disappearance of self-consciousness that occurs in immersion opens the door to a new and blissful world, which is usually not accessible in normal life.

Dedication

Dedication is ordinarily defined as a feeling of strong support and loyalty towards a special ideal or activity. It refers to being enthusiastically involved in and engaged with one's work.[5]

Dedication is the quality of being deeply or uncommonly committed to a task or purpose. It is an internal contract that guarantees the continuance of effort with regularity—even in the presence of apathy, hopelessness and demotivation. Dedication is accompanied by passion. It provides energy to make things happen.

Dedicated people demonstrate a determination to do their best and persist in the face of obstacles. They find ways to succeed rather than reasons to fail. Dedication underpins the person's sustained capacity to act in the identified direction, above and beyond the call of duty.

The Flow Phase

At the level of behaviour, 'efficacy' refers to the belief in one's ability to succeed in specific situations or to produce the desired result. In the domain of the psyche, 'mastery' is the possession or display of superlative skill or technique. On the affective plane, flow is characterized by a feeling of *fulfilment*—a state of gentle happiness and deep satisfaction.

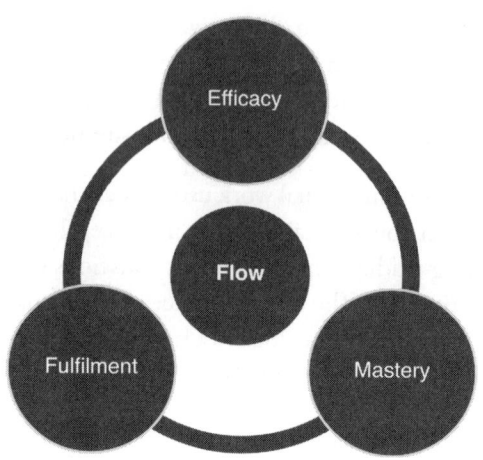

The Flow Phase

Source: Samatvam Academy

Efficacy

Efficacy refers to the capacity for producing the defined amount of the desired effect.[6] It is the quality of being successful in producing an intended result by expending effort. The 'capacity to produce effects' is how Lord Buddha has defined the phenomenon of truth.

Self-efficacy refers to an individual's confidence in her ability to organize and execute a course of action, towards the achievement of the necessary task or to succeed in a specific situation. A person's efficacy is influenced by previous experiences of success, availability of role models, social persuasion, personal strengths and vulnerabilities, health and vitality and deeply held values and beliefs.[7]

A strong sense of efficacy leads the individual to approach difficult tasks as a challenge to be mastered.

Mastery

Mastery refers to the possession of comprehensive knowledge or understanding of a subject, consummate skill in some area or rectitude during an action that allows a person to do or use something very well.

Mastery is the capacity to produce outstanding results through the development of psychological expertise in the principles that underlie those outcomes. A master demonstrates *competence* (the ability to perform a range of skills), *contextualization* (knowing when to do what), *contingency* (the flexibility to cope, adapt and respond when things go wrong), as well as *creativity* (the capacity to solve novel problems).[8]

According to Hubert Dreyfus, individuals pass through six stages of learning in the course of gaining mastery in any endeavour. These are as follows: (a) novice, (b) advanced beginner, (c) competent, (d) proficient, (e) expert and (f) master.[9]

A novice learns the basics of a subject by rigidly adhering to rules, plans or instructions. The advanced beginner connects the rules and facts to relevant contexts, but has very little sense of practical priority. A competent performer is able to contextually select rules or perspectives and formulate an approach towards problem-solving.

A proficient performer can take a holistic view of the situation, perceive deviations from the normal pattern and select the best course of action by supplementing reasoning with intuition.

The expert transcends the reliance on rules, guidelines and maxims. He/she tailors the method and approach through an intuitive grasp of situations, based on a deep and tacit understanding.

The master creatively synthesizes the available methods and tools, in order to develop her own unique style and approach. She also contributes to the development of new domain knowledge.[9]

Fulfilment

Fulfilment is the state, process or act of bringing oneself to flourishing completion. It relates to the fullest possible expression of the innate potentialities of a person. Fulfilment results in a feeling of intense satisfaction and happiness.

The capacity of the fulfilled individual for accurate perception of people and situations is heightened. The tendency for gaining false impressions is diminished. The activity that arises from a fulfilled state of being is perennially fresh and authentic. It is characterized by a unique and distinctive quality.

In a fulfilled state, the different dimensions of the individual personality get reintegrated. This leads to an existential sense of completeness. True fulfilment is marked by a return to the subjective principle of consciousness, which is at the core of the human self as well as the very foundation or ground of universal reality. The person operates effortlessly and lives spontaneously from moment to moment.

Fulfilment is characterized by fearlessness. The psychological defence mechanisms that previously served to prop up a partial, incomplete or false sense of identity are now no longer required.

The Bhagavad Gita (chapter 2, sutra 50) describes the phenomenon of excellence as *Yogah Karmasu Kaushalam*. This translates, 'The performance of the allocated work in an excellent manner is Yoga'.

Excellence, thus, represents the acme of human work and achievement on the individual plane. It can be effortlessly achieved through a simple and elegant process.

The pursuit of excellence may appear esoteric to some people and as a luxury to others. However, the truth is exactly the opposite. The achievement of excellent results has a transformational impact upon the individual, the organization and the society itself.

As an illustration, the next case study explores the legendary story of how Steve Jobs inspired excellence at Apple Inc. He thereby helped the company to create history in ways more than one.

References

1. ScienceDaily. How does body temperature reset the biological clock? *ScienceDaily*. Available at: www.sciencedaily.com/releases/2012/08/120823143051.htm (accessed: 16 December 2015).

2. James W. *The Principles of Psychology*. New York, NY: H. Holt and Company; 1890. p. 404.

3. Seligman M. *Authentic Happiness*. New York, NY: Free Press; 2002. pp. 13, 160.

4. Ataria Y. Mindfulness and trauma: Some striking similarities. *Anthropology of Consciousness*. 2018; 29(1): 44–56.

5. Bakker A & Demerouti E. Towards a model of work engagement. *Career Development International*. 2008; 13(3): 209–223.

6. Bandura A. Self-efficacy: Towards a unifying theory of behavioral change. *Psychological Review*. 1977; 84(2): 191–215.

7. Bandura A. Self-efficacy. In: Ramachandran V. (Ed.) *Encyclopedia of Human Behavior*, Vol. 4. New York, NY: Academic Press; 1994. pp. 71–81.

8. Attri R. Defining competence, proficiency, expertise, and mastery. *Androidgogy*. Available at: https://androidgogy.com/2012/09/16/skill-proficiency-expertise-and-shuhari/ (accessed: 16 December 2015).

9. Dreyfus S. The five-stage model of adult skill acquisition. *Bulletin of Science, Technology & Society*. 2004; 24(3): 177–181.

CASE STUDY
APPLE INC.

The people who are crazy enough to think they can change the world...are the ones that do.

—Apple's 'Think Different' commercial, 1997

BACKGROUND

Apple Inc., formerly Apple Computer, Inc., is a multinational corporation that creates consumer electronics, personal computers, computer software as well as communication and media devices.[2] It is also a digital distributor of media content. Through its products and services the company serves individual consumers, enterprises, educational institutions and governments worldwide.

Apple is the largest publicly traded corporation in the world by market capitalization. With annual revenues of US$ 229 billion in 2017, it was valued at US$ 927 billion as of May 2018.[1]

Apple Computer was co-founded by Steve Jobs, Steve Wozniak and Ronald Wayne on 1 April 1976 in Cupertino, California. However, Wayne stayed only a short time—leaving Jobs and Wozniak as the primary co-founders of the company.

The company's co-founder Late Steve Jobs was a famous creative entrepreneur. His dream to create a computer for the 'rest of us' sparked the personal computer revolution. Steve's ferocious drive and passion for perfection eventually revolutionized six industries: (a) personal computers, (b) animated movies, (c) music, (d) telephony, (e) tablet computing and (f) digital publishing.

Riding upon a missionary spirit, Apple remains a global business icon. For the first quarter century of its existence, the company was predominantly a manufacturer of personal computers. These included the Apple II, the Macintosh and the Power Mac series.

However, with the introduction of the iPod music player in 2001 and the iTunes Music Store in 2003, Apple established itself as a world leader in the consumer electronics and the media industries too.

Apple is presently famous for its iOS range of smartphone, media and tablet computer products. These include the iPhone, the iPod Touch, the iPad and the Apple Watch.

PRODUCT DESIGN AND DEVELOPMENT

The personality and philosophy of Apple's co-founder Steve Jobs deeply influenced the product development function at the company. This was true while he was alive, and remains valid even after he passed away.

Jobs was passionate about product design. He insisted that Apple's computers look perfect on the outside as well as inside. Steve's vision of design was succinctly captured in the statement, 'Simplicity is the ultimate sophistication.'

However, sophistication arising out of simplicity did not imply an inherent trade-off between the two attributes. Beauty did not imply the absence of functionality. In fact, the search for elegance often led the company to develop prescient and unanticipated features that appeared in the competitors' product offerings only much later.

Exquisite, neat and beautifully designed products were Apple's hallmark. The company's guiding tenet of design simplicity required herculean efforts to learn deeply about the essence of every product, the function of each of its components and the nuances of their engineering. The stunning appearance and performance of Apple products resulted from original thinking and painstaking attention to detail in all aspects of design and development.

At Apple, design simplicity and ease of product use were achieved by eliminating things. The company's products were noteworthy for what they did *not* contain.

For instance, the slot for inserting diskettes was eliminated from the Macintosh computers. While the iMac started out in an array of colours and in one determined shape, it subsequently came to be offered exclusively in white colour and in vastly varied configurations too. Even the iPhone, which was originally designed as 'hermetically' sealed, was later accompanied by a developer platform and a host of dedicated applications. And in the MacBook Air, many features that were hitherto assumed to be indispensable were likewise 'missing'.

When the smallest details were scrutinized, it became easy to discover what could be lived without. However, taking 'out' features did not automatically result in the appeal that Apple strove to create. Rather, products were allowed to evolve such that they sometimes went on to include things that were previously eliminated.

Given the popularity of Macs, iPods, iPhones and iPads over the years, Apple's success could be attributed to an ability to tap into a sense of that which is trendy at the moment. The reverse was actually the case. Rather than design around what was currently popular, Apple created products that defined or established what was considered to be fashionable at any point in time.

THE DESIGN PHILOSOPHY

Steve Jobs believed that when the underlying challenges of a design were carefully comprehended, the resulting products became simple, elegant and beautiful. Design simplicity translated into intuitive ease of use rather than sleekness that intimidates.

For instance, the design of the original iPod was intimately connected to its pristine white colour and the polymer finish that accomplished the look. A two-layered polycarbon plastic coating over the layer of solid white provided the iPod with a beautiful, snow-coloured 'skin'. This was then laid on to the rear steel cladding in order to get a sort of halo around the product. Its development was considered to be technically impossible, but Apple managed to pull it off.

When the iPod Mini was introduced a few years later, the design philosophy remained exactly the same. However, the Mini utilized the new hard drive technology and was released in multiple colours. To facilitate these, the polycarbon plastic and 'snow' of the original gave way to an alumina metal casing that could be 'blasted' and then anodized (the equivalent of dyeing). The Mini became wildly popular.

The company's passionate championship of pristine white, and the advocacy of colour within a couple of years with equal enthusiasm, indicated that Apple remained keenly receptive to new technology, materials and processes. The company eschewed a static approach that assumed a single conclusion. It adopted a dynamic approach to innovation. No product feature or facet was considered sacrosanct.

Apple's ability to retain its design philosophy, while it adapted to new technology and materials, was evident in the iPod Nano and Shuffle too. The cost, the physical size and the amount of music that could be stored on these derivative products were progressively pruned. The idea was that people would want a 'portfolio' of iPods. And so they did![2]

Thus, Apple embraced a constructive approach towards capitalizing upon new and varied design possibilities. However quirky and contrary an idea might initially appear, it was gladly adopted if it served the broader mission of creating 'insanely great' products for the rest of the world to use.

THE DESIGN PROCESS

Jobs believed that when a design problem appeared to be simple at first glance, this was a sign that its complexity had been poorly understood. The resulting solutions were inadequate and unsatisfactory.

People would then begin to appreciate and grapple with the true complexity of the issue. Fuzzy solutions were developed, and even operationalized for a while. Soon, the world would move on and get interested in something else. The matter often rested there.

However, Jobs had a distinct vision of design perfection and excellence across the board. He considered a great designer to be one who kept the search on, until the key underlying principle of the problem would be located. The design solution that finally emerged would be beautiful, elegant and functional.

The goal of the original cadre of Apple developers was to design computers that people could fall in love with. This was actually a necessity since the machines were otherwise expensive to purchase and complex to operate. For the users to choose Apple products, their design needed to be functional, user-friendly, aesthetic and exquisite enough to be regarded as a work of art. And so it came to be!

Apple adopted a relatively unstructured and iterative approach towards product design. The process would commence with an abstract notion of that which was to be created and delivered. Slowly, it would get better defined and start to assume a concrete shape. A further refinement would take it to a point where the prototype would begin to deliver something.

It might then occur to the design team that they had missed the mark completely. The entire software code or product scheme would be set aside. A cleaner model would then be built from scratch, and perhaps get a little lopsided once again with further additions.

Things would progress iteratively thus, until an insight would suddenly emerge (as if) out of thin air. The exact form of the product would then take shape, almost magically. The designers would now craft a simple, elegant and appropriate solution to the design 'problem'.

Product design requires the courage and confidence to repeatedly set things aside, and build from scratch. Apple often designed products whose utility and appeal were unquestionable, even when the technology to build these had not yet emerged.

The designers created a target, and then worked with the engineering and the manufacturing teams to reach it. Both sides applied a lot of creativity, ingenuity and innovation in order to make the 'impossible' happen in actual practice.

USER CENTRICITY

Apple believed that its products needed to be simple, interactive and intuitive enough for users to closely integrate their work along with the device. The company paid careful attention to the most minute of details, which the users may not otherwise notice or consciously care about. This significantly contributed to the product's appeal as well as utility.

For instance, the iPod appeared to be a simple and friendly device that merely allowed people to store and navigate their music. However, the simplification that went into its design had been very well thought through. The fact that no other company managed to duplicate the capabilities of iPod for a long time meant that the building blocks of its design were difficult to come by.

Apple products were designed to be personal tools that facilitated individual efforts for problem-solving. After all, a device was merely a tool that helped people to experience or accomplish something. The company, thus, integrated customer experience into its design and development processes in order to create user-friendly products. Direct user inputs helped to proactively identify any problems or glitches, and facilitate the smooth functioning of the actual product.

While Apple took great care to understand what the people sought in the first place, it would go on to envisage what more the device could potentially do for its users. Extra capabilities that users may not even have dreamt about usually took root in the mind of Apple's design team, years in advance. The beautifully designed products of the company took shape in this extraordinarily aspirational milieu.

For instance, the Macintosh exemplified the intuitive way in which people could work with a computer. Leveraging the instinctive and habitual ability of the users to shuffle the papers lying on their physical desks, the graphical screen of the Mac was modelled on the metaphor of the desktop. This enabled the users to handle the documents on the computer screen in a similar fashion.

BOLD EXPERIMENTATION

Steve Jobs once noted that Apple's explosive growth was not an excuse to play it safe, but to actually get bolder. A salient example of this line of thought was the company's audacious decision to move into retail, against near-universal received wisdom.

The idea of Apple Stores was quite controversial at the time when the company opened its first Apple Store at McLean, Virginia, in May 2001. Physical stores were then being derided as 'bricks' that were sure to succumb to Internet 'clicks'. Similar attempts by Gateway Computers had been a spectacular failure. It was not apparent as to who would come to visit the Apple Store and why. Since the iPod was still a few months away, and the fanatical fan base of Macintosh computers represented a minuscule 3 per cent of the market, Apple's bet on 'foot traffic' was deemed ridiculous.

On the other hand, Dell's hallowed web-based purchasing approach was considered as the 'best practice' of the day. The company allowed customers to create their own products by providing various combinations that could be swiftly built and dispatched through efficient manufacturing and delivery processes. Customers used the company's website to design the exact configuration of the hardware and the software they required, and immediately found out how much it would cost. Further, Dell needed only 36 hours after the receipt of an order before it shipped a computer out of the door.

In contrast, customers visiting an Apple Store found only a few products and a limited amount of software for sale. The available machines were of a specific, predetermined configuration. Further, they were priced distinctly higher than those available at Dell and other websites.

Yet foot traffic is exactly what the Apple Stores generated. Curious non-Apple customers were drawn into elegant surroundings, in upscale locations that hosted beautiful as well as useful devices. Technical repair and support was publicly undertaken at 'genius bars' within the store.

This helped seal the company's 'cool' image. By 2008, Apple Stores had become architectural statements that attracted a huge number of 'destination' shoppers.

As another example of counterintuitive experimentation, Apple insisted on developing and integrating its own hardware and software. Its backward migration into designing chips for iPods and iPhones initially appeared to be out of step with the evolution of the industry.

In a world that celebrated the open source movement, third-party developers, community design and transparency, Apple clearly seemed to be an outlier. Yet the company regularly managed to create 'insanely great', award-winning devices that were loved and adored by the users. At the same time, these products created handsome profits for the company.

LESSONS AND INSIGHTS

Apple and Steve Jobs are deeply intertwined in the minds of most people. Insights about Apple may, thus, be gleaned by appreciating the style and personality characteristics of Jobs himself.

Steve Jobs was an artist as well as an engineer. He was an ardent Buddhist and a hard-nosed businessman at the same time. A seamless integrator of opposites, Steve was an optimist and a pessimist rolled into one. A rugged individualist who appealed to the masses, he was also a prickly and somewhat difficult leader who inspired enormous loyalty among his troops. Jobs stubbornly guarded privacy and secrecy, even as Apple provided the world with the tools of transparency.

Brilliance, insight and courage were the hallmarks of Steve Jobs. His 'satori' leaps of genius redefined the technology landscape forever. Jobs could hold two completely disparate ideas and values in the mind at the same time, and then synthesize these in order to create simple, elegant and intuitive outcomes.

Steve's biographer Walter Isaacson considered the following attributes as the key to Apple's success, particularly during the time that the company was under the active stewardship of Jobs.[3]

WHEN BEHIND, LEAPFROG

The hallmark of excellence is not only to emerge with new ideas first but also to leapfrog when one has fallen behind.[3] When Apple built the original iMac, the focus was upon helping the user manage photos and videos. The music was relatively neglected. On the other hand, the IBM PCs facilitated song downloads and the burning of CDs.

Instead of merely catching up by upgrading the CD drive of the iMac, Apple created an integrated system that would transform the music industry. The result was the trio of iTunes, the iTunes Store and the iPod that allowed users to seamlessly buy, share, manage, store and play music.

PUT PRODUCTS BEFORE PROFITS

Apple's mandate to the Macintosh design team in the early 1980s was to make an 'insanely great' product with remarkable capabilities without worrying about profit maximization or cost trade-offs.

At his first retreat with the Macintosh team, Steve Jobs began by writing a maxim on his whiteboard 'Don't compromise'. The machine that resulted was very costly, and led to his ouster from Apple. Nevertheless, it accelerated the home computer revolution.[4]

In the long run, Apple got the balance right. It created legendary products and reaped unprecedented fame and success as a result.

THINK AHEAD

Steve Jobs believed that caring deeply about the customer's needs and wants required an instinctive feel for the desires that had not yet formed in their minds and hearts. Instead of relying on market research, Jobs honed his own version of empathy and intimate intuition about how best the customers and their needs could be served.[5]

Steve often invoked the words of Henry Ford, 'If I would have asked customers what they wanted, they would have told me, "A faster horse!"'

BEND REALITY

Steve Jobs had the capacity to inspire people to achieve the 'unachievable' and to innovate the 'impossible'. His colleagues dubbed it as Steve's reality distortion field.

For instance, Steve Jobs complained to Larry Kenyon (the engineer responsible for the Macintosh's operating system) that the machine was taking too long to boot up. Brushing off Kenyon's protestations, Jobs asked him, 'If it would save a person's life, could you find a way to shave 10 seconds off the boot time?' Kenyon accepted that he probably could.

Steve then showed that if 5 million people were using the Mac, and it took 10 seconds extra to turn it on every day, this added up to around 300 million hours an year. That was the equivalent of at least 100 lifetimes. This interaction had the desired impact. Kenyon was able to programme the machine to boot up 28 seconds faster within a few weeks.

PUSH FOR PERFECTION

During the development of almost every product, Steve would repeatedly go back to the drawing board because he felt that the conception was not perfect.

For instance, the initial design of the iPhone had the glass screen set into an aluminium case. The device felt too masculine, task-driven and efficient.[3] Jobs mandated the team to design afresh. 'We are all going to have to work nights and weekends. If you want, we can hand out some guns so that you can kill us now', he exhorted.

Instead of balking, the people agreed. This became one of his proudest moments at Apple.

Steve's perfectionism extended even to the parts unseen. As a young boy, he had helped his father build a fence around their backyard. They employed as much care on the back of the fence as on its front. In response to the lad's complaint that nobody will ever know what is on the back, Jobs replied, 'But you will know'. It was the mark of a true artist to have such a passion for excellence and perfection.

STAY HUNGRY, STAY FOOLISH

Steve Jobs was influenced by two cultures during his early life: the hippie movement of the San Francisco Bay Area and the high-tech, entrepreneurial culture of the Silicon Valley.

An admixture of these cultures was found in publications such as Stewart Brand's Whole Earth Catalog.[4] On its first cover was the famous picture of Earth taken from space, indicating that technology could be friendly. The final issue carried a photograph of an early morning country road with the words, 'Stay Hungry. Stay Foolish' written beneath it.

Steve Jobs stayed hungry and foolish throughout his career. He complemented the business and engineering aspects of his personality with his nonconformist and artistic streaks.[4]

Since the death of Jobs seven years ago, Apple remains without a landmark new product. The Apple Watch is a limited success, while the Apple TV is yet to make its mark.

Yet the company is soaring in ways that it never did before. Its revenues and profits continue to hit new highs.

Without the physical presence and the 'wow' factor that Steve Jobs provided to the company, it remains to be seen if Apple shall continue to be as successful in the new regime. As the company celebrated its 42nd birthday, the key question is not whether Apple can continue to stay ahead of Samsung, Google and others. Rather, the world seeks to know if it has the capacity to reinvent itself successfully for 'life after Steve Jobs'.

The jury is still out!

REFERENCES

1. Sommer J & Russell K. Apple is the most valuable public company ever. But how much of a record is that? *Nytimes.com*. Available at: www.nytimes.com/interactive/2017/12/05/your-money/apple-market-share.html (accessed: 8 May 2018).

2. Thomke SH & Feinberg B. *Design Thinking and Innovation at Apple*. Boston, MA: Harvard Business School; 2009.

3. Isaacson W. *Steve Jobs*. 1st ed. New York, NY: Simon & Schuster; 2011.

4. Isaacson W. The real leadership lessons of Steve Jobs. *Harvard Business Review*. Available at: https://hbr.org/2012/04/the-real-leadership-lessons-of-steve-jobs (accessed: 14 March 2016).

5. Gregoire C. The unexpected source that inspired whole foods, apple's sleek design and the white album. *HuffPost India*. 2013. Available at: www.huffingtonpost.in/entry/famous-inspiration-from-meditation_n_4297598 (accessed: 16 March 2016).

VIDEO REFERENCE

Samatvam. (2016, March 30). *Apple Inc.—The Missionaries of Excellence*. YouTube. Available at: https://youtu.be/Z2FRoRIKpe8 (accessed: 26 November 2018).

SUPERVISORY ACUMEN

8

Rank does not confer privilege or give power. It imposes responsibility.

—*Peter F. Drucker*

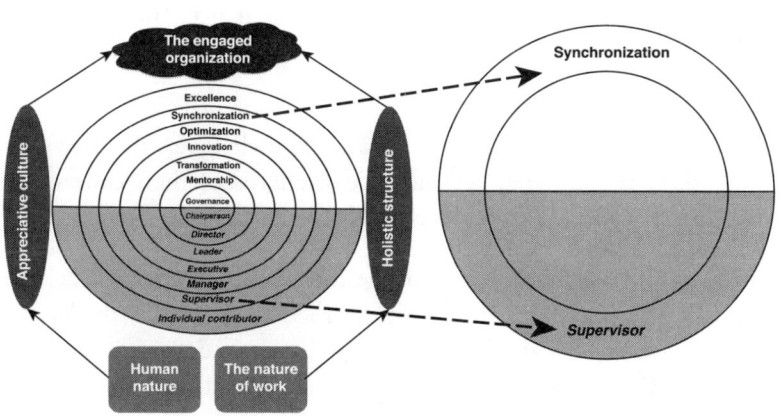

The Supervisory Mandate of Synchronization
Source: Samatvam Academy

Supervision refers to the act of overseeing the activities performed by other people. It is concerned with observing, guiding and monitoring a group of people as they apply themselves towards the performance of the assigned responsibilities—within time, cost, quality, safety and other stipulated parameters.

The term supervision arises out of a combination of the two words 'super' (meaning over and above) and 'vision' (the act of seeing). On the other hand, the term 'acumen' refers to the possession of keen insight. Thus, supervisory acumen is the ability to educate a team of people about the job requirements as well as expectations and then purposefully coordinate their efforts towards accomplishment.

The core supervisory mandate is to achieve collective results by:

1.   Implementing the performance agenda for a group of individual contributors.

2.   Harmonizing and integrating their efforts.

3.   Providing guidance and counsel as necessary.

This mandate places the supervisor at the second rung of the accountability hierarchy. In contemporary parlance, the supervisor is also variously referred to as the departmental head, team leader or project incharge.

Supervisors usually have strong working knowledge of the activities under their charge. They leverage the strengths of their colleagues, give clear directions and provide timely feedback to the people.

Effective supervisors are known to be considerate, supportive, democratic, flexible and development-oriented. They respond with alacrity to contingent events and reciprocate sensitively in delicate situations. Their creativity lies in managing the overall context within which the workgroup operates.

The Transition from Individual Contributor to Supervisor

When meritorious individual contributors produce good results and also demonstrate an ability to collaborate with other people, they are usually promoted to a supervisory role. This is the first occasion when they assume professional responsibility for coordinating the work of other colleagues.[1]

Moving from doing an assigned task well (e.g., playing the violin) to synchronizing the efforts of other people (e.g., conducting the music orchestra) constitutes a daunting upward shift in responsibility.

This situation is akin to marriage or parenthood. The focus shifts from fulfilling one's own desires and aspirations towards satisfying the needs and wants of other people.

This transition is something for which their previous 'individual performer' role does not prepare them. Thus, freshly promoted supervisors often experience their new role as a 'stretch' assignment. Most new incumbents also fail to appreciate the reality of how the supervisory duty differs sharply from individual work.

There are at least five common myths and misperceptions that lead to mistakes in their early days.[2]

First, supervisors expect their commands to be complied with on account of the formal authority invested in them. In actual practice, the colleagues obey only after the supervisor has won their respect and trust. Team leaders need to demonstrate good character, competence as well as an ability to care for others before the group members willingly accept their directions.

Second, supervisors erroneously believe that a significant amount of authority comes from their new job and title. In actual practice, they find themselves enmeshed in a web of interdependent relationships with colleagues and associates—inside as well as outside of the organization. Supervisors are thereby required to negotiate and navigate their way ahead. Linda Hill quotes a new promotee as saying, 'Becoming a [supervisor] is not about becoming a boss; it is about becoming a hostage'.[3]

Third, authority flows from the formal organizational position of the supervisor. When team leaders authoritatively direct a colleague to do something, the latter does not necessarily respond. In fact, the more talented the person, the less likely she is to simply follow the orders. The supervisory cause is best served by seeking a strong sense of commitment rather than compliance.

Fourth, supervisors mistakenly believe that they must build friends and forge good individual relationships at the workplace. This is mandatory, but inadequate for supervisory excellence. The actual fact is that the supervisor must harness the concerted power of the group. By shaping the team culture around diversity of talent, progressive norms and shared values, the supervisor unleashes the collective problem-solving prowess of the workgroup.

Finally, the mandate of the supervisor is considered to be that of ensuring that things run smoothly. This is certainly necessary, but by no means sufficient for supervisory success.

Supervisors must proactively initiate the necessary changes that can enhance the performance of their workgroup. In doing so, they sometimes need to challenge certain organizational systems and processes that lie beyond their locus of direct control.

Supervisory Work

Supervisors are required to perform three distinct roles at work[1]:

1. An *operational* role, wherein the workflow is managed through problem-solving and decision-making—so as to meet the targets in terms of output, timeliness, cost and quality.

2. A *communication* role, whereby the supervisor serves as a two-way conduit between the management and the frontline employees.

3. A *supportive* role, wherein the team members are encouraged and motivated to do their best.

The Development of Supervisory Acumen

Supervisors guide and enthuse groups and teams of employees or associates on the operational front. Because human beings learn and grow chiefly by imitation, the behaviour patterns of the supervisor set the tone for the interpersonal interactions within the entire workgroup.

In order to become an effective supervisor, a person thereby needs to:

1. Demonstrate *personal credibility*, which is the quality of being trusted and believed by others—through the demonstration of personal clarity, hope and authenticity.

2. Build *interpersonal commitment*, which is the act of inspiring the involvement, enthusiasm and dedication of other colleagues.

3. Enable *collective collaboration* by aligning and empowering the employees to work together at the intersection of common goals.

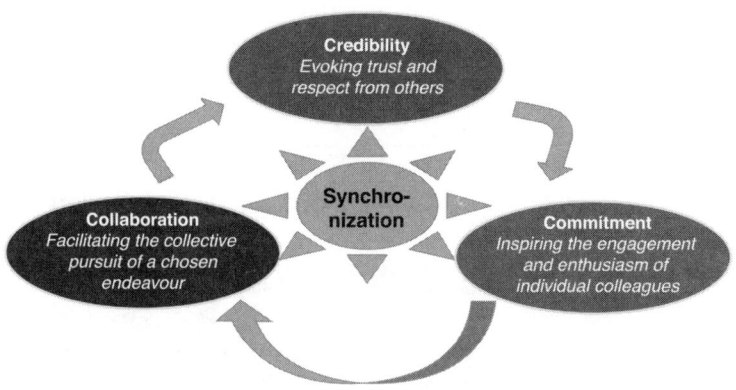

Technology of Supervisory Acumen

Source: Samatvam Academy

The Supervisory Acumen Framework

Supervisory acumen is developed by means of an active and iterative progression through the three stages of credibility, commitment and collaboration. Each stage operates concurrently across the behavioural, cognitive and affective dimensions of the human personality.

On the behavioural plane, the phenomenon of *authenticity* (the unobstructed operation of one's core self in daily operation) naturally facilitates *empathy* (the ability to identify and understand another person's situation and feelings without making value judgements) that eventually leads to collective *alignment* (affective agreement or cooperation among persons in a group).

At the affective level, *clarity* (lucidity of understanding about one's inherent strengths, sense of purpose as well as vision of the future) facilitates *motivation* (the condition of having a strong desire or enthusiasm to accomplish something) that eventually culminates into *mobilization* (the act of marshalling, organizing and assembling resources for deployment) on the collective plane.

With respect to the cognitive dimension, *hope* (the expectation that something desirable shall occur in the future) leads to *adaptability* (the ability to adjust oneself readily to different conditions) that facilitates *synchronization* (the systematization of activities such that a system can operate harmoniously, and in unison).

The framework may be succinctly represented as follows.

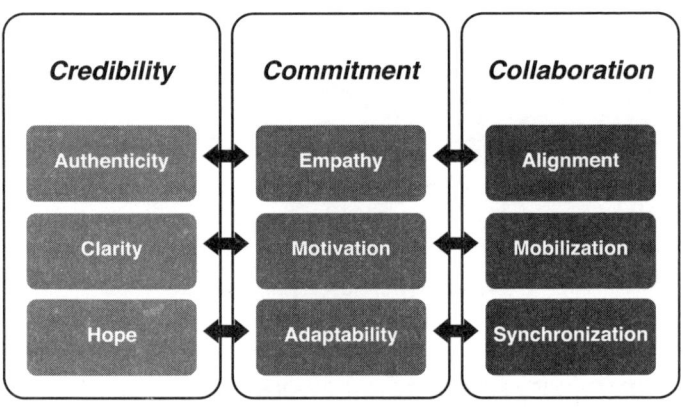

The Supervisory Acumen Framework
Source: Samatvam Academy

Authenticity is the starting point of the supervisory pilgrimage. Unless the person has the courage to politely (but firmly) call a spade a spade, he/she is unlikely to ever succeed in genuinely guiding and working effectively with others.

Motivation is the fulcrum of the supervisory endeavour. A simple test of supervisory competence is to assess whether people feel elevated after an interaction with the incumbent or they feel dissipated. Lifting human spirits is the key task of the supervisor.

When this is done well, the results manifest themselves by way of people working co-operatively together. Synchronization of efforts is the fundamental goal and outcome of the supervisory endeavour.

The Credibility Phase

Credibility is the quality of being personally worthy. It refers to the objective and subjective elements of the trustworthiness of a person and the impeccability of judgement by way of doing the right things at the right time for the right reasons. A sense of credibility evokes respect and trust from other people.

Human beings put forth their full vitality into an effort only when they truly believe in it. Likewise, they repose their trust and faith in a person whose thought, word and deed they can rely upon. Thus, credibility is the foundation of supervisory acumen.

The Credibility Phase
Source: Samatvam Academy

Authenticity

Authenticity represents the unobstructed operation of one's core self in daily operation. It is the degree to which the person remains true to one's own personality or character, despite external pressures to the contrary.

Authenticity is the state of being worthy of acceptance, trust or belief on account of genuineness or conformance to known facts or experience. Authentic people act in ways that are consistent with their deepest values and beliefs.

An authentic person pays close attention to the signals originating from the inner being. He/she emphatically aligns her external actions with these intuitive whisperings—regardless of contrary external forces, pressures and influences.

Authenticity also involves striving to achieve sincerity, openness and truthfulness in interpersonal relationships. An authentic person faithfully represents one's true values and assumptions to others.[4]

Clarity

Clarity refers to the lucidity of perception and understanding as well as a relative freedom from ambiguity.

Every human being seeks to live effectively and also to achieve fulfilment in life. Fulfilment is the capacity to express oneself fully in the course of life's activities. On the other hand, effectiveness requires the person to continuously learn, grow and acquire knowledge and skills so as to carry out the functions of life properly. Both of these attributes require the development of personal clarity.

Innate individual strengths and talents constitute the foundation upon which self-understanding may be developed. Further, every human being aspires for a larger sense of purpose and meaning in life beyond one's narrow and limited self. The desire to make a positive difference in the lives of other people is fundamental to human existence. Finally, the crystallization of a personal dream or vision provides a direction to one's life, and offers guidance for decision-making.

Thus, strength, talent, sense of purpose and vision of the future are the elements of personal clarity.

Hope

Hope is an optimistic attitude that is based upon an expectation of positive outcomes related to events and circumstances in life. Hopeful thinking comprises the twin beliefs that one can (a) find pathways to the desired goals and (b) muster the motivation to use these pathways appropriately.[5]

Pathway thinking entails the perceived ability to generate routes connecting the present to the imagined future (goal achievement). *Agency* is the perceived ability to use pathways to reach the desired goals. Agency thinking is important in all goal pursuits because it helps people to apply the motivation that is necessary for movement along an alternate pathway.

The Commitment Phase

Commitment refers to the consistent pursuit of a chosen course of action over an extended period of time. It is also the state of being emotionally pledged towards a relationship or a course of action. Commitment is an intrinsic force that binds a person towards a person, role or aspiration.

The Commitment Phase
Source: Samatvam Academy

Empathy

Empathy is the ability to comprehend another person's situation, feelings and motives or concerns in a non-judgemental manner. Being genuinely understood by another person ranks among the deepest and the most basic of human necessities. Empathy provides insights into what others are feeling or thinking, and helps to explain the how or why of their behaviour.

Motivation

Motivation is the drive that accounts for an individual's intensity, direction and persistence of effort towards attaining a goal.[6]

Motivation is the process that initiates and guides goal-oriented behaviours. It is a complex mix of active influences that arouses a person to action towards a desired goal. Motivation occurs as a continuous cycle wherein thoughts influence behaviour which in turn drives performance that eventually impacts the nature of the thoughts.

Extrinsic motivation arises from influences that are external to the individual, such as money, power or prestige. On the other hand, intrinsic motivation arises from an interest or enjoyment in the task itself.

Intrinsic motivation represents the desire to seek out new challenges, to analyse one's capacity and to gain knowledge or capability. Doing this yields a sense of meaningfulness, competence and progress.[7]

Adaptability

Adaptability is the ability to adjust oneself readily to different conditions and to respond effectively to changing events in the environment. It involves cognitive, emotional and dispositional flexibility. Cognitive flexibility is the capacity to use varying thinking, strategies and mental frameworks. Emotional flexibility is the ability to alter one's approach towards dealing with emotions. Dispositional flexibility is the capacity to remain optimistic as well as realistic.[8]

In their classification of talent themes, Buckingham and Clifton describe an adaptable person as one who,

> lives in the moment, sees the future as a creation of the choices made every moment (and not as a fixed destination), has plans but responds willingly to the demands of the moment even if this pulls away from the plans, does not resent sudden requests but expects and even looks forward to them, flexible, can stay productive even when faced with demands pulling in different directions.[9]

The Collaboration Phase

Collaboration is the process of jointly working together with another person or group in order to carry out or achieve something. It is marked by the integration of multiple efforts towards the generation of valuable output. Collaboration blends together the strengths of different people in order to reach a decision or goal that an individual would be incapable of accomplishing when working alone.

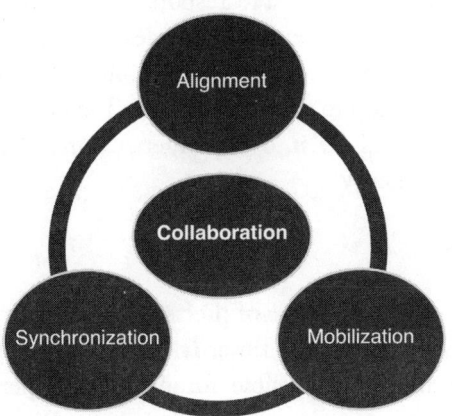

The Collaboration Phase
Source: Samatvam Academy

Alignment

Alignment is the state of cooperation among persons in a team or group or an emotional agreement with a way of thinking. An aligned workgroup is marked by the fusion of individual energies, commonality of purpose and the presence of cohesive emotional bonds amongst the people.

The emergence of a sense of mutual respect helps to generate positive energy and enthusiasm. The group then functions as a 'whole'. In order to maintain alignment, the supervisor or team leader facilitates participatory decision-making through dialogue, discussion and debate. He/she also mediates when the group members need help in transcending mutual differences that emerge from time to time.

Mobilization

Mobilization is the process of organizing and coordinating the work of a number of people towards the achievement of a specific purpose or goal.

A state of mobilization is characterized by the assembly of required resources, allocation of roles and responsibilities and assumption of accountability for the various tasks. A clear articulation of expectations encourages people to take responsibility for their respective individual contribution to the overall effort. The knowledge of exactly where each individual fits into the larger scheme of things helps to release collective energy.

Synchronization

Synchronization is the process of precisely matching multiple activities or processes together in time. It refers to the systematization of events that makes it possible for people to operate in mutual concert and unison. Synchronization becomes visible as the keenly coordinated action that characterizes a good surgical unit, a pit stop team in car racing or a sports team.

Every workgroup takes its own time to get synchronized. People initially come together as an aggregation of individuals who share a common setting. Diversity is accepted, and even appreciated, as a potential strength. Slowly, the development of acceptance facilitates the opening up of deeper feelings. Members become more expressive, impulsive, frank and spontaneous. Data and information flow quickly and easily through the group. This enables people to behave in productive ways. Finally, the group members begin to work and play together in flow.

Synchronized workgroups are high-performance teams that deliver outstanding results, qualitatively as well as quantitatively. Synchronization results when people function together like the multiple limbs of a single, unified organism. Simultaneously, such groups and forums are very fulfilling for their individual members.

Supervisors or departmental managers are the life and blood of any organization. They are instrumental in helping achieve the results that lead to the realization of the organization mission and vision.

Ample proof of this fact is provided by the case of Narayana Health, which is the subject of the next case study. This innovative institution was founded by the genius cardiologist Dr Devi Shetty. He built it upon the principles and practice of credibility, commitment and collaboration.

The blazing trail of Narayana Health is likely to help restore compassion and affordability into the practice of modern health care, and thus bring vitality as well as cheer back to human life across the globe.

References

1. Charan R, Drotter S & Noel J. *The Leadership Pipeline*. New York, NY: John Wiley & Sons; 2012.

2. Hill L. *Becoming a Manager*. 2nd ed. Boston, MA: Harvard Business School Press; 2003.

3. Hill L. Becoming the boss. *Harvard Business Review.* 85(1). Available at: https://hbr.org/2007/01/becoming-the-boss (accessed: 10 May 2015).

4. Kernis M & Goldman B. A multicomponent conceptualization of authenticity: Theory and research. *Advances in Experimental Social Psychology.* 2006; 38: 283–357.

5. Snyder C. Hope theory: Rainbows in the mind. *Psychological Inquiry.* 2002; 13(4): 249–275.

6. Robbins S & Judge T. *Organizational Behavior.* 13th ed. New York, NY: Custom Publishing; 2009.

7. Thomas K. *Intrinsic Motivation at Work.* 2nd ed. San Francisco, CA: Berrett-Koehler; 2009.

8. Junarso T. *How to Become a Highly Effective Leader: Ten Skills a Leader Must Possess.* Bloomington, IN: iUniverse Inc.; 2009.

9. Clifton D & Buckingham M. *Now, Discover Your Strengths.* New York, NY: Simon and Schuster; 2001.

ENGAGE!

NARAYANA HEALTH

Most of the things worth doing in the world had been declared impossible before they were done.

—*Louis D. Brandeis*

BACKGROUND

Narayana Health (formerly Narayana Hrudayalaya; NH) is a large Indian hospital chain. It was established by Padma Bhushan Dr Devi Prasad Shetty in 2001 with the objective of providing affordable cardiac care to the masses.

NH presently comprises a network of 25 hospitals, 7 heart centres and 19 primary care facilities spread across 31 Indian towns and cities. It has over 5,800 operational beds. Over 2 million patients from all parts of India and across the world avail of its facilities every year. As of December 2017, NH had 15,906 full-time employees and associates—including 3,388 doctors.[1]

In FY 2018, NH clocked revenue of ₹2,280 crore. The earnings before interest, taxes, depreciation and amortization (EBITDA) stood at around 10 per cent. Around half of its inpatient revenue is derived from cardiology and cardiac surgery. However, NH provides advanced levels of care in over 30 medical specialties that include oncology, neurology, orthopaedics, ophthalmology and gastroenterology.

THE GENESIS OF THE INSTITUTION

Dr Devi Prasad Shetty was born in the Kinnigoli village in the Dakshina Kannada district of Karnataka in 1953. He was the eighth of nine children in a family that revered doctors.

In the fifth grade at school, the young boy heard from his teacher about Dr Christiaan Barnard—the South African surgeon who had performed the world's first heart transplant. He was deeply inspired and instantly resolved to become a cardiac surgeon when he grew up.

Dr Shetty completed his undergraduate medical degree and post-graduate work in general surgery at the Kasturba Medical College, Mangalore. The seeds of his sensitivity to health care costs were sown in this preliminary phase of his career.

Medical students in India are usually educated at 'teaching' hospitals that are frequented mainly by large numbers of poor people. The young intern's interactions with patients taught him much about the grim economic situation of rural India, and how that adversely affected the health of the people.

Dr Shetty went for further training in cardiac surgery at Guy's Hospital in London. This was one of Europe's top medical facilities. He returned to India in 1989 at the invitation of the Birla family in order to take charge of the newly established BM Birla Heart Research Centre in Kolkata.

Dr Devi Shetty rose to fame when he successfully performed the country's first neonatal heart surgery on a 9-day-old baby in 1992. His reputation spread quickly. Patients began to throng to his heart clinic for consultations. However, very few of them returned for heart surgery because of the astronomical price tag attached to the procedure.

Sometime later, Dr Shetty operated upon Mother Teresa when she suffered a heart attack. Subsequently, he served as her personal physician. Meeting Mother Teresa was like an encounter with the divine. It set the direction for Dr Shetty's aspirations in the field of health care.

His interactions with the famed humanitarian not only allowed for the close observation of her charitable work but also caused Dr Shetty to ponder upon how quality health care may be made affordable and widely accessible. 'Hands that serve are more sacred than the lips that pray', were the words of the Nobel Laureate that had a profound effect on the young doctor.

Upon reflection, Dr Shetty came to the conclusion that the medical fraternity needed to redesign its processes. Instead of a magic pill, faster scanner or a newer procedure, he surmised that the health care industry was required to reinvent its very methods in order that medical care may become available more cheaply and widely.

In the 1990s, Dr Shetty and his erstwhile colleague Dr Alok Roy established the non-profit Asia Heart Foundation (AHF) in Kolkata. The AHF assisted in the commissioning of the Manipal Heart Foundation at Bangalore in 1997. It also established the 150-bed Rabindranath Tagore International Institute of Cardiac Sciences in Kolkata in the year 2000.

In 2001, NH came into being under the AHF umbrella—with the aid of a generous contribution by Dr Shetty's father-in-law. The latter's firm Shankaranarayana Constructions built NH's original two-storey hospital building that was situated upon 25 acres of land on the outskirts of Bangalore. It housed five OTs and 280 beds.[2]

At this juncture, Dr Shetty and Dr Roy parted ways on account of some mutual differences. Nevertheless, NH progressed and soon began to attract patients from around the world.

THE GROWTH OF THE ENTERPRISE

During the first three years, NH employed internally generated funds in order to expand into a six-storey building. It accommodated 500 hospital beds that were serviced by a team of around 90 highly experienced and reputed cardiac surgeons and cardiologists. This allowed the institution to handle complex and high-intensity clinical cases.

Patients from across the Indian subcontinent as well as parts of Africa thronged to NH. This helped the organization to gain critical mass, and then expand rapidly by deploying external capital.

Over a period of 17 years, NH has developed an extensive network of health care facilities across India in order to serve patients from more than 50 countries around the world. It also ventured abroad to establish a 140-bed hospital in the Cayman Islands, just across from the United States.

All the NH hospitals are fitted with modern medical equipment, follow well-defined safety protocols and adhere to internationally accepted clinical standards of patient handling and care. Fourteen of them are also accredited with India's National Accreditation Board for Hospitals and Healthcare Providers.[3]

Around 12 per cent of all the cardiac surgeries done in India are performed at NH hospitals. The paediatric intensive therapy unit at NH is one of the largest in the world. The mortality rates within 30 days of coronary bypass graft surgery (1.27%) and infection rate (1%) at NH are as good as that at hospitals in the United States. Further, the incidence of bedsores after a cardiac surgery (that globally ranges between 8% and 40%) is virtually non-existent at NH.

Over the last five years, NH has maintained a robust annual revenue growth of about 25 per cent. Its reputation for clinical excellence, competitive salaries and ethical practices have enabled NH to attract quality doctors and medical support staff within India as well as from among the returning NRI (non-resident Indian) medico fraternity.

THE STRATEGIC PILLARS

NH seeks to revolutionize health care in India by bringing together quality, affordability and profitability. It has been able to do so in the tricky field of health care, which includes sophisticated, delicate and risky medical procedures such as cardiac surgery. An innovative strategy has been framed to support the accomplishment of NH's mission and vision.

The institutional strategy rests upon four main pillars: (a) process innovation, (b) economies of scale, (c) deployment of information technology and (d) supply chain efficiency.

PROCESS INNOVATION

NH has innovatively transformed the complex process of open-heart surgery in order to significantly bring down the cost while enhancing the quality. Many of the principles and practices of the modern industrial organization have been deployed in doing so.

NH leverages the hierarchy of medical talent in optimizing its surgical procedures. Its doctors operate in medical teams that comprise of a specialist, junior doctors, trainees, nurses and the paramedical staff.

A bypass surgery typically takes about five hours. The nurses and the paramedics help to prepare the patient for surgery. The junior doctors harvest the veins/arteries, open and close the chest and carry out the suturing. The critical surgical process of grafting takes only one hour, and is carried out by the specialist. This arrangement saves the specialist's time and leaves him free to perform more surgeries.

The general industry norm is that the cardiac specialists are paid on a per surgery basis. However, NH invites its staff surgeons to work for fixed salaries. While the remuneration is handsome and competitive, the doctors are required to work much longer hours and perform more surgical procedures. At an average of 24 surgeries a week, the typical NH surgeon is far more productive than his counterparts across the globe. Thus, NH spends only 22 per cent of its revenues on staff salaries. The comparable ratio for the hospitals in the West is up to 60 per cent.

Specialization is NH's mantra for achieving high quality. On account of the large number of cases they handle, NH doctors acquire world-class expertise in particular clinical areas and operations. In order to facilitate the development of expertise by the doctors in their specialty area, NH provides for ample support staff and facilities to assist them. It also offers a series of structured capability building programmes that every staff member is required to attend.

NH has been innovative in other ways too. When it set up a 104-bed hospital in the Cayman Islands in the Caribbean, it employed the cold water available from the sea in place of the energy-intensive refrigeration system. The resultant energy savings were to the tune of 90 per cent. This is very significant, considering that the cost of power in the Islands is three times that in the United States. Also, NH decided to set up an oxygen plant locally rather than source the gas supply from the mainland.

ECONOMIES OF SCALE

NH is able to actively leverage the economies of scale because its huge hospitals attract a large number of patients. The high volumes help to reduce the unit cost of surgery and also lead to improved clinical outcomes because the doctors gain expertise and specialization in specific types of operations.

Frugality is the watchword at NH. The institution implements cost-saving methods such as the use of digital X-rays rather than the more expensive films. The use of infrastructure is also maximized in order to serve a large volume of patients, resulting in lesser unit cost.

For instance, while most hospitals employ their CT scanners, MRI and other machines for only eight hours a day, NH uses them for 14 hours each day. The proper maintenance of the equipment is also emphasized, so that its life may be extended to the maximum.

Further, NH designs and executes its hospital projects with a view to maintaining a very tight control on the construction costs. Instead of buying expensive medical equipment outright, NH pays the supplier a fixed monthly rent in addition to the cost of the reagents that are necessary to run the tests on these machines. Equipment suppliers make a reasonable profit on account of the high volumes. They also project the successful deployment of the machine in NH's demanding operational environment as the ultimate proof of its robustness.

To achieve the scale that it is looking for, NH also engages in collaborations and associations with other institutions. For instance, it entered into a management contract with respect to the MMI Hospital at Raipur in Chhattisgarh. After taking over, NH increased the number of beds, introduced health packages to enhance preventive health care, equipped the radiology department with the latest equipment and also upgraded the emergency and trauma care centre at the facility.

West Bengal's Durgapur Medical College is now entirely managed by NH. The institution has also set up embedded heart centres in other hospitals such as Chinmaya Mission, MS Ramaiah Mission and St Marthas—on a revenue-sharing basis.

DEPLOYMENT OF INFORMATION TECHNOLOGY

NH has invested in technology, both for clinical purposes as well as for integrating its systems and processes. The institution has implemented an Oracle ERP on-cloud system that provides detailed, real-time information to all its important stakeholders.

The extensive use of information technology ensures rapid transmission of disease data, quicker diagnostic analysis and prompt disease management. The inventory and the processing times are also reduced through the use of comprehensive hospital management software.

NH has also deployed technology in order to clearly define its systems and processes. Besides the clinical area, the protocols also cover the manner in which a patient is received and transferred from one place to the other and even how the medicines are to be indented. The streamlining of operational procedures has helped to achieve better quality and reduce the error rates. This translates into reduced cost and greater satisfaction, since the patients get back home sooner.

NH also mines data extensively to raise its quality levels. Its business intelligence model throws up real-time information on 30 different parameters that the institution's management may want to track for the improvement of efficiency. NH also maps out the performance of each doctor in terms of clinical outcomes as well as financial data such as the consumables used during surgery, the time spent by the patient in the ICU and the total duration of stay in the hospital.

SUPPLY CHAIN EFFICIENCY

NH operates its supply chain with a focus upon streamlining its administrative and clinical functions, continuous process innovation and economies of scale. The institution does not sign long-term contracts. Major purchases are negotiated afresh every week in order to avoid getting locked in with potentially expensive suppliers.

The institution also procures the requisite consumable items in bulk. For instance, it saves about 40 per cent on the cost of surgical gloves by importing them in container loads directly from the Malaysian manufacturer. This way it saves on the distributor margins too.

Given its large scale, credibility and high patient volumes, NH drives a hard bargain when negotiating prices for everything from basic supplies to sophisticated medical equipment.[4] For example, the cancer hospital purchased two linear accelerators (for producing X-rays) for the price of one machine. Further, the interest-free payment schedule was spread out over seven years.

HEALTH CITIES

India currently has around 0.7 hospital beds per thousand people. In order to align that abysmally low number with the huge population of the country, NH is creating a chain of very large, self-sufficient 'health cities' situated on the outskirts of some of the major cities in India.

Each health city is conceived to comprise of a set of well-equipped multi-specialty hospitals with a total capacity of around 5,000 beds. Every constituent hospital would have its own OTs and ICU, but would draw upon common facilities such as the laboratory and the blood bank.

The logic for the health city is two-fold. First, it enables NH to extend its concept and brand of affordable health care to other specialty areas by building upon the reputation and experience that it has gained in cardiac care. Second, NH had reached a plateau in cost reduction because some of its medical equipment and facilities such as the blood bank remained underutilized. The newer specialty units within the health city shall utilize these facilities, and thus enable further reduction in unit costs.

For instance, the Institute for Bone Marrow Transplant (BMT) at NH's Bengaluru facility has managed to reduce the cost of bone marrow transplants by two-thirds from the national average of ₹12 lakh.

The blood bank previously discarded unused blood after 10 days, as it was unsuitable for cardiac surgery. It is now able to utilize the blood for BMT procedures up to 26 days after its collection.[5]

The first health city has emerged around the original NH facility at Bommasandra in Bengaluru. The non-cardiac specialty units have been housed in new buildings that are constructed in an area of 35 acres adjacent to the cardiac hospital. The medical complex now houses a 1200-bed cancer hospital, a 500-bed orthopaedic hospital, an eye hospital as well as medical education and research facilities.

AWARDS AND RECOGNITION

Over the years, NH has received numerous awards. These are a testimony to its strong brand value and work ethic. These include the 'Healthcare Excellence Award for Addressing Industry Issues' in 2012, 'ArcelorMittal Boldness in Business Award' in 2013 and the 'Health Brand of the Year' in 2017.

In addition, Dr Shetty has personally received a number of national and international awards. This includes the Padma Bhushan (India's third highest civilian Award) in 2012 for his contribution to the field of affordable health care. He has also received The Economist's 'Innovation Award for Business Process' in 2011 and The Economic Times 'Entrepreneur of the Year' award in 2012, among others.[6]

NH weds noble intentions with a sound economic model. The institution is able to tie together high quality with affordability in a manner that is surprisingly profitable too.

The doctors at NH are so committed to the institution's vision and lofty sense of purpose that hardly any of them leave or go away. Like all organizations that pursue bold dreams, NH manages to inspire its employees and associates to routinely achieve the impossible—day after day.

REFERENCES

1. Narayana Health. Investor presentation. *Narayanahealth.org*. Available at: www.narayanahealth.org/sites/default/files/announcements/InvestorpresentationandcallinviteQ3FY18.pdf (accessed: 17 May 2018).

2. Alloubani A, Taktak W, Hussein A, AlZanoun R, Rabadi H & Feeney L. Narayana hrudayalaya cardiac care hospital for the poor: Leadership case study analysis and key lessons for Jordan. *European Scientific Journal*. 2014; 10(25): 474–484.

3. Medical Buyer. Narayana health. *Medicalbuyer.co.in*. Available at: www.medicalbuyer.co.in/index.php/hospital-update/17991-narayana-health (accessed: 17 July 2016).

4. Knowledge@Wharton. Narayana hrudayalaya: A model for accessible, affordable health care? *Knowledge@Wharton*. Available at: http://knowledge.wharton.upenn.edu/article/narayana-hrudayalaya-a-model-for-accessible-affordable-health-care/ (accessed: 9 July 2016).

5. Khanna T, Rangan VK & Manocaran M. Narayana Hrudayalaya heart hospital: cardiac care for the poor (A). *Courses.edx.org*. Available at: https://courses.edx.org/asset-v1:HarvardX+SW47x+2T2017+type@asset+block/12-page_505078.html (accessed: 9 May 2018).

6. Narayana Health. Dr Devi Prasad Shetty. *Narayana Health*. Available at: www.narayanahealth.org/leadership/board-of-directors/dr-devi-shetty (accessed: 9 July 2016).

VIDEO REFERENCE

Samatvam. (2016, July 12). *Narayana Hrudayalaya*. YouTube. Available at: https://youtube/QfR9mWQUvsc (accessed: 26 November 2018).

MANAGERIAL EFFICACY

9

A manager is not a person who can do the work better than her
people; she is a person who can get her people to do the work better
than she can.

— *Frederick W. Smith*

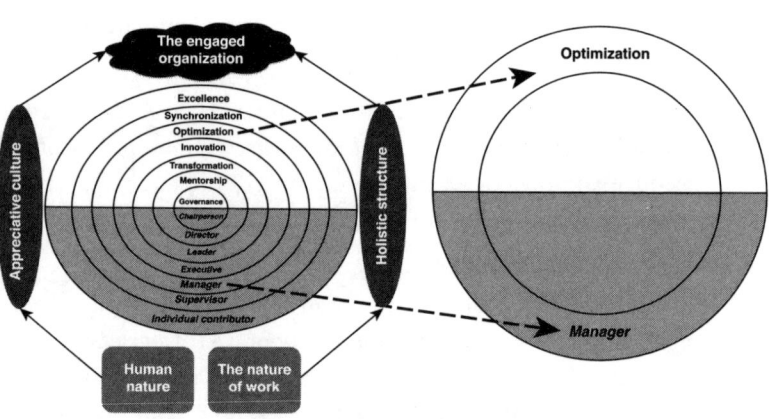

The Managerial Mandate for Optimization
Source: Samatvam Academy

A manager is any person who provides directional and operational inputs to several groups of people and is held accountable for the quality and quantity of their collective output.

The process of management involves the use of knowledge and skill in the exercise of judgement and decision-making. Judgement may be about reality (assessment of the facts in a situation) or about the value (the significance of those facts).

Managers reside at the third rung of the hierarchy of accountability. They direct the operations of a functional area or regional unit. In doing so, managers are expected to integrate their respective activities with the mission and vision of the larger organization.

Managers navigate the interaction between the situational variables in order to achieve the planned output. A manager works at peak effectiveness when the overall performance of the work unit moves close to its full potential.

Managers are tasked with generating progressively increased output from the deployment of minimal resources. They balance and utilize the available resources and also develop systems, processes and procedures that enable the most productive accomplishment of work. People development is also an integral feature of managerial work.

Effective operational work units are marked by a resolve for excellence, tremendous energy, rapid learning and quick-paced problem-solving. In practice, these favourable conditions usually occur only when the system is faced with extraordinary challenges such as the development of a new product offering or the commencement of a new operation. The managerial ideal is to achieve such efficacy even under the normal, day-to-day conditions of organizational functioning.

The Challenges of Managerial Work

Managers solve challenging problems that are usually operational and concrete in nature. Since real-time access to operational data is slowly becoming the norm, managerial performance is closely monitored by senior management.

This reduces the autonomy available to the manager and adds to the complexity of the work at the same time. The stress and challenge of the managerial role are also increased due to an imbalance between the high expectations and the relatively low degrees of freedom available.

While the supervisors, team leaders and other Stratum II role holders that assist a manager are usually capable and competent, they sometimes work reactively. With increasing levels of professional expertise, these employees also prefer to focus on their narrow individual domains. They display initiative, but only in the areas of their personal interest.

Also, employees often resist managerial efforts to integrate their work with that of their other colleagues due to the unfounded fear of losing autonomy. Further, people typically become defensive when confronted with issues and concerns.

The composite impact of these factors is that the manager needs to unceasingly follow-up with colleagues within and outside the system in order to secure timely results.

Since the managerial tasks are complex, specialized and interrelated, a diverse group of people comes up with better solutions. Managers must, therefore, cooperate with peers who are in charge of other functions.

Of course, they have also to secure the enthusiastic cooperation of their immediate colleagues in the work unit. This becomes possible only when the individual interests of the people have been synchronized with the collective needs of the function/region in a 'win-win' fashion.

Residing as they do at the middle level of the spine of accountability, managers feel squeezed in from all sides. They work with a perennial sense of the 'lone ranger' pushing uphill. Despite strenuous efforts, achievements do not come by easily. There persists a significant gap between their potential capacity and the actual performance.

The Development of Managerial Efficacy

Managerial efficacy is the capacity to deliver the optimal output by synergizing the effective achievement of tasks and the building of constructive relationships. Through the judicious use of all the available inputs, managers help the organization to deliver more with less.

The key to managerial efficacy lies in recognizing that high task productivity is not necessarily in opposition to the development of meaningful relationships. These are complementary values that are actually symbiotic in nature, much like the two sides of the same coin.

An ancient proverb holds that 'Whatever we pay attention to, grows'. This perspective is key to the development of a constructive managerial approach. Managers fully leverage the available strengths and talents. Successes are celebrated, before the manager moves to resolve any outstanding issues and concerns.

The managerial goal of optimization is achieved through an active progression across a three-step cycle of stakeholder engagement. The stages are named as *affirmation*, *amalgamation* and *accomplishment*.

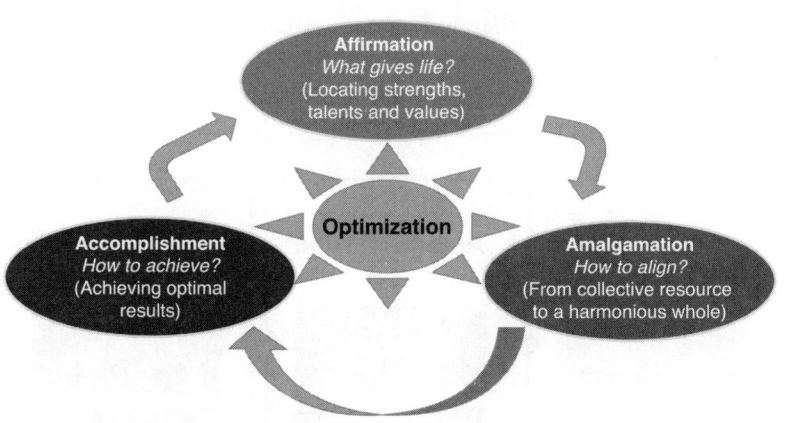

The Technology of Managerial Efficacy
Source: Samatvam Academy

The Managerial Efficacy Framework

The three stages of affirmation, amalgamation and accomplishment operate concurrently across the affective, cognitive and behavioural dimensions of the human personality.

On the cognitive plane, the individual sense of *purpose* (a desire to achieve something important and satisfying) gets crystallized into a common *goal* (a measurable end result) that culminates in the development of a *plan* (a forward-looking process of deciding in advance what, when, where, how and by whom things are to be done).

At the behavioural level, managerial efficacy progresses through the identification of *strength* (a natural capacity for behaving or thinking in a particular way) that determines the appropriate assignment of individual *roles* (the function that each person performs within the group as a whole) that eventually results into *achievement* (carrying an initiative through to successful completion).

With respect to the affective dimension, managerial efficacy commences with the articulation of individual *values* (fundamental principles that act as the yardstick by which particular actions are judged as appropriate). These shape the development of progressive *norms* (shared beliefs that indicate acceptable ways for people to interact and behave in a social setting), leading to *optimization* (the process or methodology of progressively making a system or decision as perfect as possible).

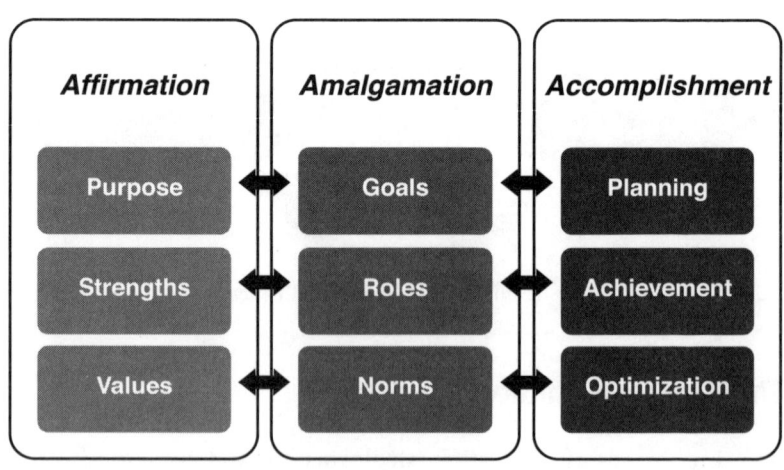

The Managerial Efficacy Framework
Source: Samatvam Academy

Articulating a meaningful sense of purpose is the starting point of the managerial journey. Appropriate role allocation, which requires the selection of the right person for the right job, is the crux of the managerial endeavour. Optimization of results is the *summum bonum* of managerial accountability.

The Affirmation Phase

In the affirmation phase, individual colleagues are acknowledged, regarded and respected as human beings in their own right. Managers explore the best of 'what is', through affirmative conversations around the *strengths, values* and *sense of purpose* of each of their direct reports, within the overall context of the organizational mission and vision.

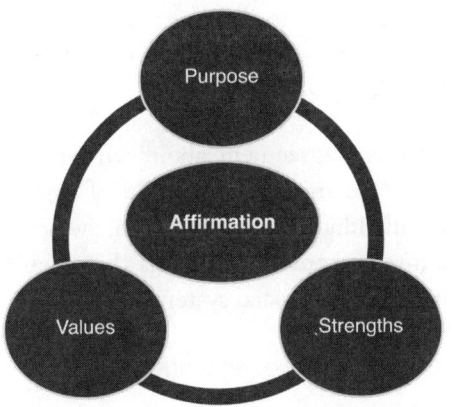

The Affirmation Phase
Source: Samatvam Academy

Strengths

Strength is the natural capacity for behaving, thinking or feeling in a way that allows for optimal functioning in the pursuit of valued outcomes.[1]

Strength is in evidence when a special natural ability or aptitude is combined with associated knowledge and skills so as to yield consistent, near-perfect performance in an activity.[2]

People experience stimulation, rather than exhaustion, when using their strengths. Further, people grow most in the areas of their greatest strength.

Values

A value is any instrumental principle, code, belief or ideal that a person considers emotionally significant, and as an end in itself. Collectively, values refer to a set of consistent principles and fundamental convictions that constitute the standard by which particular actions are judged as good, appropriate or desirable.[3]

Values represent a person's enduring beliefs about how things should be accomplished.[4] They are the cognitive and affective processes that help people to decide what to do, or not do. In this manner, values are the deep-seated, pervasive standards that set the parameters for human decision-making.

Values are also a social agreement about what is right, appropriate and good. They enable the self-regulation of impulses that would otherwise bring individuals in conflict with the society. Values help to facilitate the interpersonal interactions that enable individuals to achieve collective goals in a social system.

Purpose

A sense of purpose is a generalized intention to accomplish something that is meaningful to the self, and is also of consequence to the world beyond.[5] It is about recognizing and fulfilling one's highest potential. A clear sense of purpose keeps people motivated, provides them with energy and confidence and facilitates coping with difficult circumstances.

Every human being is driven by an internal sense of purpose, which may be about what she wants to do or the kind of person she wants to become. A sense of purpose helps the person to find a direction in life, while its absence can leave one in a rudderless and confused state.

ENGAGE!

The Amalgamation Phase

The term 'amalgamation' refers to the act of helping a group of individuals to join together into an organic whole, without sacrificing their sense of individuality. This is similar to a set of luminous stars coming together to form a majestic galaxy.

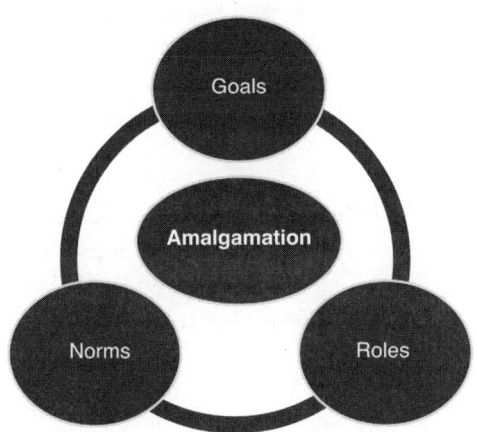

The Amalgamation Phase
Source: Samatvam Academy

Goal

A goal is an observable and measurable end result that is comprised of one or more objectives to be achieved, within a relatively fixed time frame.

A goal describes what the work unit is striving to accomplish and why. It helps people to connect their everyday work with the larger organizational mission.

A true goal has four essential characteristics. First, it reflects the core purpose of the work unit. Second, it is compatible with the requirements and expectations of the workgroup's internal customers. Third, the goal is commensurate with the internal capabilities of the workgroup. Finally, the goal is challenging enough to stretch and draw the people out of their comfort zones.

Roles

In social structures, every individual is required to perform a certain function. This is known as the role that is played by the person. The best way to structure the functioning of a human system is to assign unique roles to each member. Each person then knows what to expect from one's own self, as well as from the other colleagues. The efficacy of a team depends more saliently upon the balance of the roles that are collectively played by its members. Roles may be assigned based on the individual strengths of the unit members or may be rotated periodically.

If a role does not allow the person to use her competence, it shall be less effective. On the other hand, a person must have the requisite knowledge, skills and the capability required for the role. Role efficacy comes about when the person is able to contribute to the evolution of the role.

Norms

Norms are a set of shared beliefs that indicate acceptable ways for people to interact and behave in a social setting. Group norms are the (usually) unwritten codes that create expectations, set standards and provide guidelines with respect to the acceptable behaviour.[6] Norms provide explicit cues towards how people may get the job done, what their level of output should be and even the acceptable level of tardiness.[7]

Most norms develop in one or more of the following four ways: (a) explicit statements by supervisors or co-workers, (b) critical events in the group's history, (c) primacy, or by virtue of their introduction early in the group's history and (d) carryover behaviours from past situations.

The Accomplishment Phase

The accomplishment phase commences with detailed *planning* that facilitates the *achievement* of aims and objectives, followed by the iterative refinement and *optimization* of the work activities.

The Accomplishment Phase
Source: Samatvam Academy

Planning

Planning is a forward-looking process of deciding in advance what, when, where, how and by whom things are to be done. It helps to bridge the gap between the present state and the desired future.

The primary step in planning is to establish definite and measurable objectives. Then, the major premises or situational assumptions upon which the plan is based are specified. The next process is to determine several alternative courses of action and then evaluate these for optimality.

The penultimate step is to select a course of action from among the different options. The timing and sequence of activities are carefully arranged, such that priority is given to critical tasks. Finally, the plan is communicated to stakeholders within and outside the work unit.

Achievement

Achievement refers to the act of carrying an initiative through to successful completion. It involves the organizing, harmonizing and monitoring of multiple resources and efforts as well as paying careful attention to 'detail' without losing sight of the 'big picture'.

Organizing alludes to the act of arranging and systematizing elements, activities and procedures. It is the process of bringing together all the required resources for the achievement of desired goals.

Harmonizing refers to the facilitation of constructive relationships amongst the people, such that they are able to leverage the collective strengths in the service of goal attainment.

Monitoring implies the regular measurement of delivered performance against the standards. Keeping a close track of the actual activities allows for the deviations to be spotted and swiftly rectified.

Optimization

Optimization is the act, process or methodology of making a design, system or decision as perfect and functional as possible. It is concerned with leveraging the existing resources to their highest potential in order to facilitate the maximization of output.

Optimization results from the concurrent maximization of resource efficiency (input/output ratio), effectiveness (match between the actual and intended outcome) and utilization (available time versus the duration of actual deployment).[8] The efforts of all the systemic components are combined, and their effects are orchestrated in order to obtain the targeted output.

In practice, there is a continuous and iterative interplay between the three dimensions of *plan-achieve-optimize*. This is because all three of them are concerned with the actual execution of the organizational intentions. In modern times, agility is the key to successful execution.

Managerial Agility

Managerial agility is the strategic and operational capacity of a manager or an organizational system to identify, capture and service the opportunities more quickly than others do. It is a way of constructively utilizing external and internal dynamism, in the service of organizational success.

ENGAGE!

Agility represents the ability to quickly transform information into insight in response to external movements. It mandates the reduction in the cycle time for managerial action. This can be broken down into three components: (a) sense, (b) decide and (c) respond.

'Sense' refers to how long it takes to register a change in needs or conditions. 'Decide' is concerned with how long it takes to make a decision. 'Respond' refers to the length of time that is required to make the necessary change, and thereafter validate the outcome of the change.

Agility is broadly marked by six characteristics: (a) 24×7 availability, (b) qualitative outperformance, (c) proactive anticipation of changes and crises, (d) speed of response, (e) causing minimal disruption and (f) continued communication and teamwork.

Across the world, management has been one of the preferred career options of bright, young people for some decades now. This is not without reason. In an increasingly resource-constrained world, managers help to make the most of the available means. In this way, they contribute to a better quality of life for everybody.

As an illustration of managerial luminosity, the next case study relates the incredible story of the visionary Dr Govindappa Venkataswamy (aka Dr V). The Aravind Eye Care System that he founded is the largest eye care provider in the world today. It offers high-quality services that often surpass western standards, but cost only a minute fraction of what people on the other side of the world pay for them.

The fact that the institution is growing from strength to strength even 12 years after Dr V passed away is a testimony to his organization building abilities and also the managerial abilities of his successors.

References

1. Linley P & Harrington S. Playing to your strengths. *The Psychologist*. 2006; 19(2): 86–89.

2. Buckingham M & Clifton D. *Now, Discover Your Strengths*. London: Pocket Books; 2005.

3. Halstead J & Taylor MJ. *The Development of Values, Attitudes, and Personal Qualities: A Review of Recent Research*. Slough: NFER; 2000.

4. Kouzes J & Posner B. *The Leadership Challenge: How to Make Extraordinary Things Happen in Organizations*. 5th ed. San Francisco, CA: Jossey-Bass; 2012.

5. Damon W, Menon J & Cotton Bronk K. The development of purpose during adolescence. *Applied Developmental Science*. 2003; 7(3): 119–128.

6. Ricketts C & Ricketts J. *Leadership: Personal Development and Career Success*. 3rd ed. New York, NY: Cengage Learning; 2011.

7. Robbins S, De Cenzo D, Coulter M & Woods M. *Management: the Essentials*. New South Wales: Pearson; 2014.

8. KPMG. Creating an optimized organization key opportunities and challenges. Kpmg.de. Available at: www.kpmg.de/docs/India_OptimizedOrganisation.pdf (accessed: 18 May 2015).

ENGAGE!

THE ARAVIND EYE CARE SYSTEM

Intelligence and capability are not enough.

There must be the joy of doing something beautiful.

Being of service means going beyond the sophistication of the best technology, to the humble demonstration of courtesy and compassion to each patient.

—*Padma Shri Dr Govindappa Venkataswamy*

BACKGROUND

Aravind Eye Care System (AECS) is a non-profit eye hospital chain in India. It was founded by Padma Shri Dr Govindappa Venkataswamy (fondly known as Dr V) at Madurai, Tamil Nadu, in 1976, with the vision of eradicating needless blindness in India.

Inspired by (and named after) the sage Sri Aurobindo, the mission of AECS is to provide compassionate and high-quality eye care that is universally affordable. Since its inception, AECS has treated over 40 million patients and performed more than 5 million eye surgeries and laser procedures.

About 40 million people across the world are blind. Nearly 80 per cent of these cases are curable. Blindness afflicts around 1.5 per cent of the population in the developing nations. Cataract is a major cause of this blindness. It accounts for about 75 per cent of all cases in Asia. A cataract forms as the natural lens of the eye clouds over time and has to be surgically replaced by an artificial one.

Over the four decades of its existence, AECS has created a major impact towards eradicating cataract-related blindness in India. Its network presently includes 10 eye hospitals, a research institute, an intraocular lens factory, an eye bank and a training institute.[1] AECS has also established an extensive outreach programme, wherein doctors reach out to remote villages to conduct eye camps that are sponsored by various charitable institutions.

To progressively eradicate needless blindness in India, Dr V studied the fast-food assembly line approach of McDonald's and then intelligently adapted it to eye care. This innovation allowed the institution to leverage the power of standardization, scale, product recognition, accessibility and service efficiency.[2]

The three pillars of the AECS business model are (a) high volume, (b) high quality and (c) affordable cost. Its operational and growth model has been widely applauded and also studied in depth by numerous internationally reputed business schools.[3]

THE GENESIS OF THE INSTITUTION

Born in October 1918 as a farmer's son in Vadamalapuram (a village 80 km from Madurai), AECS' founder Dr Venkataswamy grew up walking barefoot to school. He tended the family buffalo and wrote his lessons in the sand. The loss of a cousin sister due to childbirth complications seeded in the young boy the conviction of becoming a doctor so as to prevent such untimely tragedies.

After graduating with a BA in chemistry from Madurai's American College, Dr V received his medical degree from Stanley Medical

College, Chennai in 1944. He joined the Indian Army Medical Corps thereafter.[2, pp. 48–50]

However, Dr V had to retire from the armed forces in 1948 after developing chronic rheumatoid arthritis and psoriasis. This severely debilitating and painful disease persisted for a long time. He found it difficult to walk or even hold a pen in his badly crippled fingers.

Dr V never married either. This noble suffering perhaps prepared him for the visionary endeavour of eradicating curable blindness.[2, p. 61]

Despite his condition, Dr V earned a diploma and a master's degree in ophthalmology. In 1956, he joined the faculty of the Madurai Medical College. Through painstaking determination and hard work, he taught himself how to cut and operate the eye with his twisted fingers. He learned how to hold a scalpel in his hand and to perform cataract surgery. Eventually, he was able to carry out over a hundred eye surgeries within the space of a single day.

In the ensuing two decades, Dr V introduced a number of innovative programmes to deal with the problem of blindness in India. He developed the outreach eye camp programmes in 1960, and a rehabilitation centre for the blind in 1966. Dr V was also instrumental in the creation of a training programme for ophthalmic assistants in 1973.

In his clinical work, Dr V personally performed over 100,000 successful eye surgeries. In recognition of these achievements, the Government of India awarded him with the Padma Shri in 1973.[2, p. 66]

As a young man, Dr V had become a disciple of the sage Sri Aurobindo. The latter's teachings emphasized that human beings must transcend into a heightened state of consciousness so as to become better instruments for the divine force to work through in life.

Thus inspired, Dr V audaciously ventured to create the Aravind Eye Hospital as a self-supporting, humanitarian institution. He was propelled less by a business strategy and much more by an intense desire and an infinite vision to offer selfless service to those in need.

After retiring as the head of the department of ophthalmology at Madurai's Government Medical College, the 58-year-old Dr V wished to continue his professional work of providing quality eye care on an even larger scale. He put his life savings on the line to establish the Govel Trust, under whose auspices a modest 11-bed eye clinic was founded in order to work towards the eradication of 'needless' blindness in India.[2,p.66]

Dr V recruited his extended family to join in this mission. His youngest sister Dr G. Natchiar and her husband Dr P. Namperumalsamy were the first to come on board. Dr Vijayalaksmi (the sister of Dr Nam) and her husband Dr M. Srinivasan soon followed. The team established three simple rules, which they seeded as the organization's DNA from the outset[2,p.61]:

1. We shall not turn away any patient, irrespective of the person's economic capacity.

2. We shall never compromise upon quality.

3. We must remain financially self-reliant so as to refrain from compromising our freedom.

This meant that all of Aravind's activities needed to embody compassion, excellence and integrity. Indeed, Dr V started the institution without raising any external funds or donations. Marketing was directed exclusively towards people who did not have the capacity to pay and 60 per cent of the services were to be given away for free. All the same, world-class quality was to be offered and maintained at all times. The organization that was founded on this seemingly absurd framework is paradoxically the world's largest provider of eye care today.

SCALING THE ORGANIZATION

AECS realized that the key requirement for rapidly scaling an organization is to standardize its key activities. The cataract surgery procedures, and even the screening activities at the eye camps, were all amenable to value-engineering techniques. The ancillary activities that supported the organization's core operations also lent themselves well to standardization.

As a result, every activity at AECS was carefully designed and neatly orchestrated. Detailed procedures governed how an AECS eye camp was to be promoted, how patients were to be brought in, how its logistics were to be organized, how medical screening was to be done and how patients were to be selected and prepared for the journey to the main hospital. The same applied to the surgical procedures as well as the preliminary and post-surgical processes.

In a spirit of learning by doing, AECS constantly innovated its delivery model. For instance, when Dr V's application for a bank loan to support free eye care for the poor was rejected, he built the ground floor of his hospital as 'fee-for-service'. However, the foundation of the building was laid deep enough for the vertical expansion of the facility at a later date.

Similarly, less than one in five potential patients were found to actually avail of the 'free surgery' offer during the initial eye camps. It was discovered that poor rural people faced many barriers in making the choice to have a surgery. The institution then added services such as food, lodging and transportation to address those constraints. As a result, the acceptance rates increased to around 90 per cent. Through a similar process of trial and error, the yield at refractive camps (where eyeglasses are prescribed and fitted) surged from less than 10 per cent in 2000 to over 80 per cent in 2006.

Unsuccessful experiments were terminated after being given a fair chance. For instance, several surgical camps were initially conducted on-site in order to make it convenient for rural people to accept the surgery. However, the medical outcomes were found to be hard to manage because of the variable quality of the surgical environment. AECS abandoned the surgical camp model and reverted to utilizing the camps only for the purpose of screening the patients.

In 2004, AECS began to establish permanent vision centres in villages in order to provide basic eye care services. Staffed by paramedical personnel and equipped with a high-speed communication link to the main hospital, the vision centre conducts eye examinations and helps to identify refractive errors. If spectacles are needed, the prescription is sent to the base hospital for fulfilment. Complicated as well as surgery cases are referred to the main hospital.[2, p. 137]

THE MANAGED-CARE HOSPITAL MODEL

All the Aravind-owned hospitals are vertically integrated medical facilities. That is, AECS directly controls all of their operations—from the design of the hospital to its physical building, and from the training of the staff to the manufacturing of key supplies (intraocular lenses, sutures, blades and instruments). All the Tamil Nadu hospitals continue to run on this model.

In 2001, with a view to expand its reach, AECS began to experiment with an alternative business model in the form of 'managed-care' hospitals. Three such medical facilities have been developed in other parts of India so far in collaboration with different agencies.

The Indira Gandhi Eye Hospital and Research Centre in Amethi, Uttar Pradesh, was established by the Rajiv Gandhi Charitable Trust.

The Priyamvada Birla Aravind Eye Hospital at Kolkata is funded and largely overseen by the MP Birla Group. Sudarshan Netralaya at Amreli in Gujarat was established in collaboration with the Nagardas Dhanji Shanghvi Trust.

These institutions are relatively independent of the main hospital system in Tamil Nadu. They are not led by an AECS-trained doctor, but are supported by a manager trained at Lions Aravind Institute of Community Ophthalmology (LAICO). The staff members at these facilities also see themselves as separate from AECS.

There is a significant difference in the degree of vertical integration between the core and the managed-care hospitals. AECS is involved in almost every operational aspect of the southern hospitals, while its scope of work at the managed-care hospitals is limited to surgery and overall management. It has little involvement in the building, financing or outreach activities.

Cultural differences also come in the way of the AECS model being effectively transferred to the managed-care hospitals. For instance, the internally trained nurses perform a wide range of roles such as assisting in the operating theatre, processing admissions and maintaining the facilities.

However, the efficiency and dedication of these 'sisters' in the managed-care hospitals is not observed to match that at the core hospitals. A few of them were deputed from Madurai to develop the local nursing staff. However, such transfers have decreased over time.[4]

THE WORKFLOW

The hospital processes at AECS, across the paying as well as the free sections, are carefully designed and well established. They play a key role in enabling high operational efficiency.[5]

Patients start to gather at the entrance much earlier than the designated hour of opening. They enter the hospital through the designated outpatient department (OPD) entrance. Patients usually drop in without any prior appointment and are often accompanied by one or two family members.

At 7 AM sharp, the first patient is registered at the reception counter. He/she fills out the basic personal information in a card and then waits in the queue in front of a registration counter. The computerized registration process takes about one minute per patient and prints an OPD patient card as well as a tag that serves as the patient passport for subsequent visits.

Patients then take their seat in the designated waiting area. Each unit has a nurse-in-charge responsible for managing the patient flow. After the preliminary checks carried out by the paramedical staff, the standard routine begins with the refraction or the vision test.

The patient then meets the resident doctor at the examination station where the diagnosis and the recommendations are recorded. Special tests (dilation, A-test, blood tests) may be necessary for some patients, while additional procedures (blood pressure, ocular tension, urine sugar) are required for patients over 40 years of age. A senior doctor examines the patient thereafter.

Finally, the patient is counselled and discharged from the OPD—often for further consultation at one of the hospital's specialty clinics. The entire process takes no more than two hours, depending upon the tests needed. At the end of the hospital visit the diagnosis is entered into a computer system.

Spectacles are prescribed to many patients after the refraction tests. They might (but are not obliged to) go to one of the spectacle shops located in the hospital. These shops are run as separate profit centres. They sell spectacles at a price less than what they would cost in an external optical shop. The grinding and fitting of the glasses are also done in-house. The entire system is geared towards enabling patients to leave the hospital with the prescribed pair of glasses within a span of four hours.

Patients requiring surgery are admitted immediately, subject to their readiness as well as the availability of rooms. The paying patients may choose specific doctors to carry out the surgery as well as the type of surgery (e.g., phaco surgery), the type of lenses (rigid or foldable etc.) and the type of rooms. Staff counsellors assist the patients in making these choices. These requests and preferences are processed on the computer and an admission or reservation slip is generated.

The workflow in the surgical wards is equally smooth and efficient. The nursing staff comes in at 6.30 AM. The names of patients to be operated on during the day in each theatre is put up by 6.45 AM. The patients to be operated upon during the day are moved to a ward adjacent to the OT. After the local anaesthesia injections, their eyes are washed and disinfected. By 7.15 AM, two patients are lying on adjacent operating tables within the OT.

The OT has four operating tables that are laid out side-by-side. Two surgical teams, each consisting of one doctor and four nurses, operate simultaneously. Every team looks after two adjacent tables. Although operating theatres usually do not allow simultaneous operations to take place due to the risk of infection, no such difficulty has been reported at AECS.

The first patient is on table #1. He is ready for the operation and the nurses are also fully prepared. The doctor commences the procedure, which takes up to 12 minutes to complete. When the first surgery is over, the doctor moves to table #2 where the second patient is ready. The microscope is already focused upon the eye to be operated upon. The instruments are ready too.

Meanwhile, the first patient is bandaged by the nurses and moved out, and the third patient is moved in (on table #1) and readied for the operation. As soon as the second patient's surgery is completed, the doctor moves back to table #1 to operate upon the third patient. The surgeon constantly shuffles between the two tables in this manner with hardly any intervening break or loss of time.

AECS is very particular about the quality of the surgery. The management keeps a very close track of the intraoperative as well as post-operative complication rates. Each case of complication is traced to the operating team that performed the surgery and the reasons are identified. Corrective action, including the training of whosoever was found deficient, is undertaken.

THE STRATEGIC PILLARS

The extraordinary success of AECS lies in the innovative design and thoughtful integration of several elements that are woven tightly together into a virtuous cycle of synergistic performance. The development of the institution has been supported by five strategic choices. These are as follows:

1. Focus on cataract treatment

2. Hybrid business model

3. Operational efficiency

4. Vertical integration

5. Spirit of service

Some of these are based upon pure economic reasoning, while the others help to align the management processes with the core mission of the organization. However, each one of them is critical towards collective success. If even a single element of the strategy was to fail, the entire system may unravel. However, when all the elements click together symbiotically, the results are there for all to see, experience and emulate.

FOCUS ON CATARACT TREATMENT

Since its inception, the unstinting focus of the organization has been on the elimination of cataract blindness. In founding Aravind, Dr V could have gone in many directions. He chose cataract blindness. That rest of the AECS strategy was predicated upon this singular choice.

Even as AECS is a multifaceted clinical and research institution with many ophthalmic specialties, it principally remains a large-scale cataract surgery 'factory'. Since cataracts are the leading cause of blindness in India, about 65 per cent of AECS surgeries are carried out for their removal.

AECS conducts several studies every year that investigate the causes of blindness. These include nutrition, lifestyle, culture and customs. However, these activities are not a significant part of its core programmes. The institution remains focused upon the surgical treatment of cataract.

HYBRID BUSINESS MODEL

The core mission of AECS is to address the eye care needs of the vast numbers of poor people who live mainly in the rural areas. To that end, the organization has improvised a 'hybrid' model whereby paying and free patients are treated together. This has allowed AECS to reach a scale of operations that matched the enormous challenge of needless blindness in the country.

The development of a clientele of paying customers seeking specialized services was initially driven by the need to secure the necessary funds for the accomplishment of its core mission. However, it soon emerged that the pool of paying patients was a very important source of market feedback for the institution too. It helped AECS to maintain the discipline of performing at very high-quality standards, which had a positive rub off on the treatment of poor patients.

To address the needs of this income-generating market segment, AECS began to offer a comprehensive variety of non-cataract specialty services such as retina, cornea, glaucoma, paediatric ophthalmology, neuro-ophthalmology, uvea, low vision and orbit etc. As a result, the AECS doctors are challenged to master new skills for these specialist disciplines. Even though cataract provides doctors with the satisfaction of serving the poor and the needy, many surgeons may not consider it to be professionally challenging or adequately remunerative.

Eye Camps

Given India's population demographics and disease incidence, AECS required a robust system to take care of the millions of rural poor who were cataract blind. During his days in government service, Dr V had pioneered the large-scale use of eye screening camps to bring those selected for surgery into the base hospital. Accordingly, AECS adopted and refined the channel of 'screening camps' as its preferred way of reaching out to the rural poor.

The institution conducts eye camps through mobile units that travel to rural locations 20 km to 200 km away from the main hospital. Medical teams work closely with community leaders and philanthropic groups much in advance so as to set up these camps that screen hundreds of people in a single day. Local organizations help with the operational and the marketing activities related to the camp, while AECS provides the staff and the medical equipment.

Each eye camp team comprises at least two doctors and seven para-medical staff. Eye exams are conducted and spectacles, as well as medication, are provided on site too. Those selected for a surgical procedure are transported by bus to the base hospital, where the operation takes place on the next day.

OPERATIONAL EFFICIENCY

Having put in place a strategy for gaining volume, the next challenge for AECS lay in building the capacity to address the massive volume of cataract surgery that was being targeted. The shortage of trained ophthalmologists in the country also was a limiting factor.

In order to sidestep these 'production' bottlenecks, AECS designed an innovative low-cost but high-quality operating system for eye care. The institution also employed IT systems to monitor patient flow as well as the workload in the different units of the hospital. This ensured that no facility, staff or medical equipment was left idle.

At AECS, the processes of preparing the patient for surgery, performing the surgery and getting the patient through recovery are all configured on the lines of a modern and efficient 'assembly' line. The factors underlying this level of efficiency are broadly as follows:

1. Steady flow of patients, which keeps the patient supply line busy

2. Surgical flow, which ensures minimal waiting time between surgeries

3. Well-trained surgical assistants and adequate staffing

4. Detailed logistics planning that ensures zero downtime for want of supplies or equipment

5. Micro-planning to match the surgical load to the staffing and supply requirements

6. The skill and stamina of the surgeons

As a result, the cost of a cataract surgery at AECS is about $18 per person, inclusive of the intraocular lens (IOL). The cost of a comparable surgery in the United States is about $1,800.

Over the years, AECS has continued to reinvest its operating surplus towards the acquisition of the latest technology and equipment—while innovating to keep costs down to the bare minimum. Studies of patient outcomes have shown that the quality of care at AECS is comparable to that at top hospitals across the world.[4, p. 23]

VERTICAL INTEGRATION

A low-cost assembly line system can produce excellent output at an affordable cost, only if the incoming components are of high quality and low cost too. This logic has led AECS to the vertical integration of its key production inputs. The two important cost elements in eye care are as follows[4, pp. 20, 21]:

1. The wages of the trained medical personnel such as doctors and nurses

2. The high-technology components in the surgery that include the IOL

Therefore, an essential facet of the AECS model is the optimal leverage of the surgeon's time through the provision of highly trained ophthalmic nurses. Since a large pool of such talent was not readily available, Aravind chose to create its own supply.

Every year, over a hundred girls are selected from the nearby villages to attend two years of rigorous training before their absorption into the system. These 'sisters' form the backbone of clinical operations at AECS. Most of these young women have barely passed high school and are unlikely to find any meaningful employment in their village. AECS steps in to hire them and then provides for their training free of cost. During this period, the interns also receive free housing and a stipend.

During the structured training programme, the emphasis is as much upon the development of skill in ophthalmic techniques as in learning to deliver care in a compassionate, patient-centric way— combined with the supervised living accommodation at the nurses' hostel; this is seen by many families as the ultimate mode of employment as well as income in a safe environment.

Most nurses serve at AECS for several years, during which time they develop valuable skills as well as self-confidence. This stint also provides them with an opportunity to earn some money for themselves, before they return to their families in order to get married and settle down.

During the 1980s, the surgical technology had evolved considerably. However, AECS still lacked a viable source for the IOL that are an essential component of cataract surgery. This led to a wide quality gap between the paying and the poor patients. The manufacturing of such lenses was considered extremely high-tech at that time. It required the latest in precision machining techniques and quality control.

In the face of adversity, AECS once again chose to innovate boldly in order to fulfil its vision. In 1992, in the teeth of opposition from the developed world and against the advice of the WHO, AECS acquired the IOL technology from the Western world with the help of supporters such as David Green of the Seva Foundation.

This led to the establishment of Aurolab, a manufacturing facility that currently produces enough quality lenses to meet the internal needs. Aurolab presently manufactures 2 million lenses an year, within a highly affordable price range of $2–$10. It also exports ophthalmic supplies to 130 other countries.

SPIRIT OF SERVICE

The bedrock of the AECS is the committed human engine that runs it. The institution's doctors and support staff work together as a highly disciplined and inspired workforce. AECS currently has over 4,000 people engaged in its mission. This includes 35 of Dr V's family members. It is difficult to run such a huge system on the philosophy of its founder, especially when that calls for sharp attention to efficiency and dedication to service quality.

To address the challenge, AECS built institutional mechanisms to motivate its people. Its doctors are encouraged and supported in research activities that involve training in cutting-edge techniques. The nursing staff is also treated with care. Keen attention is paid to their development. Given its size and reputation, AECS attracts doctors from leading academic institutions around the world to visit and spend time in training its personnel. AECS is often the lead user for advanced technologies or treatments from leading equipment suppliers.

All of this supplements the satisfaction of providing people with the gift of being able to see again.

To paraphrase Abraham Lincoln, an institution of the people, by the people and for the people shall never perish from this earth. The AECS appears to be destined to serve humanity for all times to come and sets an example for others that is eminently worthy of emulation.

REFERENCES

1. Center for Global Development. *Millions Saved—CASE 19: Treating Cataracts in India.* Washington, DC: Center for Global Development. Available at: https://www.cgdev.org/page/case-19-treating-cataracts-india (accessed: 5 April 2016).

2. Shenoy S & Mehta P. *Infinite Vision.* San Francisco, CA: Berrett-Koehler Publishers; 2011.

3. Clyde P. *Growing Pains: A Ross School Perspective on the Evolution of the Aravind Eye Care System.* Ann Arbor, MI: Ross School of Business University of Michigan; 2005. Available at: www.aravind.org/content/aravindmediapdffiles/journalcasestudies/Growingpains.pdf (accessed: 6 April 2016).

4. McKinsey & Company. *Driving Down the Cost of High-Quality Care: Lessons From the Aravind Eye Care System.* Health International; 2011. Available at: https://www.mckinsey.com/~/media/mckinsey/dotcom/client_service/healthcare%20systems%20and%20services/health%20international/issue%2011%20new%20pdfs/hi11_18%20aravindeyecaresys_noprint.ashx (accessed: 26 November 2018).

5. Manikutty S & Vohra N. *Aravind Eye Care System: Giving Them the Most Precious Gift.* Ahmedabad: Indian Institute of Management; 2003. pp. 7–10.

VIDEO REFERENCE

Samatvam. (2016, March 1). *Aravind Eye Care System: An Inspired Institution.* YouTube. Available at: https://youtu.be/bNHtDMkvor4 (accessed: 26 November 2018).

ENTREPRENEURIAL SYNERGY

10

People who say it cannot be done should not interrupt those who are doing it.

—*George Bernard Shaw*

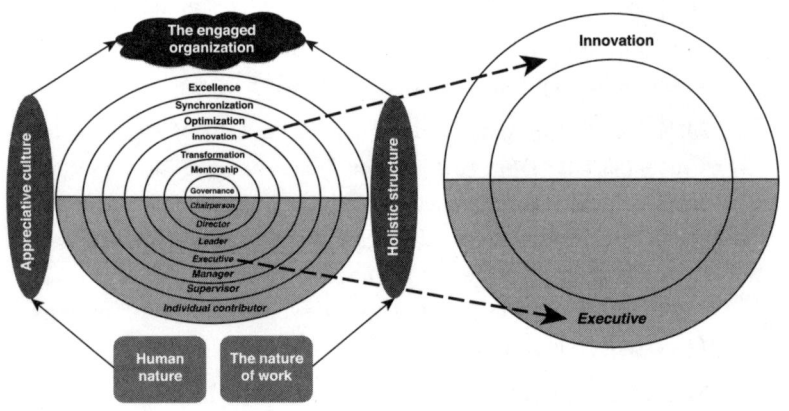

The Executive Mandate of Innovation
Source: Samatvam Academy

Large business organizations are usually structured as a set of interrelated divisions or business units that come together to form an integrated enterprise. Each division is typically placed under the charge of a senior executive, who usually reports to the chief executive officer of the enterprise. Executives are placed at the fourth rung on the hierarchical ladder of accountability.

The executive role demands excellence from a functional as well as a business perspective. While functional maturity translates as the ability to think about the function from multiple perspectives, business maturity involves the development of a holistic view of the business.

Seasoned executives always keep the big picture in mind even as they pay close attention to the details. They transcend the 'silo' mentality and evolve from a narrow dedication towards their own business unit to the success of the entire organization. Executives also collaborate with their colleagues across divisions and support the accomplishment of one another's strategic work. Considering the impact of local decisions upon the larger institution is the key to executive success.

In order to serve customer needs and create extraordinary value from limited resources without antagonizing any of the stakeholders, executives adapt as well as innovate their way along. They assume significant personal and organizational risk in doing so. In effect, corporate executives adopt an entrepreneurial approach to their work.

The process of entrepreneurship involves uncovering, seizing and developing an opportunity to create value—regardless of the adequacy of the material, capital and the human resources available with the enterprise. Entrepreneurs are social architects who foster creativity and facilitate the development of new ideas. They adopt an innovative approach in order to create radically new products and services.

However, the task of business executives is relatively more complex than that of individual entrepreneurs. Executives operate within an organizational setting that is characterized by diverse stakeholders with widely varying and conflicting needs, values and perspectives. These corporate entrepreneurs (also known as *intrapreneurs*) are, thus, required to grapple with several mutually opposing ideas or priorities at any given time.

Always keeping the big picture in mind while they work on the individual segments of a problem, entrepreneurial executives search for creative resolution in convoluted circumstances. They reconcile all the disparate and competing aspects in a situation, without selecting one extreme at the expense of the other. When at their very best, executives manage to synergistically fuse together numerous contrasting perspectives towards a collective benefit.

This synergistic approach helps to create an integrated solution in a dichotomous situation such that no value is compromised, lost or given up. The true executive is, thus, an alchemist who innovatively transforms conflict into synergy, in the manner of a classic entrepreneur.

The Executive Challenge

The primary challenge faced by business executives is that of achieving sustained organizational vitality in a fractured and dynamic environment. Modern enterprises demand stability and growth, long-term planning and short-term decisions, tradition and innovation, collaboration and competition, order and freedom—all at the same time.

Therefore, executives confront new challenges and unfamiliar conflicts every day. They are often called upon to do things that appear to be mutually exclusive at first glance. For instance, executives need to focus on the future even as they must pay close attention to the present at the same time. 'Command and control' is often necessary, even as 'empowerment and delegation' is almost mandatory in order that the enterprise may serve complex market needs in real time.

Even as they seek to protect the stability and continuity of the organization, executives are required to encourage innovation and risk-taking as a survival tactic. And then, they must find a way to evoke intense cohesion and collaboration among their colleagues in a competitive landscape where long-term job security can no longer be promised.

In order to excel, executives must, thereby, embrace a diverse set of competing values, priorities or perspectives that appear to be in mutual conflict—even as they are simultaneously critical for the accomplishment of organizational objectives. This makes it imperative for executives to navigate judiciously in a world that is replete with paradoxes and dilemmas, which are situations wherein two seemingly inconsistent values or contradictory ideas are both true at the same time.

ENGAGE!

Transcending such paradoxes requires a serious reconsideration of some popular reductionist beliefs and assumptions. Executives need to adopt a more balanced and integrative approach to their work. Research confirms that executives who balance competing roles are evaluated as being more effective.[1]

The key to executive success perhaps lies therein!

Framing the Executive Challenge: The Competing Values Framework

Executive success is a function of the recognition that the opposition between apparently conflicting polarities is merely a screen that veils their complementary nature. Robert Quinn's time-tested competing values framework (CVF) offers a robust formulation that highlights this phenomenon in the form of two pairs of dimensions of organizational vitality that appear to be in mutual conflict.[2]

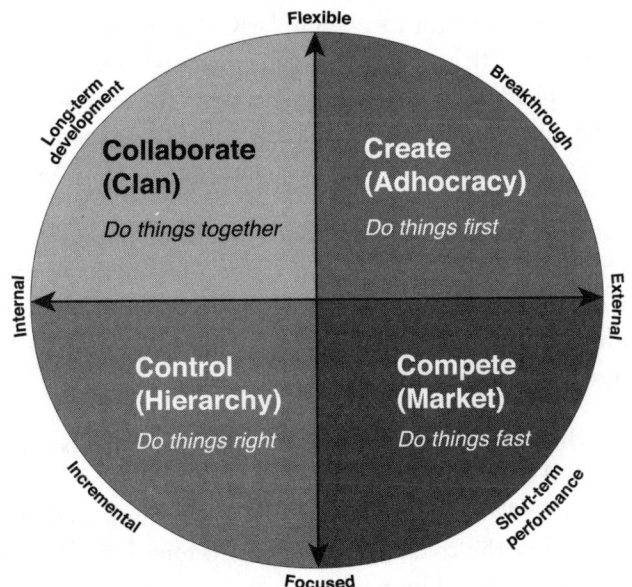

The Competing Values Framework

Source: https://www.toolshero.com/leadership/competing-values-framework/ (accessed: 20 December 2018)

The first dimension of CVF contrasts an emphasis on 'flexibility, discretion and dynamism' from the emphasis on 'stability, order and control'. This continuum ranges from versatility and pliability at one end to steadiness and durability on the other. The second dimension differentiates an internal orientation with a focus on 'integration, collaboration and unity' from an external orientation with a focus on 'differentiation, competition and rivalry'.[2] This particular continuum ranges from cohesion and consonance at the one end to separation and independence on the other.

When these two dimensions are juxtaposed with one another, they form four quadrants. Each quadrant highlights a core value that is opposite to the value on the other end of the continuum, that is, flexibility versus stability and internal versus external focus.[2]

The upper left quadrant identifies values that emphasize an internal, organic focus, whereas the lower right quadrant identifies values with an external, control focus. Similarly, the upper right quadrant identifies values with an external, organic focus whereas the lower left quadrant emphasizes internal, control values.[2] The values represented by any one quadrant are not necessarily superior or more preferable than those symbolized by the other quadrants.

The 'create' and the 'control' persuasions usually do not see eye-to-eye. If their writ were to run alone, the 'create' proponents might easily become mavericks who do not relate with the rest of the organization. On the other hand, the 'control' proponents may similarly become static bureaucrats when they are left unfettered.

Likewise, the 'compete' and the 'collaborate' proponents are also at loggerheads. However, in actual practice, the 'compete' proponents mitigate the 'collaborate' tendencies of groupthink and irrational enthusiasm while the 'collaborate' proponents tone down the 'compete' traits of impatience and immediacy.

These opposing values, thus, represent competing assumptions that are actually interdependent (like the two sides of a coin), but may nevertheless result in constructive conflict. The salient executive challenge is to synergistically leverage the tension between these pairs of symbiotic forces, in order to innovate entrepreneurial solutions that capture the 'best of both' worlds.

The Business Executive as a Corporate Entrepreneur

Executives promote innovation by challenging rigid mindsets and effectively managing various kinds of risk. This enables them to create a proposition that delivers superior value to the customer and simultaneously fulfils the strategic objectives of the organization.

In order to flourish, executives emulate the approach of independent entrepreneurs. Working from an internal organizational perspective, they promote creativity and innovation of various kinds. In the executive context, innovation refers to a multidimensional effort that yields a new concept, design or outcome through a symbiotic or synergistic integration of existing knowledge and techniques.

Innovation can be radical or incremental. While radical innovations may be revolutionary, discontinuous, original and pioneering, incremental innovations are small improvements that serve to enhance and extend the established processes, products and services.

Innovation may relate to a product or to a process. Product innovation reflects a change in the end product or service offered by the organization, whereas process innovation represents some changes in the way that the firm manufactures or creates the end product or service.[3]

Innovation is often technological. However, it may also be administrative in nature. Technological innovation relates to the endorsement of a new idea that directly influences the basic output processes, whereas administrative innovation includes the changes that affect the policies, allocation of resources and other factors associated with the social structure of the organization.

Entrepreneurially oriented executives examine situations from previously unexplored perspectives, take significant risks and remain operationally nimble. They craft a strategy after carefully assessing the challenging situation or potential opportunity and then bring together the necessary resources for securing favourable outcomes.

Corporate entrepreneurs work broadly within the ambit of organizational policies and procedures, but often become the revolutionaries who work towards change and renewal from within the system. While the organizational context implies restrictions, it also provides them with a considerable amount of support, security and leverage towards balancing competing values, achieving stakeholder delight and guiding their respective businesses towards excellence.

The Executive Mandate: Generating Entrepreneurial Synergy

Modern business enterprises are complex and dynamic relational systems that are run by entrepreneurially oriented executives. Their success hinges upon a demonstrated capacity to:

1. Organize for the creation and refinement of a variety of new products, services and solutions.

2. Translate this output into superior value for the end customer.

3. Adequately meet the concerns and requirements of the numerous stakeholders of the enterprise.

The act of creating value through innovation is accomplished by the creative transcendence of dichotomy. This was hitherto considered as *de rigueur* only for independent entrepreneurs. Now, it has become mandatory for corporate executives too.

Outstanding executives do not view pairs of opposing values or conflicting priorities as competing, zero-sum games that call for compromise. Rather, they seek to maximize both the polarities before ingeniously integrating them together. This allows them to harness synergy from their partnership. Instead of accepting a trade-off between the diverging elements, the synergistic approach works on a logic that integrates differences at every opportunity.

The term 'synergy' describes the capacity of two persons, forces or structures to work together in a mutually fruitful way so as to produce a combined effect that is significantly greater than the sum of their individual effects. Synergy is accomplished by transforming the competitive relationship between potentially opposing values into a complementary one. In such a situation, doing (more of) any one must increase the returns from doing (more of) the other.

The integrative effort involved in generating synergy requires dynamism in perception, divergence in thinking, affective flexibility and the capacity for behavioural complexity.

Perceptual dynamism is the capacity for reframing situations, such as the viewing of problems as opportunities. Divergent thinking is the ability to spontaneously draw upon ideas across domains in order to reach a deeper understanding so as to generate multiple answers to a given problem.[4]

Affective flexibility is the ability to easily switch back and forth between processing the emotional and non-emotional aspects of a situation in order to make decisions. Behavioural complexity refers to the capacity to conceive as well as perform multiple roles simultaneously.

Synergistic integration yields a dramatic sense of achievement as well as an experience of satisfaction for all the stakeholders involved.

The Development of Entrepreneurial Synergy

Entrepreneurship is the process of innovatively endowing existing resources with additional value. For instance, according to a mathematician, one and one may equal zero, one or two—depending upon whether they are subtracted, divided or added. However, an agile entrepreneur would recognize that these could be synergistically combined to make eleven too!

The fable of 'The Blind and the Lame Man' provides an anecdotal illustration of the phenomenon of synergy. It recounts how two people utilized their individual capability in an effort to overcome their respective disabilities. The blind man carried the lame person on his back, and thus lent him the use of his feet while utilizing the benefit of the latter's eyes. The outcome was mutually beneficial.

In the business domain, the Swedish furniture retailer IKEA achieved international success by creatively combining excellent product design and display with low-cost manufacturing, sourcing and storage. The company was, thus, able to deliver inexpensive furniture that was highly elegant and of good taste. Similarly, the Indian automobile industry harnessed the total quality management paradigm during the 1990s in order to synergistically enhance quality as well as affordability.

The development of such synergy entails a three-step process sequence, which helps people to arrive at a harmonious solution or an innovative outcome in any situation of divergence. While the three stages are sequential, the progress happens iteratively. These phases are as follows:

1. **Respect:** Acknowledge merit in each of the respective values

2. **Reconcile:** Integrate and harmonize the apparently competing or conflicting values

3. **Realize:** Harness the benefits that arise from the complementarity of these values

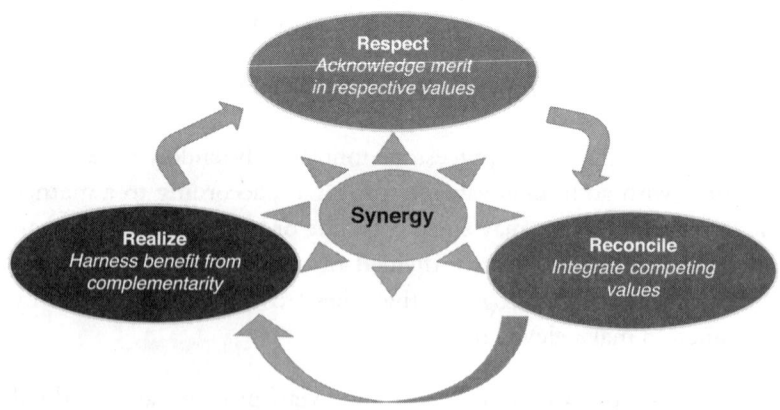

The Technology of Entrepreneurial Synergy
Source: Samatvam Academy

The Entrepreneurial Synergy Framework

Entrepreneurial synergy arises from an active progression through the three distinct stages of respect, reconcile and realize. Each stage operates concurrently across the affective, cognitive and conative dimensions of the human personality.

On the affective plane, the phenomenon of *inclusion* (a felt connection between individuals or groups) facilitates *integration* (assimilation of divergent needs and views of the people) in due course of time. This eventually leads to the development of *resonance* (a felt sense of energy and rhythm).

At the conative level, the process of synergy progresses through *inquiry* (respectfully asking questions) that facilitates genuine *dialogue* (exchange of ideas with a view to reaching an amicable understanding) and culminates into *resolution* (incorporation of contradictory options into a unitary scheme) of the conflict or dilemma.

With respect to the cognitive dimension, synergy arises from multiple *insights* (understanding of a specific cause/effect) that facilitate *retroduction* (adoption of a provisional hypothesis that can be experimentally tested), leading to the capacity for *innovation* (creative breakthrough that leads to a novel solution).

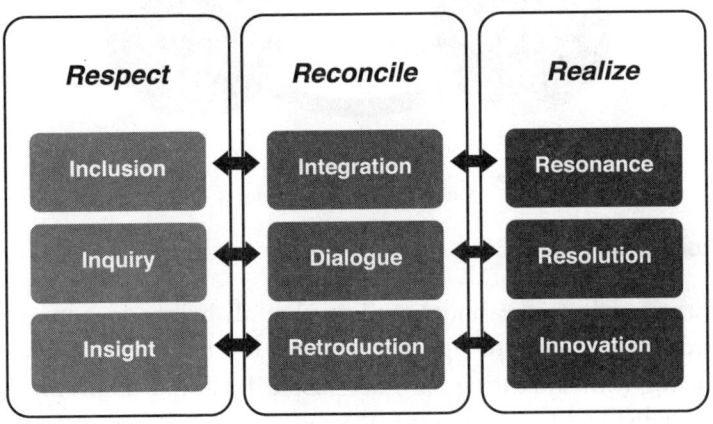

The Entrepreneurial Synergy Framework
Source: Samatvam Academy

The Respect Phase

The term 'respect' denotes a particular way of looking at or thinking about some object or situation. The idea of giving proper attention to the object is, thus, central to the phenomenon of respect. In the respect phase, the phenomenon of interdependence as a feature of life entails the inclusion of other people into one's own sense of identity. Subsequently, the mode of respectful inquiry is adopted to learn about the uniqueness of the other person or the circumstance. Finally, paying keen attention helps to generate insight into the other person or situation.

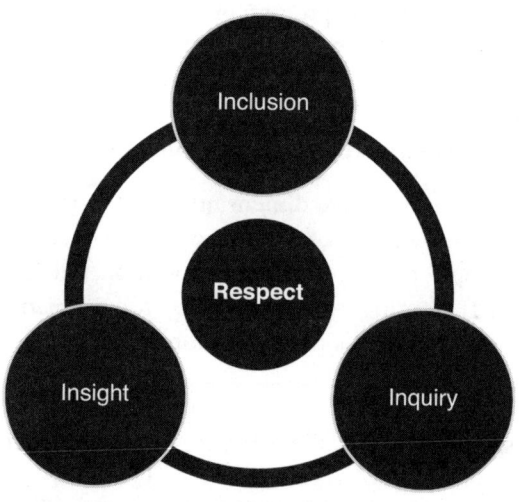

The Respect Phase
Source: Samatvam Academy

Inclusion

Inclusion reflects the understanding that all beings in nature are interdependent, even though not identical. It refers to the practice of affiliating with and caring for other people. Inclusion entails inviting every individual to engage with the social process in the fullness of his/her capacity.

A relationship begins when two (or more) people come into each other's experienced presence. Inclusive relationships develop as a result of congruent and empathic attunement between two or more individuals. This calls for the individuals to get along, while recognizing their respective faults as well as gifts. Effective inclusion involves sensitivity towards individual needs and differences.

Inquiry

Inquiry refers to the seeking after knowledge, information or the truth of a matter of one's interest, through a systematic investigation. It is the process of respectfully asking about or examining something in order to get more information. Inquiry involves asking questions in order to unlock essential information that is vital towards the resolution of the situation.

Inquiry presupposes listening with the intention of genuinely understanding the thoughts and feelings of the other person. The inquirer suspends judgement and tries to comprehend how and why the other person has progressed from the data of her experiences to arrive at a particular interpretation or conclusion. At its best, the process of inquiry yields a true picture or an authentic reflection of the situational reality.

Insight

The term 'insight' refers to a sudden comprehension that solves a problem or resolves an ambiguous percept. When people unexpectedly see the connections that had previously eluded them, they are said to have a flash of insight.[5]

Insight is often acquired through the process of conducting a non-judgemental inquiry. However, it may also arise from an understanding of the inner nature of things or by means of intuition and even introspection. In their extensive research, Kounios and Beeman[5] found that insight appears to pop into awareness seemingly out of nowhere. It literally yields a different way of looking at things.

The Reconciliation Phase

Reconciliation refers to the process of enabling two apparently conflicting objects, values, perspectives or interests to become congruous or consistent with each other.[6]

The process of reconciling a conflict is initiated with the *integration* of polarities on the affective plane, accompanied by conscious *dialogue* at the behavioural level. It culminates into a plausible new hypothesis or plan of action that incorporates all the available insights by means of the process of *retroduction*.

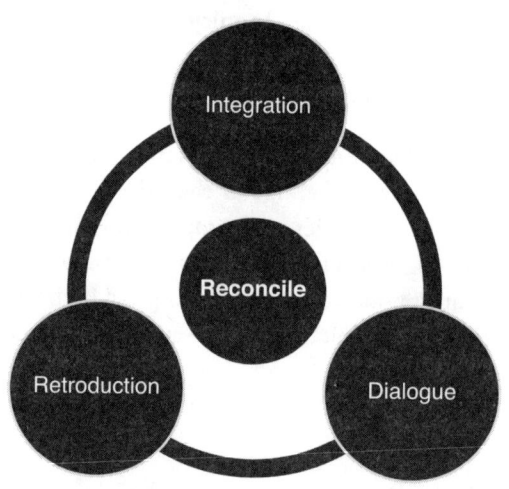

The Reconciliation Phase
Source: Samatvam Academy

Integration

Integration is the act of organizing a set of disparate elements into a unified pattern.

Integration is the capacity to simultaneously hold two diametrically opposite ideas or values deep within. This helps to generate a synergistic outcome that is superior to either of these opposing views.

Integration involves facing the tension of clashing perspectives constructively and generating a new viewpoint that contains elements of both the former perspectives. It not only employs a 'both/and' approach that sees a factor to be true but also looks upon a contradictory factor to be simultaneously true.[7] This creates value by way of a coherent synthesis of seemingly opposed values, through the transcendence of conceptual limitations.

Integration unifies opposing values as symbolized by the Chinese pictogram of 'Yin-Yang'. It collates many small components into a single, unitary and comprehensive system.

Dialogue

Dialogue refers to a written or conversational exchange of ideas and opinions between two or more people with a view towards reaching an amicable understanding or agreement. It is a collaborative exercise, wherein participants work together to explore common ground that eventually leads to a shared understanding. Dialogue is designed for situations in which people have fundamentally different frames of reference.[8]

One of the cardinal principles of dialogue is the surfacing and questioning of underlying assumptions that are usually buried deep beneath the surface. In any effective dialogue, much time and effort is spent in uncovering and excavating these hidden aspects of the dispute. The use of 'them' and 'us' gradually transposes into a credible and durable 'we'. The energy evolves towards the transformation of the dichotomous situation. The stage is then set for a breakthrough.

Retroduction

Retroduction is a form of logical inference. It leads to the formulation of a theory or hypothesis that provides the simplest, best and most likely explanation for a set of observations.[9] Retroduction facilitates the development of new explanations by means of a cerebral process that is relatively unhampered by logical rules.

Retroduction is a leap of the mind that brings together ideas that may never have previously been associated with one another. It has a *logical* as well as an *innovative* character that extends into profound insight.

The first step in the retroductive process is to find or develop a hypothesis, by means of abduction. The second step consists of deriving predictions from the hypothesis, which is deduction. The final step consists of the search for facts that will 'verify' the assumptions through induction. This cycle of abduction, deduction and induction is iteratively repeated, until all the facts finally fit together.

The legendary Sherlock Holmes and other detectives of his ilk extensively employed retroduction. They were thus able to 'magically' solve crimes that remained as conundrums for the investigative agencies.

The Realize Phase

Realize refers to the capacity to bring something into concrete existence or to carry out an act or process to completion or fulfilment.

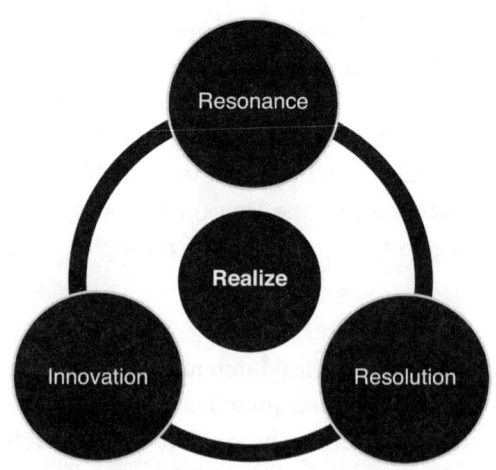

The Realize Phase
Source: Samatvam Academy

To realize synergy, executives begin by developing affective *resonance* across the organization. Competing perspectives are brought to a mutually satisfactory *resolution*. The process culminates in the generation of *innovative* and synergistic solutions.

Resonance

Resonance represents a physical phenomenon, wherein vibrations are transmitted from one vibrating body to another in the absence of any physical contact between the two. Resonance is the amplification of effect that occurs when the respective energy of two or more entities get in step or phase with each other.

When human beings exist in close physical proximity with one another, the first level of interchange usually occurs at the rational or the cognitive plane. An exchange of ideas takes place. The next level of interaction occurs as an energetic connection between the people concerned. Finally, the level of connection that is felt intuitively constitutes resonance.

Resolution

Resolution is the phenomenon of having something settled. It refers to a situation where no problem or conflict exists. Resolution is an interactive process of collecting all the different (or even contradictory) principles, values and perspectives and incorporating these into a single, unified whole that yields a voluntary agreement or solution.

Resolution represents a transformation of the relationship between the entities involved. It employs a win-win approach, which is a conscious and systematic attempt to maximize the goals of both parties through collaborative problem-solving. The focus is upon the needs and constraints of all the parties involved rather than emphasizing strategies that are designed to conquer.

Resolution, thus, represents a methodology that channelizes the energy and momentum of mutual differences towards creating common ground so as to arrive at mutually beneficial outcomes.

Innovation

Innovation refers to the generation and application of creative solutions in order to meet new or existing needs.[10] It is the process of translating an idea or invention into a solution that creates quantifiable value. Innovation involves the deliberate application of information, imagination and initiative so as to help derive greater value from the resources.[11]

Innovation thrives upon the constructive leveraging of the differences between individual values, personalities, cultures, roles as well as perspectives. When differences are viewed as complementary qualities, they may be suitably assimilated in order to yield innovative results in ways that are fair, honest and mutually beneficial. Depending upon its use and application, an innovative solution may take on different forms—a product, a service, a process or a breakthrough.

Synergy has an alchemical quality to it. People who have been brought up on zero-sum arithmetic find it difficult to surmise that an interaction can simultaneously satisfy the needs of all the stakeholders.

There is the oft-repeated story of the father with two young children, but only one orange in hand. Both the kids wanted to appropriate the entire fruit. In this circumstance, the father decided to pursue the course of respectful inquiry rather than the usual tactic of negotiation.

He asked the first child why he wanted the orange. Pat came with the reply, 'I like its sweet and juicy taste'. When the same question was asked of the second one, the father discovered that this child needed the peel of the entire Orange in order to play the prank of squeezing its pungent juice into the eyes of his classmates. Lo and behold, the problem was solved to everybody's satisfaction!

Synergy is actually that simple!

On the other hand, innovation is the endeavour of finding a way to gainfully utilize the different attributes of a resource in previously unanticipated ways—towards the resolution of a problem or the generation of a new solution. It requires a widening or deepening of one's perspective so as to look beyond the usual assumptions and horizons. Innovation is the fruitful outcome of a synergistic approach to business.

Entrepreneurs, by their very definition, need to engage with both of these constructs. Executives in modern times are also fast discovering their utility and value, towards their own benefit as well as that of the corporation they represent.

Ray Anderson was one such executive leader, who had founded the American corporation Interface Inc. in the manner of a classic entrepreneur. After two decades of successful run and the attainment of industry leadership, he asked himself how an enterprise could be profitable and environmentally restorative at the same time.

Interface Inc. is a remarkable story of what a courageous man with a vision to boot can accomplish for himself, his colleagues and the world at large. It forms the subject matter of the next case study.

References

1. Denison D, Hooijberg R & Quinn R. Paradox and performance: Towards a theory of behavioral complexity in managerial leadership. *Organization Science*. 1995; 6(5): 524–540.

2. Quinn R. *Beyond Rational Management Mastering The Paradoxes and Competing Demands of High Performance*. San Francisco, CA: Jossey-Bass; 1988.

3. Smith D. *Exploring Innovation*. London: McGraw-Hill; 2006.

4. Hennessey B & Amabile T. Creativity. *Annual Review of Psychology*. 2010; 61(1): 569–598.

5. Kounios J & Beeman M. The aha! moment. *Current Directions in Psychological Science*. 2009; 18(4): 210–216.

6. Nadler A, Malloy TE & Fisher J. (Eds.) *Social Psychology of Intergroup Reconciliation*. Oxford: Oxford Scholarship Online; 2008.

7. Lewis M. Exploring paradox: Towards a more comprehensive guide. *The Academy of Management Review*. 2000; 25(4): 760.

8. Gerzon M. *Leading Through Conflict*. Boston: Harvard Business Review Press; 2015.

9. Josephson J & Josephson S. *Abductive Inference*. Cambridge: Cambridge University Press; 2009.

10. Rangaraju M & Kennedy S. *Innovation in Management*. New Delhi: Allied Publishers; 2012.

11. Kraemer-Mbula E & Wamae W. *Innovation and the Development Agenda*. Paris: OECD Publishing; 2010.

ENGAGE!

INTERFACE INC.

We have a choice to make during our brief visit to this beautiful blue and green living planet: to hurt it or to help it.

—Ray C. Anderson

BACKGROUND

Interface Inc. is the world's largest manufacturer of modular carpet, with annual revenues of over US $1 billion. Founded by Ray C. Anderson in 1973 at Atlanta, the company presently employs around 3,100 people. Its production facilities are spread across four continents, while the sales offices are located in 110 countries. Interface has been named by Fortune as one of the 'Most Admired Companies in America', and ranked among the '100 Best Companies to Work For'.

Being heavily reliant on fossil fuels for the manufacture of its products, Interface operated instinctively for two decades, under the traditional industrial model of 'take-make-waste'. However, a series of events in 1994 led Ray Anderson to guide the company towards a more sustainable mode of existence. He catalysed Interface's transformation into the world's first industrial enterprise that is devoted to sustainability in the strictest sense: taking nothing from the earth that is not rapidly and naturally renewable and doing no harm to the biosphere.[1]

Interface formulated a bold and inspiring vision of achieving a zero environmental footprint for itself, within the space of 25 years. Over the course of its challenging journey towards this goal, this exceptionally pioneering corporation has been successful at incorporating sustainability into the very core of its being. The company has reinvented its products, operations as well as the business model, and reaped a diverse range of benefits in the bargain.

During the period 1996–2009, Interface trimmed greenhouse gas emissions by 94 per cent, pared fossil fuel consumption by 60 per cent, improved total energy efficiency by 43 per cent, cut waste to landfill by 80 per cent and reduced water use by 80 per cent. Half of its raw materials are now recycled, or bio-based. During this period, the company saved over $433 million in costs and also doubled its profits.[2]

By 2020, Interface aspires to become the first corporation that can comprehensively demonstrate (by its own example) to the entire industrial world the truth and logic of sustainability in all its dimensions: (a) people, (b) process, (c) product, (d) place and (e) profit. In doing so, Interface eventually hopes to become a restorative organization through the power of influence.

THE GENESIS OF THE ENTERPRISE

Ray Anderson graduated in 1956 as an industrial engineer from Georgia Tech, and spent the next 17 years climbing the corporate ladder so as to gain business experience. As vice president at Callaway Mills Company in 1966, Anderson was passed over for the job of divisional head. Feeling wounded and helpless, he began the psychological journey towards entrepreneurship.

In April 1968, the Deering Milliken Company acquired Callaway Mills. Ray was reassigned as the director of development for Milliken's floor covering business.[3,p.28] He was sent abroad to research the technology for manufacturing carpet tiles, which came as 18-inch squares of carpet. While offering the flexible functionality of modularity, carpet tiles could be installed without adhesive to gain the appearance of the broadloom carpet.

In carpet tiles, Ray also found the niche product that would finally fulfil his entrepreneurial dream. In January 1973, he persuaded the British company Carpets International (CI), to join him in a business venture to bring their patented carpet tile technology to the United States.[3, p. 29]

The fledgling firm managed to capitalize upon the office building and furnishing boom in the US during that period. As a result, the sales of the enterprise tripled to $2.4 million in 1975, rose to $11 million by 1978, galloped to $57 million in 1982 and leaped to $80 million in 1983. The company went public that year, and raised $14.4 million in its initial offering. CIGI controlled nearly 30 per cent of the growing US carpet tile market when its revenues climbed to $107 million in 1984. Its international business also began to pick up around this time, particularly in the Middle East.

Interface generated revenues of $623 million in 1990. After shrinking to $582 million in 1991 on account of the global recession, these rebounded to $625 million by 1993 and paced to $802 million in 1995. Two decades after it was founded, the company appeared to be in great shape. But was it?

THE ECOLOGICAL AWAKENING (1994–1997)

Even as it was spectacularly successful, Interface was deeply flawed in practice. Ray Anderson arrived at this counterintuitive conclusion after experiencing an epiphany in August 1994.

It started with a persistent customer query about Interface's environmental policies and the amount of recycled content in its carpets. In order to frame the answers to these questions and also to formulate Interface's environmental position, it was decided to constitute a company-wide global task force. Ray was requested to make the keynote remarks at its kick-off meeting.

Anderson had not really given much thought to the environment as a concern up till that point in time. While Interface had indeed taken steps over the previous decade to reduce interior air contamination, its policy as such was simply to comply with the law. Ray, thus, accepted that invitation very reluctantly and sweated for three weeks over what to say to that task force.

Serendipitously, the 1993 book *The Ecology of Commerce* by Paul Hawken came to Ray's attention. It persuasively decried the industrial model under which Interface and its peer corporations were operating. The book detailed how this mode of working was contributing to the plundering of the Earth as well as the eradication of resources that rightfully belonged to the future generations.

As Anderson perused the text, Paul Hawken's message struck him as a spear in the chest. It provided him with a new sense of purpose and a clear moral imperative. The trigger may have been a subconscious search for a personal legacy or perhaps the whispers of conscience. Either way, Hawken's book helped Ray to appreciate the need for Interface to operate more sustainably. It also served as the basic source from which the contours of a bold, new direction emerged.[4]

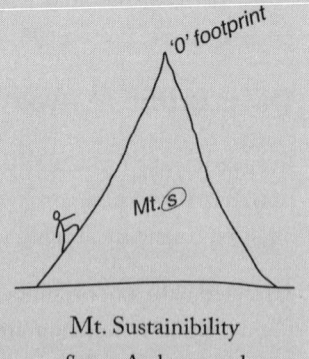

The pioneering and expansive vision that Ray shared with the task force in August 1994 was, 'Interface, worldwide the first name in industrial ecology—through substance, not words'.

Anderson also gave that group a mission: '(a) To convert Interface into a restorative enterprise—first to reach

Mt. Sustainibility

Source: Anderson and White[2, p. 6]

242

sustainability and then to become restorative; (b) To put back more than we ourselves take, and doing good to Earth (not just no harm) by helping or influencing others to reach towards sustainability'.[5] Finally, he suggested a strategy: 'Reduce, reuse, reclaim, recycle and redesign. Adopt, advance and share best practices. Develop sustainable technologies and invest in them when it makes economic sense. Challenge our suppliers to do the same'.

Ray likened the journey towards a fully sustainable Interface to the quest for summiting a mountain 'higher than Everest.' He considered the endeavour to be difficult, but not impossible if a careful and attentive plan could be put in place. He even coined a name for this effort: *EcoSense*.

This comprehensive mandate was initially received by Interface managers with a measure of fear and uncertainty that was blended with scepticism and a sense of guilt. At the time, there was a shortage of corporate sustainability frameworks and economically viable green technologies.

Since prior success stories were hard to come by, people considered it impossible for Interface to survive without the use of any sort of fossil fuel. The absence of any 'burning platform' that could trigger a transformational change also contributed to the sense of initial confusion.

The tone changed once the discussion was reframed around the professional obligation of demonstrating that an oil-dependent company like Interface could also potentially transform itself. In Ray's view, corporate sustainability would serve as a source of competitive advantage.

Ray Anderson took an impassionate view of the deceit built into the market economy. From his perspective, the economic concept of 'externalities' represented all those costs of doing business that never got charged to any one organization's bottom line. Instead, these were thrust upon society.

The 'free' market appeared to be opportunistic and dishonest in the pricing of exchange value, without regard to cost or use value. It allowed the externalization of any cost that an unwary, uncaring or gullible public would permit to be externalized.

Even though he had recently stepped down as CEO while retaining the chairman's role at Interface, Ray possessed a lot of clout within the company. He set out to reinvent its industrial practices to include a sharp focus on sustainability, without sacrificing its business goals.

Realizing that external help was needed in progressing towards sustainability, Interface drew upon the diverse expertise of a group of environmental luminaries and progressive thinkers. Known within Interface as the Eco Dream Team, this group included Paul Hawken, Amory and L. Hunter Lovins, John Picard, Bill Browning, Karl-Henrik Robèrt, Bill McDonough, Janine Benyus, Robert Fox, Jonathon Porritt, Daniel Quinn, Bernadette Cozart, John Warner, Walter Stahel and David Brower.

These ecologists inspired the revised direction of Interface. They took part in the process of redefining and promoting the company's new vision.

A preliminary set of ideas and actions were formulated to help the company progress towards the vision. These were focused upon waste reduction (physical waste, energy usage, greenhouse gas emissions and water consumption) and the introduction of recycled materials into the manufacturing process.

In the first three and a half years, the company managed to reduce total waste by 40 per cent and realize savings to the tune of $67 million.

This kitty helped to fund Interface's subsequent initiatives towards sustainability. Linking employee bonuses with waste reductions also helped to put the 'meat' on the bones of Interface's business case for sustainability.

THE SEVEN FRONTS OF MOUNT SUSTAINABILITY

The seven fronts of Mount Sustainability collectively served as the pivot around which Interface's reinvention journey was orchestrated.[1] Their salient features were as follows:

FRONT ONE: ELIMINATE ALL FORMS OF WASTE IN EVERY AREA OF BUSINESS

Interface redefined waste as anything that was not essential for the performance of a product and also did not add any value to the customer. This definition included waste in its traditional (off-quality, scrap) as well as non-traditional (overuse of materials, inventory losses, misdirected shipments, energy usage and inefficient processes) form.

There is the story of a facilities manager from a very large corporation who came to visit Interface for an assessment of the genuineness of its sustainability efforts. An Interface guide took him on a tour of the company's Georgia factory. At one place, the visitor spotted stacks of taped-up 'used' cartons that looked very old and battered. He sarcastically enquired from his host if that was the image that Interface wished to send out to the world. 'Absolutely', replied his guide, 'We use these cardboard boxes over and over again, for as long as possible'.

To the visitor, those cartons instantly became the most beautiful boxes he had ever seen!

FRONT TWO: ELIMINATE TOXIC SUBSTANCES FROM PRODUCTS, VEHICLES AND FACILITIES

The second front was concerned with the elimination of molecular waste emissions. All emissions from the smokestacks as well as the effluent pipes were required to be innately harmless to natural systems. If not, they were to be rendered benign.

The dye-house manager at an Interface fabric facility in Maine felt that too many anti-static chemicals were being employed to dissipate static electricity from the fabric. He collaborated with his suppliers and managed to switch to a more benign anti-static agent. The use of acetic acid was eliminated entirely. Unnecessary materials (waste) were thus minimized, chemical pollutants (in the effluent pipes) were cut and operating costs were slashed. All of this happened through a single, unified initiative.

FRONT THREE: OPERATE FACILITIES WITH 100 PER CENT RENEWABLE ENERGY

The objective of the third front was to reduce the company's total energy consumption and to substitute fossil fuels with renewable sources of energy. The company expanded its renewable energy sources to include solar energy, biogas as well as reclaimed gas from landfills. Eight out of ten Interface production plants presently operate on 100 per cent renewable electricity.

The LaGrange City Biogas Plant

In a beautiful illustration of public-private partnership, Interface teamed up with the city of LaGrange in Georgia to build a biogas plant that converted the waste methane stream from the city landfill site into a source of fuel for two of the boilers at the local Interface factory.[6]

This provided a revenue stream of over $300,000 per year for the city, and also extended the life of its landfill site by an estimated 15 years. At the same time, burning methane instead of natural gas came out to be a 30 per cent cheaper proposition for Interface. Further, with the elimination of the noxious smell of leaking methane, the site area became safer and more pleasant for the residents of the local community. It was truly a 'win-win' proposition.

FRONT FOUR: REDESIGN PROCESSES TO FACILITATE THE USE OF RECOVERED/BIO-BASED MATERIALS

The fourth front was oriented towards imbuing Interface's concept of design with a sense of purpose. Products were now required to be recycling-friendly and manufactured either from homogeneous materials or with components that were amenable to easy separation.

Redesigned processes allowed the reclaimed resources to return as inputs to the 'industrial' cycle (going back to the factories to create new carpets) or to the 'natural' cycle (returned to the earth in a form that was not harmful to natural systems).

FRONT FIVE: RESOURCE EFFICIENT TRANSPORTATION

Interface's operations relied extensively upon the movement of people, products and resources. This transportation resulted in extensive emissions of greenhouse gases. A life cycle assessment revealed that 8 per cent of the carbon footprint of carpet tiles came from their shipping alone. The goal then was to make all kinds of transportation (including commuting) as efficient as possible.

Trees for Travel™

Begun in 1997, the Trees for Travel programme facilitated the planting of trees to offset the air miles travelled by Interface business associates. In addition, the Cool Fuel™ and Cool CO2mmut™ programmes were introduced to balance the carbon emissions of the Interface corporate fleet, and also to apply carbon offsets towards the daily commute of its employees.

Since 1997, Interface has planted over 118,000 trees through the Trees for Travel™ programme. An additional 45,000 trees have also been planted since Cool CO2mmut™ began in 2002.[6]

FRONT SIX: SENSITIZATION OF ALL THE STAKEHOLDERS

A stakeholder was defined as anybody with an interest (or a stake) in what Interface did. This included the employees, customers, investors, suppliers, interior designers and members of the business as well as the social community.

An oft-repeated story relates to the CEO of a giant American food company who was visiting the Interface FLOR factory in Georgia. Her objective was to understand how Interface actually made money by shouldering its environmental responsibilities. She was initially quite sceptical about what a carpet manufacturer could teach them in this regard.

During a break in the conference proceedings, the lady went walking around the factory floor—and happened to lose her way. James Wisener, a forklift driver who was transporting a big roll of carpet, stopped to offer assistance. She asked him, 'What do you do here?'

James said, 'Ma'am, I come to work every day to help save the Earth'.

Startled by his answer, she asked more questions.

Finally, James said, 'Ma'am, I don't want to be rude. But if I don't get this roll of carpet off to the next process right now, our waste and emissions numbers are going to go up. I have to go'.

The CEO returned to the conference room, visibly different. She finally shared her story, saying that she had never before seen such a deep alignment of vision within an organization.

The only word she could use to describe the phenomenon was 'love'.

FRONT SEVEN: CREATE NEW BUSINESS MODELS TO SUPPORT SUSTAINABILITY-BASED COMMERCE

To get even close to achieving its sustainability objectives, Interface needed to develop innovative business models to replace the fundamentally unsustainable ones that were hitherto dominant.

These new models were largely grounded in the provision of user-friendly services, instead of tangible products and materials.

TileExchange and TileCare services offered to treat or replace individual carpet tiles. Carpet life was extended through proper maintenance, for which Interface assumed responsibility. This also led to a reduction in the environmental impact as well as the client costs. At the same time, it ensured a constant stream of reclaimed material input into the ReEntry 2.0™ programme.[6]

Restorative Impact: Net Effect Collection™

Net Effect Collection™ represents carpet tiles that are partly made from the fishing nets collected through the Net-Works programme.[7]

A fine instance of commerce redesign, this product helped to generate a new source of income for the local community while simultaneously restoring the environment. It also had a positive impact on the biodiversity of the region at the same time.

THE CULTURAL TRANSFORMATION

Interface is a showcase for a step-wise approach to radical change and innovation. The company went through a process of cultural transformation in five distinct phases.[8]

The initial 'awakening' to the sustainability imperative, coupled with the definition of a vision, comprised the first stage of change at Interface. The second stage of 'cocooning' was concerned with creating the roadmap for translating that vision into action. This mandated the formulation of goals and timelines, allocation of resource and the development of metrics.

The third stage of 'metamorphosis' was concerned with the arduous process of driving widespread change in systems and structures across the organization. This entailed the creative destruction of entrenched processes as well as mindsets, along with the provision of the necessary financial and human resources. Innovation was accelerated, even as tolerance was maintained for the associated risk of failure. Initiatives that supported organizational learning were also celebrated so as to sustain and reinforce the organization's commitment.

The fourth stage of 'emergence' was concerned with progressively engaging a larger number of people across the organization into the sustainability journey. Early successes stirred further innovation. Accurate metrics gave rise to positive and circular feedback loops of learning, action, measurement and recognition. Sustainability began to get fully saturated into the company's identity and the associated beliefs and behaviours became ingrained into its DNA.

The final stage of 'engagement' involved the process of influencing others. As the Interface organization became increasingly more committed to sustainability, the education and influencing of outsiders also became an important part of the change process.

InterfaceRAISE was formed as a consulting subsidiary to help other organizations climb the learning curve and progress through the phases of the transformational journey. This advocacy role helped to build the company's image and also led to additional learning through the process of teaching others.[9]

Interface's belief systems also evolved simultaneously, from initial scepticism to a fuller understanding that graduated to belief and strengthened into commitment before culminating in passionate advocacy. This psychological progression worked in tandem with strategic decisions (vision, roadmap, alignment, integration and influence). A deep shift in values and assumptions about 'how we do things here' moved Interface to a new view of purpose and performance, within the larger context of environmental and social responsibility.

As the organization reconstructed its collective identity, the activities associated with the new perspective slowly became embedded in its culture. This paradigm shift produced technological innovations and sustainable business practices. It also sharpened a sense of pride among the people.

The second innings of Interface, thus, began with the recognition of the opportunities as well as the challenges of greening. The organization finally made sense of Ray's vision of sustainability and embraced it wholeheartedly. The company's business model was reconfigured. The odyssey culminated into a collaborative endeavour towards the transmutation of the larger commercial ecosystem so as to facilitate wider adoption of sustainable business practices.

THE ENGAGEMENT DRIVERS

The five key ingredients that helped Interface to successfully unfold its deeply engaging initiative towards full sustainability were (a) pioneering spirit, (b) expansive vision, (c) constructive approach, (d) credible communication and (e) radical innovation.[6]

PIONEERING SPIRIT

In 1994, Interface was quick to recognize the rising level of eco-logical awareness among its customers as a paradigm shift. The company courageously stepped up to the challenges associated with being an early adopter. It engaged in bold experimentation and risk-taking towards the development of a new model of commerce and industry.

Making an early commitment to sustainability was crucial to Interface's success. Collecting the 'low-hanging' fruit helped to free up resources for investment into further exploration of sustainable processes and practices. The occasional failures too were embraced in a spirit of learning and development. The organization, thus, generated new internal capabilities as well as external opportunities, which eventually led to the development of competitive advantage.

EXPANSIVE VISION

Soon after Ray first brought his sustainability message to a group of Wall Street investors, an analyst called Interface to inform that one of its biggest investors was dumping the stock because Anderson clearly appeared to have gone 'round the bend'. Ray later explained that it was part of his job as CEO to be 'round the bend', so he could see what was coming up next.

Sustainability offered a remarkably different way for people to see the world. Stakeholders were proactively invited to imagine a future that was based on their positive core. This helped to inspire and align the people of Interface towards a shared vision that was never too distant, but always far enough to be challenging. Slowly but surely, people grasped the invitation for them to contribute towards something higher than mere profit maximization. This led to a progressive change in the mindset. People began to explore the existing as well as potential capabilities that could help actualize the vision.

Sustainability was also remarkably effective in engaging the caring and nurturing side of the people within Interface. Individuals brought more creativity and vitality to their mandates. They worked harder, because their emotional energy was channelized. The cultivation of participatory leadership also stimulated their contribution to the shared effort.

CONSTRUCTIVE APPROACH

In order to progress towards a zero environmental impact, Interface inquired whether customers really needed to buy petroleum in the shape of a carpet. The answer that emerged was in the negative. Though this could have been perceived as a barrier for a modern carpet-manufacturing company, Interface chose to shift perspective and view this as an opportunity.

The focus then shifted to the role that carpets played in lives of customers: (a) interior design, (b) comfort underfoot and (c) noise control. This resulted in the creation of new products and services (such as Intercell™) that were more about 'flooring', rather than 'carpets' per se.

CREDIBLE COMMUNICATION

Interface always remained keen to learn how people viewed its sustainability paradigm. It maintained several platforms to capture feedback, which was then distilled and incorporated into action plans. Positive feedback amplified the resolve of the associates to continue with their 'pilgrimage' up the slopes of Mount Sustainability.

The company remained committed to the maintenance of integrity and transparency in the communication of its progress towards sustainability. The organization undertook third-party verification and certification of its sustainability-related claims so as to maintain the integrity of its results. Transparent sharing of knowledge and insights was critical for Interface to progress towards its avowed aim of becoming restorative through the power of influence.

The sincere and deep alignment between the company's stated sustainability objectives and its actions on the ground helped Interface to gain credibility in the eyes of its stakeholders.

RADICAL INNOVATION

Interface is deeply rooted in the belief that it is possible to find a better way to operate in any and every situation. This probably arose out of Ray's training as an industrial engineer.

The organization demonstrated a phenomenal appetite for implementing radical, but practical, solutions to mundane as well unfamiliar problems. Humbly recognizing that not all smart people work in the same place, the company looked for guidance and inputs from outside.

Interface also invested in managerial capabilities that allowed it to conduct research, recognize opportunities and revolutionize the carpet industry. Its culture of discovery created the conditions for research and development in product ideas as well as manufacturing processes.

For instance, after a decade of experimentation, Interface was able to pioneer the ReEntry 2.0 programme in 2007—in partnership with Aquafil. This enabled the company to fully recycle any manufacturer's carpets. It was a major improvement over the original ReEntry programme introduced in 1996 that allowed for only partial recycling of the end-of-life carpets.

Subsequently, the same partnership also helped to turn discarded fishing nets into brand new carpet tiles. Such inventiveness necessitated long development cycles, substantial financial investments as well as risk-taking related to materials, business models and technologies.

Also, Mother Nature embodies millions of years of trial and error. Thus, research into how nature deals with challenges inspired creative solutions to design and many other kinds of problems. Contact with nature through sunlight, fresh air and living plants is also found to have a positive impact on human health. This conviction led to the development of many innovatively designed and patented products at Interface. The company reoriented its product designs to help create interior spaces that were restorative to the human spirit while being environmentally responsible too. It sought to create flooring that combined visual appeal and functional performance with biophilic design.

The finest ideas actually came from the employees of the company, in the course of their regular work. After attending the company's sustainability training programme, many people were keen to align with what they had just learned. Interface provided them with a safe milieu in which to experiment with their ideas. In turn, they emerged with creative and innovative solutions.

THE CHALLENGES FACED

Interface started in 1973 through the good offices of an entrepreneur with a fine idea as well as a keen desire to follow a path of his own. The organization charted out a unique path for itself and enthusiastically marched down the 'road less travelled'. The journey was deeply fulfilling for its people and brought out the very best from the company and all its associates.

Nevertheless, it was not always smooth sailing for Interface after it initiated the transition to sustainability. The process of developing and validating Interface's sustainability-centric business model was marked by steep learning curves as well as periodic setbacks.

The carpet industry faced recessionary conditions in 1998 (corporate preoccupation with the Y2K problem), 2001 (the dot-com bust) and 2008 (the subprime crisis). Interface was deeply affected too. Its revenues and profits swung along a sinusoidal trajectory. Survival itself would have been in peril, had it not been for the benefits that accrued from sustainability-led innovation.

An early 'failed' approach to recycling involved the dissolution of whole carpet tiles in a chemical solution, in order to reclaim materials. Another process involved specialized, energy-intensive facilities in two countries. Both were discontinued because they were unduly expensive, and were eventually found to increase the company's environmental footprint. However, Interface's recycled backing technology emerged only after the tough lessons of these failures.

Some product innovations took forever before they saw the light of the day. Interface made a multi-million dollar investment in a technology that attempted to recycle nylon 6.6 that did not fructify. The company's nylon supplier Aquafil took a full 13 years after the sustainability meeting at Hawaii before it emerged with 100 per cent recycled nylon carpet fibre.

Solenium, a lightweight and composite floor covering with zero nylon content, did not click either. While its environmental footprint was low, the product failed due to its poor durability.

The shift from carpet being purchased as a disposable product to being managed in a closed loop as a service was another big idea that proved to be well ahead of its time. The adverse tax laws around leasing carpet, combined with the challenge of changing how customers did business with Interface, forced the company to shelve its Evergreen Service Agreement.

Without an overwhelming belief in Ray's vision, the economic downturns that Interface had to weather might have led the company to abandon sustainability. However, the organization never even entertained such thoughts. It had progressed past scepticism and experimentation towards actively employing the learning and insights in the service of its own transformation.

AWARDS AND RECOGNITION

Apart from being invited to serve as the co-chair of the President Clinton's Council on sustainable development and receiving 12 doctorates from various universities, Ray Anderson received a host of other sustainability-related accolades throughout his lifetime.

In 1996, Mikhail Gorbachev presented Ray with the Inaugural Millennium Award from Global Green while Ernst & Young named him as the Entrepreneur of the Year. In 2001, he received the George and Cynthia Mitchell International Prize for sustainable development.[10]

In 2007, Ray Anderson received the International Quality of Life Award from Auburn University and was named as one of *Time*'s Heroes of the Environment. Numerous awards also came his way in the year 2010. These included Design for Humanity Award of The American Society of Interior Designers, Lifetime Achievement Award from GreenLaw, the inaugural Global Sustainability Prize from the University of Kentucky, and the Sustainability Award from the Women's Network for a Sustainable Future.

In 2006, GlobeScan listed Interface #1 in the world for corporate sustainability. In 2012, the company received the UK Queen's Award for Sustainable Development for the second time.

In August 2011, Ray Anderson died of cancer. Daniel T. Hendrix, who had been the company's CEO since 2001, was nominated to succeed him as the chairman of Interface Inc.

In March 2017, Jay D. Gould took over as the president and CEO at Interface Inc. Dan remains as the chairman of the board of directors of the company. Jay is wholeheartedly continuing Ray Anderson's sustainability legacy. This includes the striking of a fine balance between being purpose driven and performance oriented.

Interface's quest is to redefine commerce, and kick-start the next Industrial Revolution. However, its impressive cumulative accomplishments now appear to have reached a 'plateau'. Looking at how far the company needs to travel before it can meet the 2020 deadline for Mission Zero, many people have begun to lament that it will take a miracle to achieve it.

However, the story of Interface Inc. is unique not only for its overwhelming success but also because the assimilation of its radical vision was firmly rooted in a company with established operations. The company went through a transformational journey and emerged as a world leader with an established reputation and a list of breakthrough accomplishments.

Ray Anderson was knowledgeable enough to put the basic sustainability principles on the table, pragmatic enough to begin approaching them step-by-step whilst improving bottom-line results and was bold enough to tell the world.[6] His practicality was his most impressive aspect. Ray would always inquire into what was possible to be done in the situation, before proceeding to do it systematically.

In the church of capitalism, Ray Anderson managed to be a faithful parishioner as well as a heretic!

REFERENCES

1. Todd R. The sustainable industrialist: Ray Anderson of interface. *Inc.* Available at: www.inc.com/magazine/20061101/green50_industrialist.html (accessed: 10 October 2016).

2. Anderson R & White R. *Business Lessons from a Radical Industrialist.* New York: St. Martin's Press; 2013. p. XIV.

3. Anderson R. *Mid-course Correction.* White River Junction, VT: Chelsea Green; 1998.

4. Anderson R. A massive shift in thinking. *Interface.com.* Available at: www.interface.com/US/en-US/about/mission/Our-Mission (accessed: 12 October 2016).

5. Nattrass B & Altomare M. *The Natural Step for Business: Wealth, Ecology, and The Evolutionary Corporation.* 5th ed. Gabriola Island: New Society Publishers; 2006. p. 107.

6. Harel T, van Arkel G, Pluijm F & Aanraad B. Interface: The journey of a lifetime. *Naturalstep.ca.* Available at: www.naturalstep. ca/sites/default/files/case_study_interface.pdf (accessed: 12 October 2016).

7. Interface. The net-works program. *Interface.com.* Available at: www.interface.com/APAC/en-AU/about/mission/Net-Works-en_AU (accessed: 15 October 2016).

8. The Natural Step. Case Study: Interface. *The Natural Step.* Available at: https://thenaturalstep.org/project/interface/ (accessed: 12 October 2016).

9. Anderson R, Amodeo M & Hartfeld J. State of the World 2010: Transforming cultures from consumerism to sustainability. Worldwatch Institute. *Social and Environmental Accountability Journal.* 2011; 31(2): 96–102.

10. George Tech. Georgia Tech Celebrates 240th Commencement. *News.gatech.edu*. Available at: www.news.gatech.edu/2011/08/04/ georgia-tech-celebrates-240th-commencement (accessed: 22 August 2016).

VIDEO REFERENCE

Samatvam. (2016, October 30). *Interface Inc.: Reinventing a Successful Empire*. YouTube. Available at: https://youtu.be/9r61FWEAtG8 (accessed: 26 November 2018).

TRANSFORMATIONAL LEADERSHIP

11

It is said of a good leader that when the work is done and the aim is fulfilled, the people will say, 'We did this ourselves'.

—*Lao Tzu*

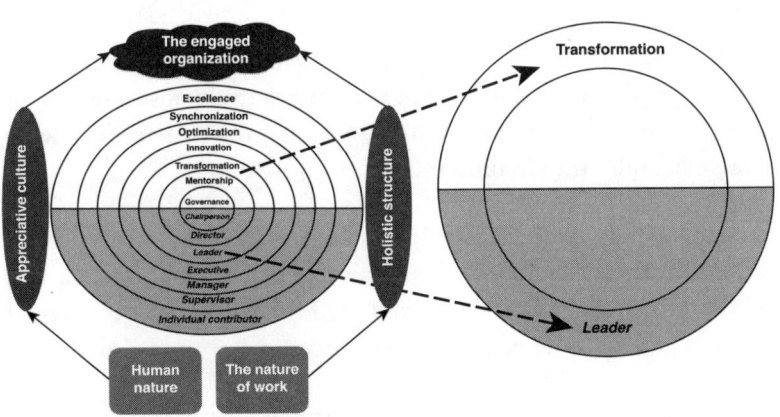

The Leadership Mandate of Transformation
Source: Samatvam Academy

Leadership has been the most discussed, but perhaps the least understood, phenomenon across human civilizations and cultures. In the twenty-first century it is considered to be more of a shared phenomenon. Leadership is now regarded as the collective capacity of a community of people to co-create and shape its own future.

The leaders of business organizations are individuals who exercise ownership as well as responsibility for the integrated functioning of a fully resourced enterprise. They occupy the fifth stratum in the organization's hierarchy of accountability.

Organizational leaders govern the value creation work of the operational and managerial facets of the institution. They connect the dots with respect to the subunits of the organization and make connections among diverse ideas, functions and people. Leaders adopt a long-term perspective.

Organizational leaders manage resource boundaries. They maintain a balancing act between present needs and future goals, between thinking broad and going deep and also between the exploration of new business opportunities and the capitalization of the existing ones.

Organizational leaders monitor the political, economic, technological and social trends on a continuous basis and assess their implications for the core business of the enterprise. When the objectives or the methods of the organization appear to be relatively unsustainable or unviable, they study the situation carefully in order to determine what is feasible under the circumstances.

The phenomenon of leadership is often juxtaposed with that of management. Leadership is about enlisting other people to join in a bold and forward-looking endeavour, while management is concerned with the judicious use of available resources in any given situation.

Managers plan, organize, direct and control in order to make the best out of the current circumstance, whereas leaders employ passion, inspiration and moral courage in order to transform the situation. Management is about working with the presently known and predictable, while leadership is concerned with working into a future that is unknown and unpredictable by its very nature.

The English word 'lead' is derived from the old English term lithan and the old French *leden* meaning 'to cause to go with oneself', and thus 'to guide or show the way'.[1] It connotes a sense of journey or movement from one place to another. Thus, leaders are individuals who proactively venture into new territory. They show the way forward for others in the face of risk, dynamism and uncertainty.

Leadership as the Navigation of Change

Contemporary society is characterized by ceaseless and disruptive change at a scale and pace that is unprecedented in human history. The turbulence on the outside, naturally, leads to turmoil within the human being. People, therefore, search for someone who can contain their anxiety and assuage their discomfort. Individuals who are able to carry out such containment are regarded as leaders.

Change is of three kinds: (a) developmental, (b) transitional and (c) transformational.[2] Developmental change is usually focused on improving skills or processes, while transitional change seeks to achieve the desired state that is different from the existing one.

On the other hand, transformational change alters the fundamental position and trajectory of the organization. It demands an extensive shift and revision of the basic assumptions held by the people.

Leaders recognize that living systems transform rapidly when they view change as the means to preserve themselves. So, they notice changes in the environment and activate the operational systems and cultural processes of the organization to innovate and adapt accordingly.

The ability to navigate a human system through profound change and renewal is thus the *sine qua non* of leadership.

Transformational Leadership

Transformational leadership is the ability to collectively formulate and realize a vision in practice.

The process commences with the identification of the core strengths and values of the organization. The institutional mission and vision are developed through a co-creative approach. A roadmap is charted out to help the organization progress towards the envisaged future. Inspiration and empowerment are the key features of the exercise of transformational leadership.

A transformational effort often begins with some rapid, short-term streamlining initiatives. These are intended to close the performance gaps and also to establish credibility towards enabling change and growth.

In the medium term, the transformational endeavour yields a fundamentally different competitive position for the organization. The operating and business models of the enterprise are examined and appropriately revised.

Over the long run, transformation requires the building of a high-performance culture. This mandates a comprehensive review of the organizational vision, mission, values, design and strategy.

Transformational leaders raise the consciousness of their colleagues by appealing to higher ideals and values.[3] They stir the people into transcending narrow self-interest for the sake of the larger good and motivate them to do more than expected.[4] Authentic relationships built upon this foundation help to develop a mutuality of trust and confidence. Deep, qualitative change is the result.

Transformational change comes about through a spiral of three processes that are performed concurrently. These stages are as follows:

1. **Appreciation:** An inspired search for the core 'heritage' in the form of the core strengths and values

2. **Visualization:** Arriving at a shared understanding of what people want to collectively be (mission) and become (vision) such that the enterprise may sustain into eternity

3. **Actualization:** Working in a spirit of service towards the realization of the organizational vision

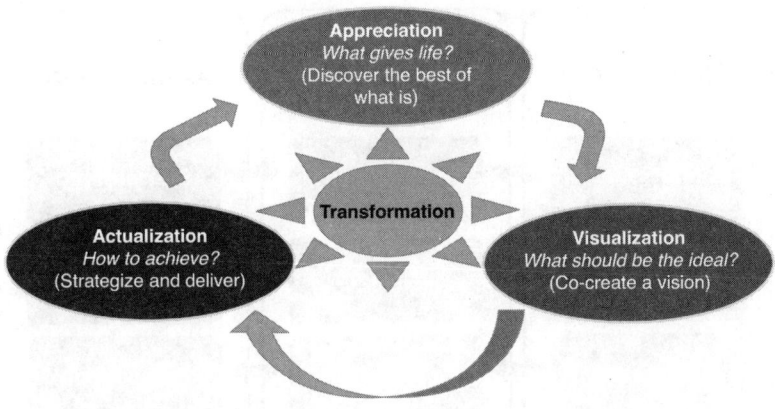

The Technology of Transformational Leadership

Source: Samatvam Academy

The Transformational Leadership Framework

The transformational leadership process moves across the stages of appreciation, visualization and actualization. The operational mechanisms that underlie these three phases are as follows:

On the existential plane, the recognition of *connectedness* (a sense of belonging to something larger than oneself) facilitates the *sustainability* (the capacity to exist for an indefinite period of time) of the enterprise because the interests of all the stakeholders of the organization are taken into account. This facilitates the adoption of *stewardship* (holding accountability for collective outcomes by empowering people) as the governing principle of the organization.

At the cultural level, the articulation of the organizational *heritage* (identifying the best attributes from the institution's past) allows for the revitalization of the *mission* (the basic function or purpose of the organization in society). A sound *strategy* (a plan of action designed to strengthen the enterprise performance) supports the fulfilment of the shared sense of purpose.

On the experiential level, the process comprises *inspiration* (brilliant and creative ideas that lead to mental stimulation) that facilitates the

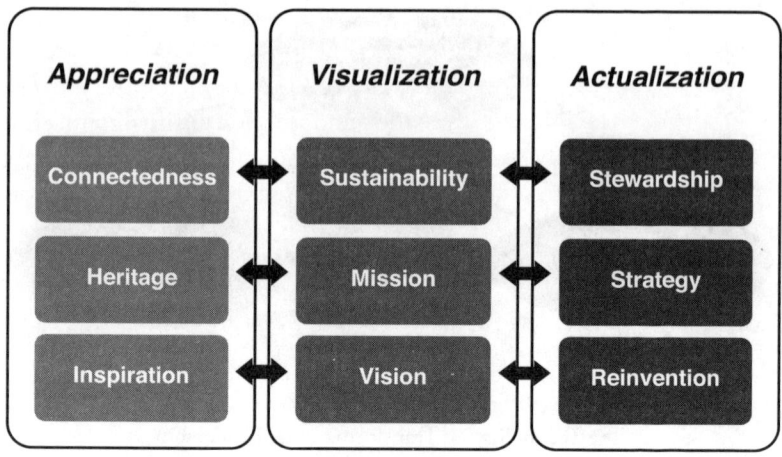

The Transformation Leadership Framework
Source: Samatvam Academy

development of a bold *vision* (a preferred future for the organization). In order to actualize such a vision in a dynamic and complex environment, the organization undergoes reinvention (dramatic changes in the business and cultural pillars).

The starting point of any transformational endeavour is a deeply felt sense of connectedness with various life forms and expressions. Unless the leader exudes an expansive and shared identity that includes all those beings around him/her, the attempt to transform shall be a non-starter.

The crux of the transformational exercise lies in the ability to articulate an exciting or elevating sense of mission or shared purpose that makes collective existence meaningful for the people. Engagement is, thus, generated and people work with their heart and soul towards a new destination.

A successful transformational initiative results into a reinvention of the collective organizational identity as well as its myriad expressions such as the structure, the culture and the business models.

The Appreciation Phase

Appreciation has been defined as the act of recognizing the intrinsic value or worth in a person or situation and feeling a positive connection to it. Accordingly, the task in the appreciation phase is to identify the best of 'what is' by focusing on the best moments or high points from the organization's past.

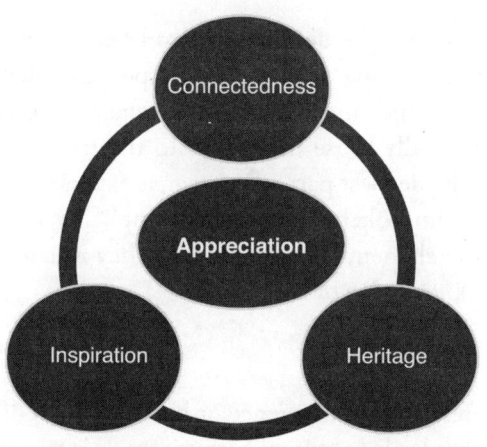

The Appreciation Phase
Source: Samatvam Academy

Connectedness

Connectedness is the sense of being a part of something larger than oneself. It represents a feeling of belonging. Connectedness also refers to the force that urges people to ally, to affiliate, to enter into mutual relationships and grow through cooperative behaviour.[5] It expands a person's sense of self to include all of mankind and beyond.

Connectedness takes away the sense of defensiveness that is inevitable when one feels in opposition to the rest of the universe. The person thus begins to feel secure, and develops a sense of positivity.

Heritage

Heritage represents anything that has been transmitted from the past or handed down by tradition. In the institutional context, heritage refers to those commonly shared and treasured assumptions, values, perspectives, norms, beliefs and core competencies that have served the organization well in the past. These constitute the essence of the unique social and psychological environment of the institution.

Cultural heritage may be detected at two levels: (a) espoused values and (b) basic underlying assumptions. Espoused values express the basic assumptions and core beliefs that are shared in common among the people, especially those that relate to the trustworthiness of an organization. The deepest part of heritage is expressed as a set of tacit assumptions or unspoken rules that are implicitly honoured by the members. These elements remain unseen. They usually exist without the conscious knowledge of the people.

Inspiration

Inspiration refers to the emergence or bursting forth of a brilliant or creative idea that leads to mental enthusiasm. It is triggered by means of a compelling internal illumination that is directed towards the realization of an idea. The inspired individual is moved by the truth, ingenuity or beauty of the trigger object and is moved to transmit, emulate or actualize those qualities.[6]

Inspiration is a motivational state that provides the power, courage, strength and resilience to overcome the obstacles that are encountered when a vision begins to be realized. It is possible to derive inspiration from one's managers, leaders, mentors, role models, heroes as well as gurus.

The Visualization Phase

Visualization refers to the employment of human imagination in order to envisage specific events and outcomes or form a mental picture of something that is as yet abstract. It is akin to preparing a map or design of the house that a person can subsequently set out to build.

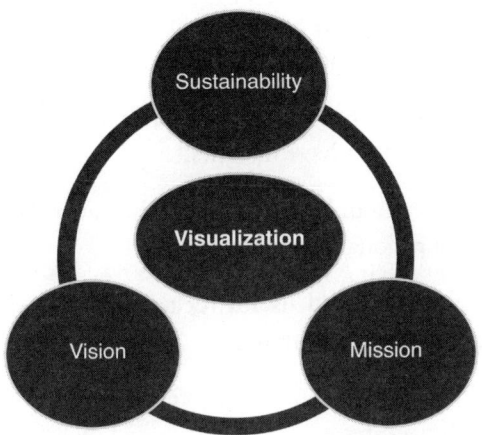

The Visualization Phase
Source: Samatvam Academy

Visualization involves challenging the status quo by envisioning a preferred future. It is an invitation for the stakeholders to go beyond what they previously thought as possible. There are three tasks during the visualization stage of the transformational journey.

Sustainability

Sustainability represents the ability to continue a defined behaviour indefinitely. It refers to a form of existence, wherein the needs of the present stakeholders are adequately met without compromising the ability of the future stakeholders to meet their own needs.[7]

Operating in an environmentally, socially and economically sustainable manner is one of the most urgent challenges facing organizations today.[8] Sustainability is an effort to improve the quality of life while living within the carrying capacity of the supporting ecosystems. Declining ecological resources, the move towards radical transparency and increasing customer expectations make a compelling case for sustainability.

The following propositions can help to guide the integration and embedding of the attribute of sustainability into business strategy[9]:

1. Quick and small wins are useful in helping generate a culture that fosters sustainability.

2. Bottom-up and top-down initiatives are both important; frontline employees have insights.

3. Sustainability should be built into the business model, while aligning the rationale to the goal.

4. Accurate, relevant and useful measurement is vital in implementing sustainability strategy.

5. Stakeholder engagement is the key to the development of a sustainability strategy.

Mission

Every institution exists in order to make a positive difference in the lives of individuals and in society at large. This represents the organization's basic purpose and its very reason for being.

The term 'mission' refers to an important goal or purpose that is accompanied by a strong conviction. This articulation often revolves around the need for economic survival and growth. It involves the maintenance of good relationships with all the major stakeholders such as investors, employees, customers, suppliers, the community and the government.

A statement of mission is intensely distinctive. It embodies the deep conviction of its creators. The mission statement conveys why the institution aspires to do what it does. The true test of a statement of mission is the actual performance that it manages to ignite and inspire.

Vision

Vision is the ability to think about the future with imagination and wisdom. It is an ideal that reveals the higher-order value preferences of the people and represents their ultimate economic, technological, political, social and aesthetic priorities.

A vision represents a unique picture of the future. It refers to the process of outlining inspiring possibilities. The vision describes the image of an ideal future state. It provides direction to human energy and results in the creation of a new internal reality.

An effective, meaningful and compelling vision is marked by the following characteristics:

1. **Future focused:** The vision paints a clear picture of the entity's desired future.

2. **Directional:** The vision clarifies the entity's focus, direction and constraints.

3. **Clear:** A clearly articulated vision provides guidance for decision-making and action.

4. **Relevant:** A credible vision is congruent with the current context of the entity.

5. **Purpose-driven:** The vision allows the people to feel a part of something bigger than themselves.

6. **Values-based:** The vision connects the people to the entity's core values, ideals and beliefs.

7. **Unifying:** The vision is an invitation to a greatness that unites people in a pursuit of high standards.

8. **Unique:** The vision reflects uniqueness as to why the entity matters and what makes it stand out.

9. **Vivid:** The vision provides an eloquent mental image that is easy to picture in the mind's eye.

10. **Inspiring:** The vision appeals to the heart as well as the mind and engages the people emotionally.

The Actualization Phase

Actualization refers to the act of realizing an articulated vision in actual practice. It involves the creation of ways and means to deliver upon an image of the future. The core values and assumptions are defined. Strategic choices are made. Finally, a carefully constructed plan of action is implemented.

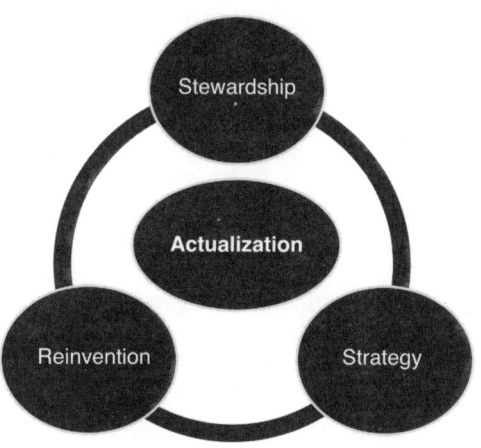

The Actualization Phase
Source: Samatvam Academy

Stewardship

Stewardship is the acceptance or assignment of responsibility to shepherd and safeguard the valuables of others. It is the willingness to operate in a spirit of service towards the stakeholders. In the practice of stewardship, self-interest is replaced with trusteeship as the basis for using social power.

A living principle that is relevant to stewardship is expressed by the Sanskrit phrase *Vasudhaiva Kutumbakam*. This translates, 'The whole planet is part of the one and the same unitary family'. It is a social philosophy that emanates from the spiritual understanding that all of humanity is made up of one and the same life energy. In the process of serving others, people thus indirectly secure their own welfare.

Strategy

Strategy refers to a high-level plan to achieve one or more goals under conditions of uncertainty. It represents the broad formula of how a business is going to compete, what its goals should be, and what policies will be needed to carry out those goals.[10] This includes identifying the combination of the ends (goals) for which the firm is striving and the means (policies and practices) by which it seeks to get there.

A strategy is a function of the ability to foresee the future consequences of present initiatives.[11] It involves the setting of goals, determining the actions required to achieve these objectives and the mobilization of resources to execute the identified actions.

The essential requirements for strategy development include the following: (a) extensive knowledge about the environment, market and competitors; (b) the ability to examine this information in a systemic and dynamic context and (c) the use of logic and imagination in choosing between specific alternatives.[12]

Reinvention

Reinvention refers to the process of revival in a different form, remaking completely, or inventing something anew. The essential core of the organization is elevated and carried forward. Everything else is let go of. Reinvention is marked by a shift in the dominant organizational paradigm. It leads to an experience of reawakening.

In the globalized economy, the life expectancy of organizations has been dramatically shortened. Organizations periodically remake and revise their own sense of who they are, what they do and how their offerings are useful for the world. This involves making significant changes in perspectives, assumptions, strategies and habit patterns.

Reinvention is a cross-functional competence that works across the short, medium as well as long term.

Transformational leadership is the adventure of a lifetime. It demands blood, sweat and tears, along with audacity, courage and tenacity.

But the results are worth it, as every newly minted mother who has delivered a baby after months of toil and exertion would readily testify.

The celebrated corporation ITC Limited stood at a precarious juncture in 1996. Its core business of cigarettes was being regarded as a 'sin' product. Takeover battles, ego clashes, accusations of ethical impropriety and charges of tax evasion were swirling around.

The manner in which the company's talented Chairman Y. C. Deveshwar led the institution out of strife and decadence and transformed it into an exemplary organization, is the stuff of which legends are made. This journey of visionary leadership is the subject of the next case study.

References

1. Low KCP & Teo TC. Tsunami leaders and their style(s) and ways. *International Journal of Business and Social Science.* 2015; 6(9): 31–46.

2. Kumar JP, Abirami A & Gowri Priya D. Essentiality and the role of transformational leadership among entrepreneurs. *Intercontinental Journal of Human Resource Research Review.* 2013; 1(10): 26–37.

3. Ackerman L. Development, transition and transformation: The question of change in organizations. In: Van Eynde D, Hoy J & Van Eynde D. (Eds.) *Organization Development Classics.* 1st ed. San Francisco, CA: Jossey-Bass; 1997.

4. Burns JM. *Leadership.* New York, NY: Harper & Row; 1978.

5. Bass B. *Leadership and Performance Beyond Expectations.* New York, NY: Free Press; 1985.

6. Hallowell EM. Connectedness. In: Hallowell EM & Michael Thomspon G. (Eds.) *Finding the Heart of the Child: Essays on Children, Families, and Schools.* Braintree, MA: Association of Independent Schools in New England; 2003.

ENGAGE!

7. Thrash T & Elliot A. Inspiration as a psychological construct. *Journal of Personality and Social Psychology*. 2003; 84(4): 871–889.

8. Munro D & Holdgate M. *Caring for the Earth*. Gland: The World Conservation Union (IUCN); 1991.

9. Hopwood A, Unerman J & Fries J. *Accounting for Sustainability*. London: Earthscan; 2010.

10. Porter M. *Competitive Strategy*. New York: Free Press; 1980.

11. Henderson B. The concept of strategy. 1981. *BCG.com*. Available at: www.bcg.com/publications/1981/concept-of-strategy.aspx (accessed: 22 August 2016).

12. Gluck F, Kaufman S & Walleck A. Strategic management for competitive advantage. *Harvard Business Review*. Available at: https://hbr.org/1980/07/strategic-management-for-competitive-advantage (accessed: 22 August 2016).

TRANSFORMATIONAL LEADERSHIP

ITC LIMITED

Sometimes, not taking a risk is the biggest risk.

—*Padma Bhushan Yogesh C. Deveshwar*

BACKGROUND

ITC Limited is a diversified Indian conglomerate that is headquartered in Kolkata, West Bengal. It has a meaningful presence in all the three sectors of the Indian economy—agriculture, services and manufacturing. With significant interests in tobacco, fast-moving consumer goods (FMCG), hotels, paperboards and packaging, agribusiness and information technology sectors, the company employs over 31,000 people across the country.[1]

During FY 2018, ITC clocked annual revenues of ₹70,852 crore and enjoyed a market capitalization of nearly ₹340,000 crore.

ITC is rooted in the philosophy of congruence between business and social purpose. At the turn of the millennium, the company redefined its corporate vision to put sustainability and inclusive growth at the top of its agenda. Supported by the bedrock of consistent financial performance, ITC crafted innovative business models that generated sustainable livelihood opportunities and simultaneously helped to renew ecological resources.

To foster sustainable and inclusive growth, ITC spearheaded an integrated rural development programme with four distinct objectives:

(a) the dissemination of information and knowledge, (b) creating access to quality inputs and markets, (c) generating supplementary incomes and (d) augmentation of natural resources. The initiative progressively led to a comprehensive development of the rural ecosystem. It empowered the farmers and raised rural incomes.

To address the challenges of environmental degradation, ITC constantly strives to minimize its environmental impact. It is the only company in the world to be carbon positive, water positive and solid waste recycling positive—all at the same time. Nearly half of the energy consumed across the corporation is derived from renewable sources.[2]

THE GENESIS OF THE INSTITUTION

ITC Limited's parent organization British American Tobacco Company (BAT) owes its origins to Mr James Buchanan 'Buck' Duke, who was in charge of a granulated tobacco factory in the United States in 1881. Buck Duke invested early into cigarette machinery. His company captured 38 per cent share of the US cigarette market by 1889. He then facilitated the amalgamation of four other companies with his own to form the American Tobacco Company (ATC).

Soon thereafter, ATC acquired a foothold in the British market. To counter the impending threat of competition, W. D. and H. O. Wills gathered all the major tobacco businesses in Britain to form the Imperial Tobacco Company (of Great Britain and Ireland).

This consolidation led to intense competition and internecine price wars in both the US and the UK markets. Dwindling profits finally brought the two companies to the negotiation table.

In September 1902, the two giants eventually consented to pull out from each other's home markets. They also jointly established BAT in an effort to establish their presence in territories outside of the US and the UK.

At that time, these two partners in BAT held separate interests with respect to the manufacturing and selling of cigarettes in India. ATC had invested into a cigarette manufacturing facility at Munger in 1907 through Peninsular Tobacco, while Imperial Tobacco Company was selling branded cigarettes in India through Dominion Tobacco and other companies.

The presence of BAT in India was formally established in 1906, when two of its employees (Jellicoe and Page) landed in the country in search of an agent to distribute their Wills and Scissors brand of cigarettes. The duo began to educate people on the 'pleasures' of smoking cigarettes. They advertised their products through roving musical trucks.

Sales soared very soon and an extensive distribution network came into being.

The Imperial Tobacco Company of India came into being in August 1910 when BAT decided to set up a full-fledged sales operation in the country. To cope with the growing demand, BAT set up another cigarette manufacturing unit in Bangalore in 1912.[7]

In July 1912, BAT also established the Indian Leaf Tobacco Company to focus upon the local sourcing and processing of tobacco. To meet with the packaging and printing requirements of the cigarette business, BAT set up a packaging and printing facility in 1925. In 1939, ITC invested in duplex board. The company entered the paper business in 1944.

THE A. N. HAKSAR ERA (1969–1983)

Born in Gwalior in 1925, Ajit Narain Haksar joined the Imperial Tobacco Company of India in 1948 as a management 'pupil'. Armed with an MBA from the Harvard Business School and a faith in market research, he institutionalized the marketing function at the company. Haksar was appointed as ITC's marketing director in 1966 and deputy chairman in 1968, before being appointed chairman in 1969.

Prior to accepting the responsibility as the company's chairperson, he is reputed to have asked the following three questions to the BAT senior management[4, pp. 198, 199]:

1. Which comes first—your company or your country?

2. Who runs the company—BAT or the chairman and the board of directors in India?

3. Will ITC be required to do what BAT wants or what its chairman and the board of directors in India consider to be more appropriate investments with relevance to India?

Upon receiving suitable answers that helped to clear his conscience, he consented to become the first 'Indian' to be placed at the helm of that flabby, foreign-owned organization with a colonial mindset. To his credit, Haksar led ITC's metamorphosis into an aggressive, outward-looking corporation that was quick to spot and capitalize upon the emerging opportunities.

In the early 1970s, a strong nationalist undercurrent swept India. It resulted in much turbulence in the economic, political and regulatory environment of the country. ITC's competitors sought to position the company as a 'foreign' enterprise that endangered indigenous firms.

The company responded by changing its name to I. T. C. Ltd in 1974. It also drew up plans to enter the core industry sectors where the Government found it otherwise difficult to attract investment.

After careful deliberation, ITC decided to diversify into hotels, paperboards and marine foods. While paperboards had linkages to the cigarette business, hotels and marine foods were potential foreign exchange earners. Being employment-intensive, the hotel business served the larger social needs of the country. It also utilized the company's marketing expertise and consumer service skills in an industry where the competition was nearly absent.

However, the parent company held strong reservations about ITC's ability to manage its diversification forays. For instance, when A. N. Haksar and his deputy Ramesh Sarin presented the plans for a paper mill to BAT, they were dissuaded from the endeavour. Nevertheless, ITC persisted in its endeavour.

In July 1979, Sarin wrote the following lines to BAT in London[4, p. 356]:

'This letter is written on the first sheet of paper produced at Bhadrachalam Paperboards Limited (BPL). It is not indicative of quality, but it does signify human endeavor and enterprise. The project has been completed before time and within the agreed budgeted cost.'

The diversification of ITC's businesses was largely successful, except for marine foods.[4, p. 433] The company managed to hold on to its leadership in tobacco while its hotels division quickly outstripped much older rival chains. The move into paperboard broke new ground in an area where no one had cared to invest for a decade. All this was accomplished with frugal resources during the 'license-permit raj' era, with the purchasing power of consumers being limited.

Haksar also sowed the seeds of ITC's transformation into a vibrant company that not only enhanced shareholder value, but also contributed to the Indian nation. Combining corporate objectives with social responsibility, ITC moved into carpet exports. The company gave training to the weaver artisans in Shahjahanpur, improved the quality of the product, provided the weavers with wool and sold the carpets abroad. The monthly income of the weavers rose tenfold to ₹2,000.

Haksar built a deep and robust professional leadership team at ITC through significant investment into human capital. Training, coaching, mentoring and the development of long-term relationships became a part of the DNA at ITC. High-potential managers were fast tracked. They were groomed for leadership roles by means of rotation across businesses and functions.

Haksar combined professional excellence with outstanding entrepreneurial qualities. His leadership philosophy was anchored in the following beliefs:

1. Putting the interest of the nation ahead of the business pays in the long run

2. Putting the interests of the people ahead of your own interests helps to build institutions

3. The building of sustainable businesses and happy teams helps to build careers

Meanwhile, the Foreign Exchange Regulation Act had been enacted in 1973. It restricted foreign equity ownership in any company to 40 per cent. BAT was, thus, forced to dilute its stake in ITC.

THE J. N. SAPRU ERA (1983–1991)

After 14 years at the helm, A. N. Haksar passed on the leadership baton in January 1983 to his brother-in-law Jagdish Narain Sapru. ITC's diversification agenda progressed under Sapru's watch, even though the company ceded some market share in its flagship cigarette business to nimble competitors.

ITC Classic Finance was set up in 1986 as a non-banking finance company. An agribusiness division was set up at Hyderabad in 1988 with the mandate to produce hybrid seeds, market edible oil and export agricultural products. In 1989, ITC acquired a 51 per cent stake in Tribeni Tissues Limited. The company also opened Bukhara restaurants in the United States.

In February 1987, the Union Government replaced the ad valorem excise duty structure with a new framework whereby excise was levied as a function of the cigarette length. With its strong portfolio of high-priced brands, ITC benefited the most from this change.

However, in a deeply embarrassing development, the Anti-Evasion Directorate of Central Excise Department issued a show cause notice to the company in March 1987. It charged ITC with tax evasion to the tune of ₹803 crore during a four-year period commencing March 1983, shortly after Sapru had assumed charge as the chairman.

It was alleged that ITC's cigarettes were being sold in the market at a price higher than the printed maximum retail price. The company contested the claim. A long-drawn legal battle ensued. ITC's professional and image reputation was significantly tarnished due to these charges.

The relations between ITC and its parent company BAT remained cordial during Sapru's tenure.

THE K. L. CHUGH ERA (1991–1995)

Krishan Lal Chugh joined ITC as an engineer at its Munger factory in 1971, after a ten-year stint at the Heavy Engineering Corporation, Ranchi. He made rapid progress up the corporate ladder. Under his stewardship, ITC's Bhadrachalam project was commissioned within budget and ahead of time.

On the strength of an impressive track record, Chugh became ITC's vice chairman in 1989 and was elevated as its chairman in

November 1991. Under his leadership, ITC repositioned all of its major cigarette brands and identified financial services and global trading as its new engines of growth. ITC partnered with Peregrine Investment Holdings and also tied up with BAT's subsidiary Eagle Star Insurance.

In international trade, Chugh's aspiration was for ITC to emerge as a leading trading house along the lines of a Japanese *sogo shosha* (general trading company). He, thus, carved out the export business into ITC Global, a fully owned subsidiary company that was based out of Singapore.

In 1993, the British Prime Minister John Major visited India as the chief guest at the Republic Day parade. The BAT officials in his entourage broached the proposal of increasing the parent company's stake in ITC from 31.5 per cent to 51 per cent.

At that time they are reported to have received positive signals from the Indian Government as well as ITC itself. However, when the BAT managing director visited India in March 1994 to progress the matter, neither of the parties supported this move. This soured the relations between BAT and K. L. Chugh.

In November 1994, Chugh unveiled ITC's plans to diversify into core sectors such as power. This did not fit into BAT's global portfolio. It was, thus, vehemently opposed by the parent company. A stormy extraordinary general meeting (EGM) that was held in March 1995 to seek the permission of the shareholders for further business diversification ended up in chaos.

On the eve of the EGM, BAT had issued a press statement that alleged 'culpable financial irregularities' by the top management of ITC. It specifically called for the chairman's resignation. In turn, Chugh accused BAT of wanting to strip ITC of its assets—in order to further its own business interests.

In his own defence, Chugh cited the impressive performance of ITC under his stewardship. Indeed, the company's revenues had doubled and its profits nearly quadrupled during the four years that Chugh was at its helm.

The political parties in India swerved to support K. L. Chugh against what was perceived as a hostile takeover attempt. What started as a battle between an MNC parent and its subsidiary eventually became a war between an individual person (Chugh) and a faceless corporation.

The company's auditors were tasked with investigating the financial irregularities alleged by BAT. Their report was a damning indictment of the way that ITC Global was managed. It held the chairman and top management of ITC Limited responsible for the wrongdoings.

These financial irregularities were confirmed by an audit committee of the Board, which later concluded that ITC's involvement in certain questionable deals had led to a drop in profits of ₹261 crore for 1995–1996. However, Chugh was personally cleared of all charges.[3]

In a surprising anti-climax in September 1995, K. L. Chugh announced his decision to step down in the 'best interests' of the company's growth. He also took responsibility for the losses suffered by ITC Global. Soon the Enforcement Directorate served a notice on ITC for alleged foreign exchange violations in its export deals.

In December 1995, after much jockeying between BAT and Indian Financial Institutions that were the two major shareholders of the company, Yogesh Deveshwar was named as the next executive chairman of ITC. An eminently forgettable chapter in the company's history, thus, came to a close. At the same time, a truly memorable one was about to begin.

THE Y. C. DEVESHWAR ERA (1996–2017)

Yogesh Chander Deveshwar was born in February 1947 at Lahore. He joined ITC as a 'management pupil' in 1968, after graduating as a mechanical engineer from the Indian Institute of Technology, Delhi. In an early career break, he was invited to serve at the ITC corporate headquarters in Kolkata in 1972 as a 'management by objectives' advisor.

In 1974, Deveshwar was appointed as the factory manager of ITC's packaging and printing facility at Chennai. He was promoted as the general manager of this division in 1978. At merely 37 years of age, Deveshwar was appointed to the Board of ITC in 1984 as the director-in-charge of the hotels division.

In 1991, Deveshwar moved on lien from ITC to serve the Government of India as the chairman and managing director of the national carrier Air India for a period of three years.

Upon returning to ITC in 1994 as vice chairman, Y. C. Deveshwar's mettle was tested in many ways. For instance, Godfrey Philips launched the Four Square Special, a brand of filter cigarettes that was making deep inroads into Gold Flake's territory. In order to stop the intruder, a feasible option was for ITC to introduce a similar variant of Gold Flake. However, this ran the risk of downgrading its precious Gold Flake franchise.

Nevertheless, against the advice of his entire divisional team, Deveshwar proceeded with the launch of Gold Flake Filter. Simultaneously, Gold Flake Kings was promoted to circumvent the possibility of brand dilution. The strategy worked splendidly and Gold Flake's volumes grew manifold over time.

Deveshwar became the ITC chairman on the New Year's Day in 1996 at a very precarious juncture. A public battle for the control of the company had ensued, amidst a huge smear campaign that battered ITC's reputation. Its weak diversification performance over a period of two decades was facing severe criticism too. The company was also being probed by the government for large-scale evasion of excise duty and for the violation of foreign exchange regulations too.

Deveshwar, thus, inherited a fractured organization that was characterized by very low morale.

In an unprecedented move in October 1996, the Enforcement Directorate arrested former ITC chairmen J. N. Sapru and K. L. Chugh as well as 12 other top ITC executives. They were charged with under-invoicing ITC's export deals so as to illegally retain foreign exchange abroad.[5] This appeared to be a sinister attempt by the parent company BAT to discredit the local ITC management team in order to take control of the company through the back door.

Deveshwar fought back valiantly. He appealed to the people as well as the authorities not to act on the basis of mere allegations and press campaigns. Deveshwar made a public offer granting authorization for any 'anybody to look at any bank account in the world'. People appreciated his sincerity. They began to see the truth and swerved to support ITC and its leadership team. Y. C. Deveshwar, thus, managed to prevent BAT from taking control of ITC.

Deveshwar also ensured that BAT officials did not interfere in its operational management. On the portfolio side, he guided ITC's exit from businesses that were not adding significant value. ITC Classic had reported huge operational losses that almost wiped out its net worth. This business was sold to ICICI. The company's stakes in ITC Agro-Tech and ITC Zeneca were sold to ConAgra. ITC Global, the company's trading arm, too faced liquidation.

On the other hand, significant investments were made in the company's core businesses of cigarettes, hotels and paperboard.

ITC's brand portfolio of cigarettes was rationalized to help the company emerge as a much stronger market leader. The company's cigarette manufacturing facilities were also significantly upgraded.

The footprint of the hotel division was revitalized through a rebranding exercise. New hotel properties were developed and the existing ones were enhanced.

In the paperboards business, a state-of-the-art 100,000 TPA elemental chlorine-free fibre line was set up. The paper and hotel divisions were also folded back into ITC's integrated structure.

In the millennium year, ITC ventured into information technology as well as apparel retailing. In 2002, the company entered the packaged foods market.

However, ITC's most significant innovation was to establish the e-Choupal mechanism for the direct sourcing of agricultural commodities from the farmers. This Internet-based intervention selectively disintermediated the middlemen, who otherwise maintained a tight hold upon the agricultural value chain in rural India. e-Choupal generated immense social capital for the company.[6]

Deveshwar, thus, did a commendable job of bringing the organization back on the rails. Over his tenure, ITC significantly widened its engagement with the community through social and farm forestry, watershed development, women empowerment, livestock development and primary education in rural areas.

The company also made significant and sustained progress with its ecology-oriented initiatives. It turned 'water positive' in 2002, 'carbon positive' in 2006 and 'solid waste recycling positive' in 2007.

Coupled with the company's continued superior business performance by way of a CAGR of 23 per cent in shareholder returns, these social and environmental achievements resulted in ITC becoming a global exemplar of triple bottom line performance.

THE STRATEGIC DRIVERS OF TRANSFORMATION

Deveshwar began the process of reinvention at ITC by working assiduously to put strong internal systems and processes in place. This was intended to put the ethical controversies of the past to rest and also preclude the development of new distractions.

An inspiring vision was developed. It forged unity amidst diversity—between the agenda of individual businesses and the broader corporate identity; between the present imperatives and those of the future; between shareholder needs and those of society. ITC's business portfolio was also restructured.

A multifarious strategy was crafted to support the transformation. It rested upon the following five key elements:

1. Diversification

2. Harnessing of internal strengths

3. Service of the national interest

4. Triple bottom line performance

5. Robust corporate governance

DIVERSIFICATION

Cigarettes were a lifestyle product in the twentieth century, but became a 'sin' product in the new millennium. The business also came under pressure from increased taxes and stronger regulation.

Deveshwar was convinced that judicious but full-throated diversification was the best way forward. The legendary distribution expertise of the company, its considerable brand management skills as well as significant cash reserves, set the stage for the development of a significant FMCG footprint.

ITC set about creating world-class consumer brands that could create and retain greater value for the Indian economy. It entered several categories of consumer goods—branded packaged foods, personal care, branded apparel and lifestyle retailing, education and stationery products, safety matches and incense sticks. Its diversification foray was characterized by a long-term focus.[7]

Thanks to the diversification exercise, ITC's non-cigarette businesses yielded around half of its revenues by 2017 even though they still yielded less than 20 per cent of the profits. Diversification also helped the company to retain talent. Its professional managers were provided with the opportunity to be entrepreneurs within the ITC umbrella. They were encouraged to create new businesses from scratch.

HARNESSING OF INTERNAL STRENGTHS

An important element of ITC's growth strategy was the creative blending of its proven core competencies such as brand building, distribution, supply chain management and customer service in order to create new engines of growth. This synergy of institutional strengths provided a tremendous competitive advantage to the company.

The packaged foods business drew upon the unique sourcing capability of the e-Choupal, the culinary expertise of a galaxy of chefs from the hotel business and the innovation capacity resident in the ITC R&D Centre. ITC's traditional marketing prowess encompassing deep consumer insight, branding skills, packaging excellence and an extensive trade marketing and distribution capacity came in handy too.

Similarly, ITC's strong presence in agricultural commodities, packaged foods and personal care products was leveraged by the company's life sciences centre to deliver products of the future aimed at nutrition, health and well-being.[8]

Further, ITC's remarkably successful *Aashirvaad* brand customized *atta* for every region of India. This became possible because the company was able to procure 18 grades of identity-preserved wheat at the farm gate through e-Choupal. These were then blended in order to meet regional preferences. Customized blending was a strength that was honed by the practice of tobacco blending over decades.

THE SERVICE OF NATIONAL INTEREST

Deveshwar held a conviction that there was no inherent contradiction between improving the competitive context and making a sincere commitment towards the society and the nation. In order to make an enduring contribution to the Indian society, he resolved to build ITC into an exemplary, value-driven enterprise that would adopt the credo of putting the country first.

Sustainability was embedded into the company's core. Innovative strategies were designed to create sustainable value chains linked to its businesses. ITC's early diversification into the hotels and paperboards businesses was also guided by national interest. The potential to generate significant foreign exchange earnings and create large-scale employment in the tourism sector were the triggers for the hotels foray.

Similarly, the opportunity to contribute to the economic development of a backward region like Bhadrachalam facilitated ITC's entry into paperboards. The e-Choupal was also born from the vision of creating greater competitiveness for Indian agriculture.

Equally, these diversifications were backed by sound strategic rationale. Paperboards was a vertical backward integration for its printing and packaging business, which had already developed a sophisticated technology and skills platform by then.

Likewise, the hotel business was premised upon leveraging ITC's deep consumer insights and marketing acumen. And the celebrated e-Choupal network helped to source farm produce worth over ₹400 crore a year for the foods business. It also became a distribution engine for ITC's consumer products.

e-Choupal

A stellar example of ITC's promotion of India's national interest was the e-Choupal initiative. This was a unique click and mortar capability that served to make the country's agricultural value chain more competitive. The intent was to create an agricultural 'market of markets' across India that would provide farmers with critical information on farm productivity, prices and markets. Their earnings could be increased through better price discovery, improved quality and cost savings. These e-hubs also provided services such as micro-credit, insurance, health and education to the farming community.

e-Choupal reorganized the farm supply chain for more cost-effective sourcing using the physical transmission capabilities of current intermediaries, while disintermediating them from the information flow and market signals. The digital infrastructure was supplemented with a phased rollout of physical infrastructure (ITC *Choupal Saagar)* that served as a hub for clusters of villages. This hub and spoke model was energized at the village level through *sanchalaks* (trained farmer) and *samyojaks* (middle man) drawn from the farming community, who represented the extended enterprise.

TRIPLE BOTTOM LINE PERFORMANCE

Besides enhancing shareholder value, ITC actively sought to create environmental and societal value. The 'triple bottom line' approach defined the company's growth path. The transformation of its paperboards division was a wonderful case in point.

The Turnaround of ITC Bhadrachalam

In the late 1990s, ITC Bhadrachalam Paperboards was a troubled enterprise. It had survived in a closed economy, despite outdated products and a globally uneconomical scale. However, the reduction in custom duties as a result of the economic liberalization process exposed the business to international competition. The energy intensity of paperboard manufacture, the high cost and unreliability of electric power from the state grid, and the challenge of absorbing modern technology in the underdeveloped Bhadrachalam region stacked the odds against it.

Further, the dwindling forest resources of the country and a national policy that did not permit corporates to engage in farm forestry operations posed a serious threat to the continuity of its access to cost-effective fiber that was its raw material. On the other hand, India needed this sector to flourish so as to support its growing sectors such as education and packaging.

The company chose to invest ₹150 crore into ITC Bhadrachalam towards acquiring competitiveness in the quality as well as the cost of manufacture at its own mill. Pulling together all the resources at its disposal, the company's insights as a consumer of value-added paperboards were fully leveraged in order to support the modernization and technological upgradation of the paper mill.

Substantial investments were also made into an ongoing biotechnology-based R&D programme to develop high yielding, disease-resistant clonal saplings that would grow at a rapid pace in relatively harsh climatic conditions. These saplings made the growing of pulpwood species on degraded wastelands a sustainable livelihood option. Marginal farmers and poor tribals in the economic vicinity of the mill were mobilized to grow these trees on their private wastelands.

This strategy implied longer gestation, substantial investment and considerable management attention in managing risk and uncertainty. There were periods of negative cash flows and low return on investment. It was an extremely difficult path, as compared with the easy option of importing pulp in an almost zero-duty regime. However, it enabled the poor and marginalized farmers to generate a sustained source of income by converting their wastelands into pulpwood plantations. ITC was a willing buyer of their produce, even as the growers were free to sell to the highest bidder in the open market.

Eventually, this strategy yielded three-dimensional success. On the social plane, it helped to create over 70 million person-days of gainful employment. A multiplicity of environmental benefits included the creation of a green cover for 160,000 hectares of land, carbon sequestration, groundwater recharge, regeneration of biomass and the nurturing of depleted soil. Simultaneously, the paperboards business became an industry leader. It was profitable as well as socially and environmentally responsible.

ROBUST CORPORATE GOVERNANCE

ITC was restructured according to a divisional framework. Robust performance measurement processes for independent 'investment' centers were painstakingly created. These were supported by an elaborate management accounting system. Further, a new three-tiered mechanism of corporate governance was introduced. Under this scheme, ITC's board of directors were mandated with strategic supervision while a corporate management committee dealt with strategic management and the divisional management committees carried operational responsibility for their respective businesses.

This arrangement allowed the company's top management to assume the character of a holding company, with the mindset of a venture capitalist. They mentored the existing businesses and created new avenues for growth by blending together various skills drawn from different parts of the ITC Group.

AWARDS AND RECOGNITION

ITC received national and global recognition for its multifaceted achievements. It was ranked as 'India's Most Admired Company' by the Fortune India magazine and Hay Group. The company was rated as the world's eighth largest 'sustainable value creator' amongst consumer goods companies by the Boston Consulting Group. As a testimony to its exemplary triple bottom line performance, ITC was also presented with the 'World Business and Development Award' at the historic Rio+20 UN Summit.

For his leadership in transforming ITC into an organization with a deep commitment to national priorities of sustainable and inclusive growth, Y. C. Deveshwar was conferred with the Padma Bhushan in 2011. Also, Harvard Business Review ranked him in 2013 as the world's 7th Best Performing CEO.[9]

Y. C. Deveshwar handed over the mantle of executive leadership at ITC to Sanjiv Puri in February 2017. However, he shall remain as the chairman of the company for another five years.

Y. C. Deveshwar had always canvassed for government support in order to maintain ITC as an independent, professionally managed company. The Government of India's ban upon FDI in tobacco is the final spoke in the wheel for any potential BAT plan to take over the company after his retirement!

REFERENCES

1. ITC. ITC report & accounts 2016. *Itcportal.mobi*. Available at: http://itcportal.mobi/about-itc/shareholder-value/annual-reports/itc-annual-report-2016/default.aspx (accessed: 4 September 2016).

2. Patil P. Environmental management information system (EMIS) for sustainable organizational development a literature review. *Proceedings of International Conference on Advances in Computer Technology and Management* (ICACTM). Available at: https://journalnx.com/papers/20150662-management-system-for-organization.pdf (accessed: 14 May 2018).

3. ICMR. The BAT-ITC tussle. *Icmrindia.org*. 2002. Available at: www.icmrindia.org/casestudies/catalogue/Business%20Ethics/BAT-ITC%20Tussle-Business%20Ethics.htm (accessed: 5 September 2016).

4. Haksar A. *Bite the Bullet*. New Delhi: Viking, Penguin Books India; 1993.

5. Business Standard. ITC—The inside story. *Business Standard*. 1996 (Vol. 5, Issue 21).

6. Bowonder B, Gupta V & Singh A. Developing a Rural Market e-hub The case study of e-Choupal experience of ITC. *The Planning Commission*. Available at: http://www.planningcommission.gov.in/reports/sereport/ser/stdy_ict/4_e-choupal%20.pdf (accessed: 19 November 2018).

7. Deveshwar Y. ITC: In pursuit of value creation. Speech presented at Kolkata, India; 2000.

8. ITC Limited. ITC Limited: Report and accounts 2017. *ITC Limited*. Available at: www.itcportal.com/about-itc/shareholder-

value/annual-reports/itc-annual-report-2017/pdf/ITC-Report-and-Accounts-2017.pdf (accessed: 19 November 2018).

9. Hansen M, Ibarra H & Peyer U. The best-performing CEOs in the world. *Harvard Business Review*. Available at: https://hbr.org/2013/01/the-best-performing-ceos-in-the-world (accessed: 15 November 2016).

VIDEO REFERENCE

Samatvam. (2016, September 29). *ITC: The Strategic Transformation.* YouTube. Available at: https://www.youtube.com/watch?v=uwD49J M3r7Q&feature=youtu.be (accessed: 26 November 2018).

MENTORSHIP MASTERY

12

The delicate balance of mentoring someone is not creating them in your own image, but giving them the opportunity to create themselves.

—*Steven Spielberg*

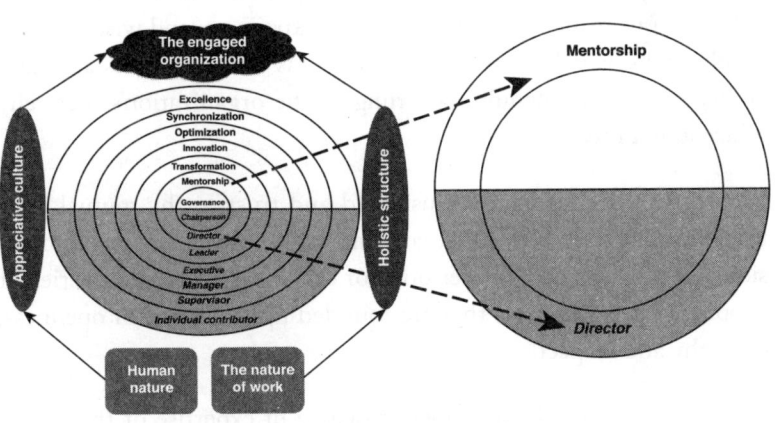

The Director's Mandate of Mentorship

Source: Samatvam Academy

Institutions employ people in order to pursue their mission and vision. The need to consistently achieve goals in a dynamic environment necessitates their continual growth and development. This statement rings more true as one ascends the hierarchy of accountability, particularly at the executive levels.

The job role of the group business head, supervisory council member or the director on the Board at the sixth stratum of the organization is a nurturing one. The mandate is to facilitate the successful conduct of the business. This includes helping the chief executive officer who actually runs the business organization to succeed in his/her role. Directors cede all direct, hands-on involvement in the running of the enterprise to the CEO and the executive team.

Divisional business executives are required to continually imbibe new knowledge, learn new skills and also appreciate diverse perspectives in order to handle the varied challenges of the business head role. A very effective method of executive development is the establishment of mentoring relationships between the organizational executives and the governing board members or directors of an enterprise.

Mentorship is a supportive relationship between a caring individual who is ready to share knowledge, experience and wisdom with another who is willing to benefit from this exchange. This accountability rests at the penultimate rung of the organization's hierarchy of accountability.

Mentorship is a structured, sustained and trustworthy mutual relationship that facilitates accelerated maturity in the personal, professional as well as social dimensions of existence. It entails a series of supportive interventions that are founded upon a spirit of openness, empathy and respect.

Mentors possess a definite area or degree of expertise of their own. They provide guidance towards the acquisition of the requisite contextual knowledge, skills, time applications and work values that are necessary for the successful fulfilment of executive responsibilities. The mentor is a guide who helps the executive to learn more quickly or develop at a faster pace.

Mentorship is a holistic developmental process that facilitates the informal transmission of knowledge, social capital and the psychosocial support. At the heart of this partnership lies an interpersonal dialogue that allows for collaborative reflection, planning and feedback towards the attainment of the mentee's desires, goals and objectives.

Mentors help to develop executive capability, confidence as well as character. Their mandate is akin to that of the guru, who plays an instrumental role in helping the pupil to transcend the perceived limitations of the personality. In this manner, mentorship is instrumental in helping to build a cadre of capable executives who can actively contribute to the realization of the institutional mission and vision.

It is not necessary that the directors must mentor the executives directly under their charge. Mentees may be cross-selected from among the entire executive population across the conglomerate entity.

The Benefits of Mentorship

Mentorship is a win-win process for all concerned. The benefits for the mentor are as follows:

1. Significant learning in the realm of self-awareness, arising from the frequent need to explain one's own intuitive reasoning to another person.

2. Satisfaction of knowing that one has made a positive difference to another individual's life.

3. Widening of one's perspective, by listening to views that arise from another frame of reference.

4. Meeting the intellectual challenge of helping to resolve unfamiliar issues, without the exercise of power or direct influence.

5. Gaining a constructive and people-friendly reputation within the organization or community.

The Discipline of Mentorship

Mentorship is about creating a legitimate and sacred professional space, wherein talented people can authentically reflect upon their past experience and fine-tune the direction for the future.[1]

The relationship begins with a contact between the mentor and the executive—often on account of a simple desire for a sounding board for ideas, but sometimes also to resolve a problem being faced. The next stage is that of exploring the degree of mutuality and compatibility between the individuals at a personal level and to know more about the other person's intents, values, attitudes and behaviour.[2]

As the mentor and the executive progressively grow in comfort and understanding, they arrive at a mutually accepted 'protocol' for their partnership. This informal code of conduct serves to clarify the boundaries and expectations within which the relationship may function. These are clearly articulated so as to eliminate the possibility of misinterpretation.

An important issue to be clarified is the very meaning of being a mentor or a mentee and the respective perceptions with regard to the two roles. Once a common understanding is reached on these aspects, the relationship is placed on a sound footing before the actual work of mentorship commences.

Mentorship unfolds as an iterative process of three phases. These phases are as follows:

1. **Esteem:** Discovery and articulation of the positive core of the mentee

2. **Envision:** Formulating a meaningful, engaging and convincing picture of one's own future

3. **Evoke:** Creating a supporting structure for translating the mentee's vision into reality

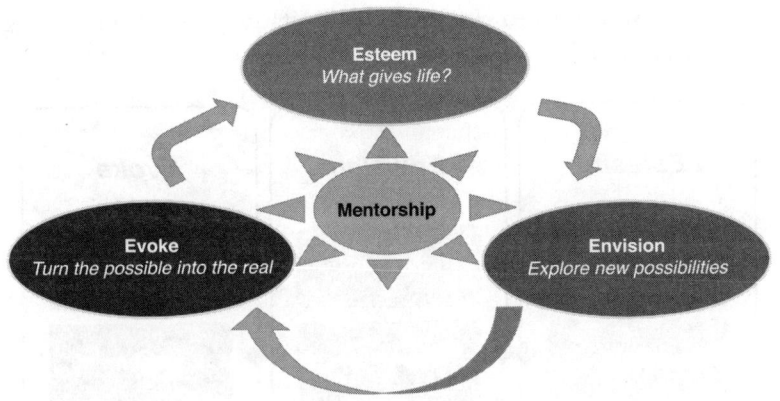

The Technology of Mentorship Mastery
Source: Samatvam Academy

The Mentorship Process Framework

The mentorship journey proceeds iteratively, through three phases. At each stage, there are certain goalposts to be crossed and objectives to be achieved.

In the esteem phase, the salient *talents*, as well as *aspirations* of the executive are identified and articulated. The constructive nature of this process facilitates the development of self-awareness. It also provides encouragement and *self-confidence* to the mentee.

The envision phase helps to crystallize the key aspirations of the executive into a cherished *dream* of the future. Talents are honed and organized into clusters of *capability*, just like the different flowers that are arranged into a beautiful bouquet. The self-confidence developed in the previous stage now matures into a sense of *conviction*.

The evoke phase is where the elements of the dream are translated into inspired action. A *blueprint* acts as the guide map for the activity that lies ahead. With the deployment of personal capability in line with the plan, an authentic sense of personal *engagement* is achieved. The amalgam of conviction and engagement gives rise to the white heat of devotion that burns up the impeding constraints.

301

The executive begins to *transcend* the limitations that were holding him/her back so far.

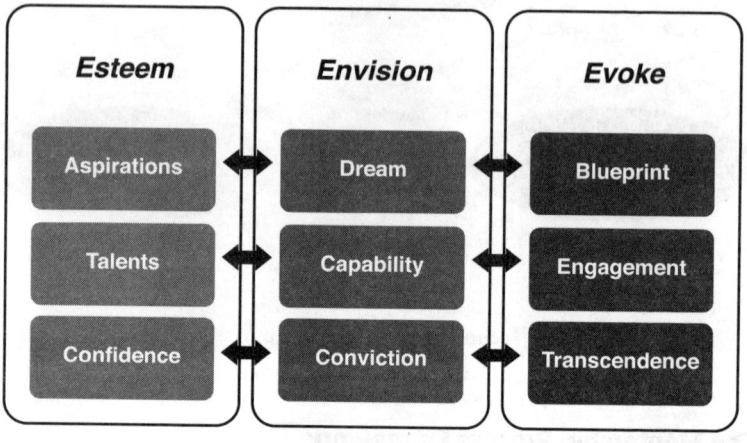

The Mentorship Mastery Framework
Source: Samatvam Academy

The work of mentorship commences with the crystallization of the executive's aspirations. These act as the central reference point all along the mentorship journey. The focal point of the endeavour is the building of executive capability. The entire mentorship effort is a developmental one, such that the executive becomes progressively more capable of realizing his/her own aspirations. The fruit that ensues from the exercise of mentorship is the development of the capacity to gradually transcend the perceived limitations or constraints that were restricting the progress of the mentee.

The Esteem Phase

The esteem phase is concerned with the discovery and articulation of the salient *aspirations* and *talents* that characterize the executive. Reflection upon critical incidents and high point experiences from the past provides the individual with an opportunity to see oneself in a new light. The recognition of talents, aspirations and strengths of character yields personal clarity and helps to impart greater *confidence*.

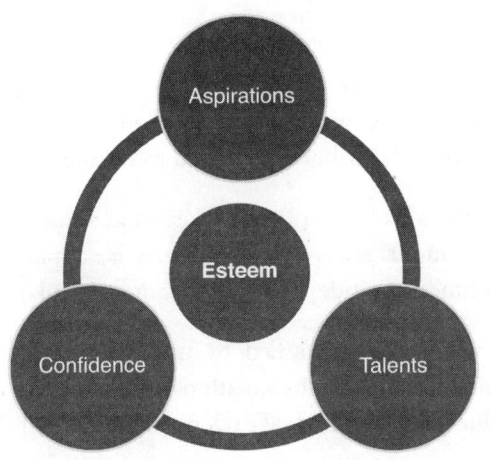

The Esteem Phase
Source: Samatvam Academy

Aspirations

Aspiration reflects the hope and wish towards the fulfilment of something that often pertains to higher values or ideals. Aspiration is accompanied by a strong will to succeed.

Aspirations are powerful human yearnings that cry out for satisfaction in the course of an individual's life. They influence the person's behaviour and encourage the application of one's strengths and talents. The pursuit of aspirations allows people to introduce a new sense of direction into their lives.

Intrinsic aspirations (such as affiliation, personal growth and community contribution) facilitate well-being to a greater degree, as compared to *extrinsic aspirations* (such as wealth, fame and image). The latter is more related to obtaining some of the external signs of worth. People who value intrinsic aspirations tend to pursue these with relatively greater zest and vigour, whereas the ones who chase extrinsic aspirations tend to be more deliberate and calculative.[3]

Talents

Talent is defined as any recurring pattern of thought, feeling or behaviour that can be productively applied.[4,p.42] It comprises the personal abilities and attributes that lead to excellent performance.

Talent represents a natural aptitude to excel at something, especially without being taught. Although talent may be applied to a specific job, it usually functions independently of any particular work context.

Personal talents may be identified by monitoring one's spontaneous top-of-the-mind reactions to the situations encountered in daily life.[4,p.59] Additional clues to an individual's talents include the following:

1. Yearnings that are felt early in life

2. Rapid learning during the acquisition of a new skill or ability

3. An experience of satisfaction during the performance of an activity[4,pp.61–64]

Confidence

Confidence is the state of certitude about something. It reflects a belief in one's ability to mobilize the cognitive, affective and conative resources towards obtaining specific outcomes.

Confidence is concerned with the quantum of faith and belief that a person has in oneself. It arises out of a combination of self-efficacy and optimism and is marked by freedom from doubt, uncertainty, diffidence or embarrassment.

Confidence implies a certain openness to challenge and the keenness to expend effort in the pursuit of a valued outcome. It is characterized by the willingness to take risks and try new things.

The Envision Phase

In the envision stage, the mentor assists in the creation of a *dream* that encompasses the executive's significant aspirations.

Next, the requisite *capability* domains that can help translate the dream into reality are visualized and enunciated. Existing talents are woven together in order to develop new capacity and competencies.

Once the dream has been articulated and the requisite capability is built, the executive requires emotional support in developing *conviction* towards the actualization of the dream.

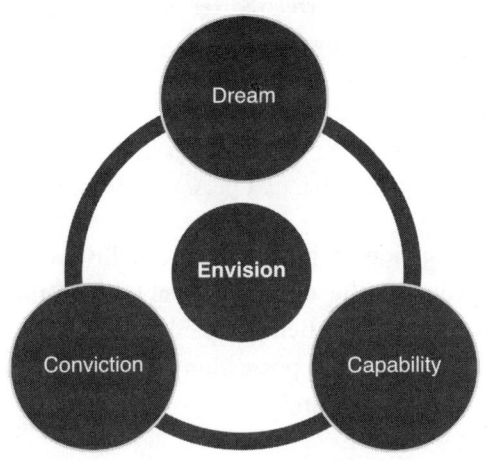

The Envision Phase
Source: Samatvam Academy

Dream

A dream is a visionary creation that stretches the person beyond the limits of the present and helps to formulate an inspirational picture of the future. The former President of India Dr A. P. J. Abdul Kalam defined a dream as 'not that which you see in sleep, but that which keeps you awake at night!'[5]

Even as a dream may span multiple years into the future, its formulation begins with an exploration of the past. The person reflects back upon her cherished experiences in life and also the factors that helped to make these as high points. This reveals themes and patterns that indicate what one is likely to find compelling in the future. As these creative expressions start to come together into an intelligible whole,

305

the person gradually comes to believe that it is within her power to bring the dream to fruition.

Capability

Capability is the natural ability, skill or power that enables a person to accomplish something, especially of a difficult kind. It refers to the capacity to leverage an interrelated set of knowledge, skill and value parameters in a functionally useful way.

Capability is a measure of the ability of an organization, person or system to achieve its objectives, particularly in relation to its overall mission. It is the wherewithal of a person to accomplish things.

Capability is a function of the individual's ability (what one is able to do), the opportunity (the options available) and the matching of capacity with opportunity. Being capable means having the 'power' to do something, while the possession of capability translates into knowing how to do something.

Conviction

A conviction is a condition of being certain about something. It is an emotional representation of an attitude that is strongly oriented towards holding something to be true.

Conviction is reflective of a strong persuasion or firm opinion. It is a state in which the person considers something to be the case, with or without the presence of empirical evidence or a verifiable foundation to prove its factual certainty.

A conviction is true and authentic only when it is consistent with the fundamental values held by the individual. Henry Ford is once reported to have quipped, 'Whether you believe you can or you can't, you are right'. That is a succinct illustration of the phenomenon of conviction.

The Evoke Phase

The task in the evoke stage is to prepare a supporting structure for translating the dream into reality. A detailed scheme or *blueprint* is crafted for leveraging the identified strengths and also addressing the areas of development. Employment of the talents, strengths, hopes, dreams and aspirations of the executive leads to a state of positive *engagement*. When accompanied by a deep sense of conviction, the executive works like a dynamo to neutralize the impediments and *transcend* any limitations that may come in the way.

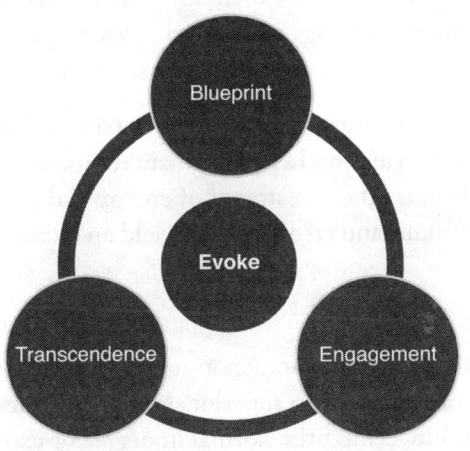

The Evoke Phase
Source: Samatvam Academy

Blueprint

A blueprint is an original design, pattern or prototype that may be followed as a guide for making or building something. It is a model that shows the possibilities for achievement and a detailed plan for doing something in order to bring about the accomplishment.

In the context of mentoring, blueprint represents a design for action that can help turn a dream into reality. It enables the executive to figure out how to gain the relevant knowledge, acquire the needed skills and imbibe the requisite values and perspectives. The mentor and the executive jointly identify the suitable ways and means for facilitating such development.

Engagement

Engagement is a state of emotional involvement or binding commitment. It is a dynamic process, wherein the person is attentive, connected, focused and integrated.

When people are engaged, they are seen to employ and express themselves physically, emotionally, mentally and intellectually in varied role performances. The engaged person remains curious, interested, motivated and persistent in the face of challenges.

Engaged individuals pursue goals with determination and vitality. They are found to yield higher performance, productivity, safety and good health. In turn, the investment of energy and attention leads to the building of skills and resources that yield an increase in capability.

Transcendence

Transcendence is the phenomenon of exceeding one's apparent limitations in order to reach a superior state. It is the act of surpassing usual limits and exceeding the normal in degree or excellence.

To transcend means to significantly extend the limits of ordinary experience by climbing over previously assumed boundaries. It is an evolutionary process that involves moving beyond prior conceptual, presumptive or behavioural limitations. Transcendence takes the form of a cognitive leap from the distinct and the particular to the complete and the whole.

At its best, mentorship transforms lives. One such 'mentor' is Nand Kishore Chaudhary, the founder of Jaipur Rugs.

N. K. Chaudhary has made a crucial and comprehensive difference to over 40,000 rural lives. His story, and that of his ingenious and compassionate enterprise, is the subject of the next case study.

References

1. Brewer A (ed). Positive mentoring: Learning to shape and nurture talent and confidence. In: *Mentoring from a Positive Psychology Perspective: Learning for Mentors and Mentees.* 1st ed. Switzerland: Springer; 2016.

2. Clutterbuck D. *Everyone Needs a Mentor.* London: Chartered Institute of Personnel and Development; 2010.

3. Rijavec M, Brdar I & Miljković D. Extrinsic vs. intrinsic life goals, psychological needs and life satisfaction. In: Fave A & Angeli F. (Eds.) *Dimensions of Well-Being Research and Intervention.* Milan: Franco Angeli; 2006. pp. 91–104.

4. Buckingham M & Clifton D. *Now, Discover Your Strengths.* New York: Simon & Schuster; 2005.

5. Gopal Bhushan. *Memories: Incredible Kalam.* New Delhi: DRDO, Ministry of Defence. Available at: http://drdo.gov.in/drdo/pub/Memories_Incredible_Kalam.pdf (accessed: 21 May 2016).

MENTORSHIP MASTERY

CASE STUDY
JAIPUR RUGS

A business is truly successful when you empower everyone involved in it.

—*Nand Kishore Chaudhary*

BACKGROUND

Jaipur Rugs is India's largest manufacturer and exporter of hand-knotted and tufted rugs as well as carpets that are manufactured from fine hand-spun wool, silk and cotton. The company has created a rich heritage of aesthetically designed, high-quality rugs with sophisticated textures in homes across 40 countries around the world.

In order to keep alive the fine traditional art of rug weaving, the company has built a network of nearly 41,000 skilled, home-based artisans across eight Indian states. Eighty per cent of the artisans are women. A large majority of them hail from the disadvantaged communities of rural India. Besides providing the rural artisans with a respectable and sustainable livelihood, Jaipur Rugs connects them with global markets and the elite icons of the world.

Jaipur Rugs was established in 1978 at Jaipur, Rajasthan. The company is a product of the zeal of its founder Nand Kishore Chaudhary (hereafter NKC) to work selflessly for the upliftment of the poor, the downtrodden and the outcast sections of Indian society. Its business model is a highly inclusive one.

Jaipur Rugs manages a highly efficient and large-scale global supply chain that attempts to match the skills of its weavers with the needs of its customers.[1,p.167] Through an innovative system of organization, the activities of numerous geographically dispersed independent workers are integrated together so as to produce a consistently high-quality product.

The Jaipur Rugs enterprise has established a robust mechanism to deal with the weavers directly so as to provide a fair return for their hard work and artistic creation. The raw material for the carpets and the wages earned for the work are delivered to the artisans at their doorstep.

By doing so, the company has virtually eliminated the role of exploitative middlemen that are otherwise deeply involved in the carpet trade. Jaipur Rugs has, thus, directly helped to improve the living standards of the artisan community at the grassroots and also facilitated their social empowerment.

Jaipur Rugs abides by the principle of equal opportunity as well as wages. It also provides the weavers with welfare services such as skill enhancement, health care and education. The company not only employs traditional weavers but also teaches the craft to people who do not hail from a weaving tradition.

Jaipur Rugs exemplifies the triumph of simplicity and determination over poverty, exploitation and ignorance. Compassion runs deep within the company's veins. NKC and his colleagues treat the artisans very respectfully as human beings in their own right and as equals.

From the owner to the weavers, Jaipur Rugs constitutes one large and happy family that annually produces more than 500,000 rugs and over ₹133 crore of revenue. Threads of love and regard, woven by deft hands and deep hearts, bind its people together in a tight embrace.

THE GENESIS OF THE ENTERPRISE

NKC was born in 1953 in a traditional Marwari family in Churu, Rajasthan. He completed his bachelor's degree in commerce and began his career in the family's shoe business.

In 1975, NKC secured a permanent position as a cashier at the United Bank of India.[2] To the surprise and dismay of his near and dear ones, he refused the job. His aspiration in life was to do something on a much larger scale, as an entrepreneur.

Meanwhile, NKC spent long hours contemplating upon the meaning of life. He read the Bhagavad Gita and also the writings of Osho, Mahatma Gandhi as well as Tagore.

NKC reflected deeply upon the nature of the business that he might engage with. In due course, he came to know that hand-woven woollen rugs and carpets of high quality were in great demand. With its blend of economic and aesthetic appeal, the carpet business appeared to be the right choice for him.

Armed with this clarity and determination, NKC borrowed ₹5,000 from his father in order to set up two carpet looms in 1978 within the courtyard of their house. He engaged nine trained, nimble and hardworking but unemployed weavers in order to commence the enterprise.[3]

NKC soon fell in love with the weaving business. He picked up the nuances of the art of carpet weaving by observing the weavers at work. NKC took time to sit, talk with and even eat his meals with these craftsmen. He forged a close relationship with them and gradually developed faith in their abilities.

This trust was duly rewarded upon the completion of the very first carpet. It had been made to order for a Jaipur-based exporter. The buyer was so delighted with the quality that he invited his own *karigars* (artisans) to inspect it. This was a tremendous confidence-building measure for the fledgling enterprise.

Thus encouraged and emboldened, NKC decided to expand his operations. Within the space of two years, six additional looms had been acquired. The enterprise was now thriving.

While the contractor supplied the raw material, NKC delivered high-quality, finished carpets in return. By 1980, this operation was yielding a net profit of over ₹30,000 per month.

ESTABLISHING THE BUSINESS

NKC reinvested a substantial portion of these earnings into the purchase of additional looms. In search of good talent he ventured into the villages located around Churu. While the village artisans were desperate for work, NKC was careful to select and engage only those who had great passion and at least some discipline towards their work. Most importantly, the individual also had to be a 'good' person.

As the number of weavers and the worksites grew, a rudimentary management system was created. One of the weavers was upgraded to the position of quality supervisor and then equipped with a motorcycle in order to travel and inspect the ongoing work at the looms. The supervisor compiled a production progress report that mapped the square feet of weaving per artisan and made payments to the workers accordingly.

After eight years of working as a contractor, with over 300 weavers and 100 looms under his charge, NKC's annual earnings touched ₹1.5 million. However, the business still rested upon the greedy shoulders of the exporters. This hampered the idealistic entrepreneur's aspiration to excel at his work and also to make a difference in the society at large.

There was a huge worldwide market for rugs that was waiting to be tapped, if only the challenge of producing high-quality handmade carpets on a large scale could somehow be surmounted. In 1986, in partnership with his brother M. K. Choudhary, NKC decided to invest in additional looms as well as raw materials so as to commence the direct export of carpets. After three years of effort, the duo received their first direct order worth about a million rupees from a German customer.

NKC now decided to make the state of Gujarat his main production base. This was because the tribal people in Gujarat were artistic as well as loyal, provided that they were treated with love and respect. Moreover, the state government provided training to the tribal artisans. It even equipped them with carpet weaving looms for free.

Accordingly, NKC shifted his entire household to the town of Pardi, Gujarat, in 1990. It took him three years to develop a deep rapport and bond with the tribal people and to train them in the art of weaving high-quality carpets.

While the Churu operation continued, the Gujarat operation gradually scaled up. In less than a decade, NKC had trained 10,000 tribal weavers with over 2,000 looms. Production in far-flung villages was tracked by means of communication over a wireless set. Two jeeps and twenty motorcycles ferried quality inspectors over rocky terrain. A truck full of carpets was dispatched to Jaipur every week for inspection, prior to their eventual export.

However, the fledgling enterprise received a tremendous blow in 1999 when NKC and his brother decided to part ways. Having focused almost exclusively upon developing weavers at the ground level, NKC had acquired very little expertise in operating the commercial side of the business.

Nevertheless, armed with a few looms apart from twenty years of goodwill, he started all over again. NKC's genius helped notch up exports of nearly ₹40 million in the very first year.

However, problems soon cropped up. NKC tried to recruit professional managers to handle these issues. But the malady turned out to be worse than the disease. These professionals came on board with massive egos and expectations of their own. The business suffered and started to make losses as a result. At one point it appeared that the company might even have to shut its doors.

In this grim situation, NKC once again turned within for answers. He read the scriptures, attended satsangs and generally remained in communion with nature. These musings helped him to discover the simple truth that all the limitations experienced by human beings actually reside within the self and not outside. Before attempting to bring about a change in the external situation, NKC realized that it was necessary to first alter one's own thinking and perspective.

The philosophy that NKC eventually adopted was that of 'finding yourself through losing yourself'. In practice, this translated as the giving up of one's own sense of ego and self-importance. The individual then becomes more sensitive to the needs and capabilities of other human beings.

This approach yielded phenomenal results. NKC's children also began to join the business one by one.

The operations of the Jaipur Rugs enterprise are handled by multiple legal entities. The Jaipur Rugs Company (JRC) is run by NKC along with his son Yogesh. JRC and its 22 branch offices take care of all the aspects of production, from raw material procurement to the export of finished goods. Jaipur Rugs Incorporated (JRI) manages the sales and distribution of carpets in the United States. Based at Atlanta, JRI is run by Asha and Archana Chaudhary.

Bhoomika Wools is the firm that is responsible for wool procurement and processing. The raw wool is inspected and cleaned at its seven warehouses in Bikaner, before it is carded and spun into yarn with the help of external partners. NKC's brother-in-law Navratan Saraf holds charge of the management of this entity.

The final pillar of the enterprise is the Jaipur Rugs Foundation (JRF). Established in 2004, this non-profit organization receives a percentage of the profits earned by the JRC. These funds are deployed towards the welfare, training and motivation of the artisans. The foundation also conducts medical camps and literacy classes for the weavers and their families.

The coordination of activities across the different operational groups provides the company with access to the necessary skills, though not their ownership. The company also maintains a significant influence over the key production processes, even though it does not control them directly. This distributed approach helps to decentralize the investment too.

THE ENTERPRISE STRATEGY

Jaipur Rugs facilitates an autonomous group of geographically dispersed artisans in processing the provided raw materials into finished rugs of the finest quality. Its enterprise strategy is founded upon four pillars: (a) innovative business model, (b) developmental values, (c) low capital intensity and (d) modern communications architecture.

INNOVATIVE BUSINESS MODEL

Jaipur Rugs is a family business that stresses upon the importance of keeping family values alive. The company empowers every lady of the house by providing her access to a sustainable livelihood within the precincts of her home. It has pragmatically aligned its operational model to align with the traditional Indian community practice of women refraining from stepping outside the household for employment.

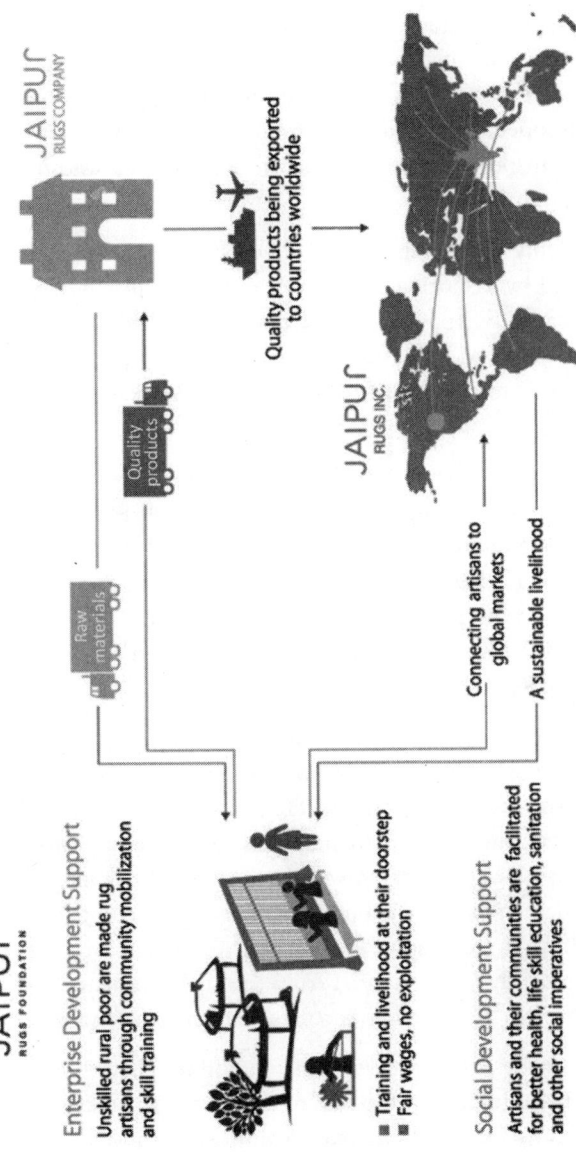

Doorstep Entrepreneurship

Source: https://www.jaipurrugsco.com/how-we-impact/doorstep-entrepreneurship (accessed: 30 November 2018).

Jaipur Rugs facilitates rural women towards carrying out highly productive work within the four walls of their home. It organizes for the business to travel to the doorstep of the weavers. Through a grassroots network that requires specialized logistical support, the raw material is dropped off at an artisan's home. Quality supervisors regularly travel to inspect the looms in order to track progress and ensure consistent output.

It is the responsibility of the supervisors to ensure that the artisans are not interrupted by a shortage of yarn or any other disruptions to their earning capacity. They also make payments to the weavers every month at their looms. When completed, the rug is picked up at the doorstep of the weavers and passed on to the next stage of the rug making progress.

The artisans are, thus, able to operate comfortably from home, at their own pace. Mothers with young children have no trouble working and weaving at the same time. Weavers also get to decide their own work hours. They can, thus, work around their family's schedules. Further, they lose no working hours in the processes of receiving and transporting material. As a result, more numbers of them can work towards financial independence.

Jaipur Rugs deploys a number of different models to engage with the weavers. It has established relationships with thousands of weavers directly. The company has also built indirect relationships with numerous other weavers through 'entrepreneurs'. These are usually former weavers who employ local villagers to weave rugs on multiple looms. In addition, middlemen facilitate about 20 per cent of the company's weaver relationships in geographical areas where enough weavers cannot be independently located. Apart from this, the company also gets work done through 'outsourcing' partners that employ artisans.

The company supports the weavers in obtaining government subsidies. It also helps to finance the cost of the looms. In deserving cases, it even lends its looms to the weavers until such time as they are able to purchase looms of their own.

The Jaipur Rugs enterprise has three kinds of field employees. A branch manager looks after the operations of each of its 22 branch offices. Most of them are former weavers, who have been promoted over the years when they demonstrated managerial potential.

Each branch has a posse of area commanders who are responsible for maintaining communication with the weavers in a given area.

Finally, the JRF motivators are responsible for recruiting the weavers, managing their skill training through various beneficial government schemes and maintaining good relationships with the artisan families in general.

DEVELOPMENTAL VALUES

The company's social values are manifested in the introduction of various developmental initiatives for the artisan community. In line with its mission to make a positive difference to the lives of rural artisans, the JRF regularly organizes health camps to provide continuous health care support to the entire village community. Apart from the treatment of general ailments, those with severe health issues are referred to specialized hospitals for proper care.

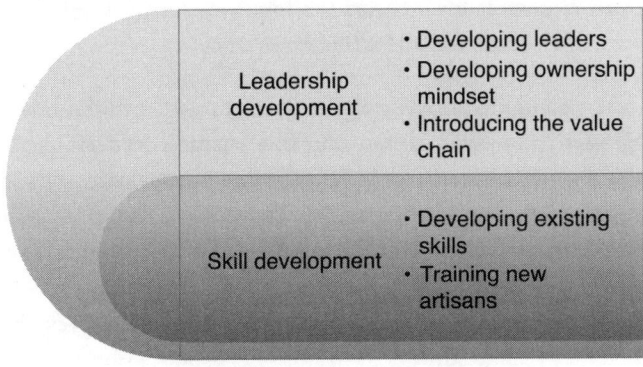

Entrepreneurship Development at JRF

Source: Samatvam Academy

JRF trains weavers who have no viable work employment available to them within their surrounding area. Potential artisans are identified through an intensive campaign. The mission of Jaipur Rugs is explained to them. Skills training is imparted to the new recruits by the JRF staff members as well as other experienced weavers. Through JRF's intervention, these artisans gain access to perennial employment that is not hampered by the vagaries of the weather or the season.

JRF conducts a six-month-long alternative education programme (AEP) for illiterate artisans and other village community members who have not completed primary education. While the core ambit of this initiative is basic literacy and numeracy skills, it also helps to generate an understanding of health, hygiene, family life, education and the environment. The AEP essentially seeks to build the confidence and self-reliance of the participants.

The JRF's Weaver Engagement Programme introduces rural artisans to the entire process of rug weaving and helps to provide them with a holistic perspective of their contribution. Members of the grassroots workforce visit the company's head office to experience the art that they create and derive pride in their work. Some of the weavers have woven carpets for 30 years without ever seeing a finished rug. They are often mesmerized by this experience.

JRF also conducts management development programmes for young women in order to tap into their natural leadership ability. Most of the women weavers have spent the greater part of their life in executing domestic chores. They have never attended school. This programme helps build the confidence of the women towards taking up leadership roles in their village and also prepares them for assuming managerial positions within the Jaipur Rugs enterprise. Further, they help to subvert the traditional gender imbalance within rural societies.[4]

Financial inclusion has been a major gap area in the development of rural communities in India. Jaipur Rugs identifies locally accessible banking services and also helps the artisans to open bank accounts.[5]

LOW CAPITAL INTENSITY

Jaipur Rugs works on very low fixed costs by decentralizing the work. Rug production is done purely on a 'pay for performance' basis. The payments are determined by the quality and the quantity produced.

Further, most of the manufacturing operations such as the dyeing, washing, machine carding, machine spinning and most weaving looms are outsourced. Besides reducing the capital requirement, these features allow for significant operational flexibility too.[1,p.173]

MODERN COMMUNICATIONS ARCHITECTURE

A combination of human talent, an electronic network and logistical infrastructure helps Jaipur Rugs to institutionalize quality and to maintain the company's influence over the entire process of rug production. An ERP system is deployed to optimize its geographically diverse supply chain. Another interesting process is the design and creation of the build sheets (known as 'maps') that provide easily understandable instructions to the minimally educated weavers.

The well-designed communication network of Jaipur Rugs facilitates the delivery of raw materials, regular communication with the weavers and the monitoring of the progress of the work that takes place in remote villages with limited resources. These communication channels help the company to manage a highly labour intensive process very effectively.[1,p.173]

ACCOMPLISHMENTS

NKC founded Jaipur Rugs upon the core principle of preservation and enhancement of human dignity. He thereby managed to subvert the antiquated social practices that shunned the poor, the women and the artists. NKC thus brought dignity back to the art and craft of rug making.

As a result, 41,000 Indian artisans as well as their clientele across 40 countries of the world subscribe to the company's philosophy of responsible manufacturing. Most importantly, the incomes of the artisan have gone up as a result of their engagement with Jaipur Rugs.

Owing to its innovative and socially beneficial business model, Jaipur Rugs has received several awards for outstanding performance in the carpet industry.

The CNBC TV18 Emerging India Award was conferred in December 2014, in recognition of the company's efforts towards the benefit of the society as well as the underprivileged. The NASSCOM Foundation presented the Social Innovation Honours Award to Jaipur Rugs in 2014 in recognition of the creative leveraging of information and communication technology by the company to create solutions that address gaps in social development. In the same year, Jaipur Rugs also won the Bihar Innovation Forum Award as well as the IndiaMART Leaders of Tomorrow Award.

NKC has ceaselessly championed the cause of the downtrodden and the socially underprivileged people in India for nearly four decades now. His personal efforts over the decades have been duly recognized too. The Ernst & Young Entrepreneur of the Year Award was conferred upon NKC in 2010.[6]

NKC also received The Times of India Social Impact Award for 2012 in recognition of his efforts to provide livelihood opportunities for people living below the poverty line in remote and distant areas.

While a business approach is the key to its success, grassroots entrepreneurship is encouraged and the workers are always given first priority. It is therefore no wonder that NKC is often referred to as the Mahatma Gandhi of the carpet industry.

REFERENCES

1. Prahalad C. *The Fortune at the Bottom of the Pyramid: Eradicating Poverty Through Profits*. New Delhi: Dorling Kindersley Pvt. Ltd; 2014.

2. Nand Kishore Chaudhary. Biography. *NkChaudhary.com*. Available at: www.nkchaudhary.com/biography/ (accessed: 15 November 2016).

3. Bansal R. *Take Me Home: The Inspiring Stories of 20 Entrepreneurs from Small Town India with Big-Time Dreams*. Chennai: Westland; 2014. p. 21.

4. Jaipur Rugs. Leadership training. *Jaipurrugs.com*. Available at: www.jaipurrugsco.com/how-we-impact/social-intervention/leadership-training (accessed: 6 November 2016).

5. Oxfam India. Jaipur rugs—weaving the lives of the poor into the global markets. An inclusive business model. *Oxfam India*. Available at: www.oxfamindia.org/blog/1174/jaipur-rugs-%E2%80%93-weaving-lives-poor-global-markets.-inclusive-business-model (accessed: 23 August 2016).

6. Jaipur Rugs. Awards. *Jaipurrugs.com*. Available at: www.jaipurrugsco.com/awards (accessed: 13 November 2016).

VIDEO REFERENCE

Samatvam. (2016, November 27). *Jaipur Rugs: Weaving Together a Rooted Empire*. YouTube. Available at: https://youtu.be/VDkejBXeZqY (accessed: 26 November 2018).

EPILOGUE

The task of organization building is a Herculean one. It starts with a shared sense of purpose. Talented individuals come together to work 'under one roof' only when the collective charter is a promising one and fulfils as many of their physical, mental and spiritual needs as possible.

Once the institutional mission has been crystallized, a vision is framed in order to provide a sense of direction to the enterprise. This requires an informed 'peep' into what lies ahead. A guide map for the future is charted out. In doing so, an overall sense of balance is maintained between the demands of the external environment and the competencies and aspirations that reside internally within the system.

Finally, a strategy to attain the mission and vision is formulated. The people of the organization work wholeheartedly, towards the implementation of the business plan. They put in their best efforts to attain the outlined goals and objectives, resulting in success.

However, in the course of doing business, several tricky choices must be made from moment to moment. Every time an employee comes to a crossroad, he/she is faced with multiple options. These call for an expression of preference for one course of action over another. The cultural and ethical values of the organization become the reference point around which the individual makes a choice from among the numerous available alternatives.

Values are the instrumental principles that guide action. The values practised by the organization from day to day serve as the frame of reference around which strategic and operational decisions are taken. They constitute the salient expressions of collective intent. In this way, values act as the pivot around which the organizational work revolves.

There is little that is wrong or right about any chosen set of values; the results that arise from their practice always speak for themselves.

The age-old natural principle applies, 'As you sow, so shall you reap'. However, transparency is important. The gap between the 'espoused' values and the values-in-action should be minimized.

Framing, implementing and championing a set of values that people can live and work by is the central task of corporate governance. The accountability for governance rests at the apex level of the organization. It is the chairperson of the governing board of the organization, institution or enterprise that holds the ultimate responsibility for corporate governance.

As the 'governor' of the institution, so to say, the chairperson provides a guiding framework of values within which the operational and strategic work of the enterprise takes place. He/she also creates a platform upon which the various role holders can demonstrate competence and channelize their talents.

Corporate governance represents the mechanisms and procedures by which corporations are directed. It denotes the principles that identify the distribution of rights and responsibilities among its different stakeholders. Governance also includes the processes through which the institutional objectives are set and pursued, within the context of the social, regulatory and the competitive environment.

Corporate governance is essentially concerned with holding the balance between economic and social goals and also between individual and communal goals. The governance framework encourages the efficient use of resources. It also emphasizes the accountability for the stewardship of those resources. The aim is to mutually align the interests of the individuals, the corporations and the larger society as closely as possible.

Values and ethics are the central concerns of corporate governance. Values are principles held for their own sake, without any particular end in mind. They act as the defining elements of the individual personality, and reside at its deeper levels that transcend the world of words and logic.

An important value that relates to organization building is whether to adopt a constructive or a critical approach to management. Another relates to whether the organization must 'make' or 'buy' talent. But perhaps the most important choice may be stated akin to Hamlet's dilemma, 'To engage or to exploit—that is the question!'

Exploitation has been practised in society across the ages and is conveniently looked upon as inevitable. But when the chairperson bats for engagement, he/she indirectly bats for the very 'humanity' that characterizes the human being.

The choice of engagement over exploitation eventually benefits all the stakeholders of the organization. In particular, the employees and associates of the organization are the most positively impacted.

In return for a wonderful and humane work context, people put their heart and soul into the enterprise. In a deeply engaged organization, the human spirit is, thus, authentically witnessed in action.

All that has been enunciated in this book relates to how the dream of building happily engaged organizations might be realized. However, building engaged organizations is ultimately a choice.

May you exercise that choice! The world will be a better place as a result. Individuals will be happy and enterprise will create prosperity.

In the words of General Colin Powell, 'A dream does not become reality through magic; it takes sweat, determination and hard work'.

EPILOGUE

ABOUT THE AUTHOR

Dr Sunil Maheshwari is the dean of Samatvam Academy—based in Gurugram, Haryana. He has facilitated executive education at a large number of corporations and institutions in India and abroad. His developmental expertise was honed in the course of an extensive corporate career with RPG Enterprises, Gillette, Wipro Corporation, the Tata Group and Ernst & Young in various human resources/organizational development roles.

Dr Maheshwari is also a graduate of the certificate programme in Yoga education from The Yoga Institute, Santacruz, Mumbai. He has comprehensively taught and researched the role of Yogic sciences in delivering health, harmony and happiness for human beings in society. He is an external assessor with the Yoga Certification Board, Government of India.

Dr Maheshwari completed his PhD on 'Relationship between Appreciative Intelligence and Leadership Capability' from Faculty of Management Studies, University of Delhi, New Delhi, and also has an MBA from the same institution. Prior to this, he schooled at Mayo College, Ajmer, Rajasthan, and emerged with flying colours in athletics, dramatics and debating. Dr Maheshwari then went on to pursue a bachelor's degree in industrial engineering from Nagpur University.

Dr Maheshwari can be contacted for any feedback and suggestions about the book at sattva@samatvam.co.in